When God was Out to Lunch

Why God won't go away

Catherine Schell

When God Was

fantom

publishing

First published in 2018 by Fantom Films
fantomfilms.co.uk

A catalogue record for this book is available from the British Library.

Hardback edition ISBN: 978-1-78196-311-1

Typeset by Phil Reynolds Media Services, Leamington Spa
Printed and bound by CPI Group (UK) Ltd, Croydon, CR0 4YY
Jacket design by Will Brooks

For Bill

Also by Catherine Schell and published by Fantom Films

A CONSTANT ALIEN
an autobiography

Contents

Chapter One

'**D**ON'T KILL HIM YET!' I SHOUTED DOWN THE PHONE to Marie-Jo in French. 'Kill him next Friday. Cut him into pieces and I'll collect him in the evening.'

'Do you want his blood?'

'I don't think so, we'll be soaking him in mustard overnight.'

'Blood is good for the red wine,' she advised.

'I'm sure it is, but not with mustard.'

We were discussing the imminent execution of a rabbit and the recipe for its corpse.

'How many will you be?' she asked.

'Eight. Is he big enough?' I was worried. I didn't want to have two dead bunnies on my conscience.

'Oh, yes. But don't come too early. I can't cut him up until he's cold.'

Gulp… and then, 'Thank you, Marie-Jo. See you on Friday.'

'*De rien*. It was your bread that made him *grosse*.' We both hung up. What dialogue! And not a scriptwriter to blame. How did I learn it? Tripping off the tongue… 'Wednesday night for dinner? Oh, I am sorry but I'll be giving an English lesson in the old abattoir'. If friends want to visit in January, 'Please! Not the middle weekend. Every room will be booked by my annual group of pig-killers.' Or having driven back down the hill, late from my bread run, to hungry clients waiting on the terrace for their breakfast, 'Forgive me! I'm late but the old peasant "Pistou"'s cows got loose and ambushed me again. They wouldn't get out of the way until I threatened them with a baguette.' Then a little later to Bill, 'Cut that bit off, it fell in some cow shit.'

'Do you think they'll notice?'

'Bill!!'

Our guests were served unadulterated bread and fresh croissants. The terrace was brilliant in the early-morning sunshine and a very pretty woman asked for a hat. I placed a spare fedora on her blonde head and gave her dark glasses lest the crow's feet which were beginning to etch themselves into the delicate skin around her eyes became more permanent. For a moment she reminded me of a life I used to know. An actress on a glamorous location having breakfast on the terrace of a four-star hotel, hiding from the sunlight, Peter Sellers waving as he called across his shoulder, 'See you on the set, kid,' before he disappeared into the luxury of his chauffeur-driven Rolls while I remained giggling with my colleagues blessed with a later make-up call. I thought those days would never end. Wrong.

I am now serving breakfasts with coffees, teas and for those hateful, inconsiderate few, hot chocolates from 8:30 to 10:00 and woe to those who arrive early! Bill is not averse to admonishing whoever dares approach with intent to breakfast before the appointed time with, 'Piss off, you greedy swine! It's not 8:30 yet!'

I am grateful that in our experience we have come across the same lack of enthusiasm for learning a foreign language amongst the French as is practised in Britain. Not understanding the words, the guests smile politely, notice the tables are not ready and take themselves for a walk.

It seems almost impossible that, in the six short years we have been occupied with our humble B&B/guest house, such an incredible assortment of human life should have found its way to our door. They have come from every continent, in all shapes and sizes, aged from eight days to 101 years old, of every complexion and practising incredibly diverse professions.

I'd lived in London, albeit in a cul-de-sac, for twenty-seven years as one of eight million inhabitants and I never knew there were so many different people out there. Some of them would have appeared in books I had read but that's passive knowledge. We had to come to deepest France, to a hamlet which, counting the two of us, consisted of nine inhabitants, to actively become acquainted with fighter pilots, NATO generals, pharmacists, musicians of extraordinary instruments, psychiatrists, doctors (specialising in all manner of bodily malfunctions), detectives, undercover policemen (we were assured they really were on holiday), owners of vineyards, atomic physicists, microbiologists, an ex-worker in an asbestos factory (I've never used an ironing board since), breeders of exotic sheep or cows, vets, organ restorers, clock repairers, all manner of bureaucrats (usually Belgian), wives of important functionaries (we are very discreet) and very important husbands with obviously not their wives, teachers, artists, social workers, opera singers, bee keepers, hairdressers, architects, clerics, pilgrims and an undertaker.

Now take five of these individuals with their partners and make a seating plan for dinner. Go on. I dare you. This is your cast: The gynaecologist is female, German. A trumpet player is male, French, with policewoman partner, also French. A breeder of long-horned cattle is Australian, with wife. A teacher of mentally handicapped children is female, French, with her friend who is an outrageously gay mortician, male, French (separate rooms) and the alcoholic heir to what was a very important French family fortune (now blown) with his acknowledged concubine. You will be relieved to know the nun cancelled. And yet, every night a small miracle happened. It is amazing how well people can communicate on neutral ground. It pleases me when I am able to witness a very important, handsome young scientist from the Institut Pasteur in Paris listen with earnest interest to a detailed description by an eighty-year-old master carpenter, who was minus two fingers on his right hand, of the intricate grain in the wood he used to fit the then Shah of Iran's kitchen in his villa on the Côte d'Azur.

Bill and I are thrilled when such incongruous dinner parties should be in animated conversation around our table, but then the inevitable happens and someone asks of either Bill or myself, 'How on earth did you find this place?' The table quietens and, if the common language that night is predominantly English, Bill relates the story; if French or German, Bill plays 'butler' while I hold forth. But whichever one of us answers, the first words are always 'by accident' or *'par hasard'*, or even *'beim zufall'*.

I have never believed in fate. Perhaps it was because my education from the age of seven to thirteen had been entrusted to a strict order of Hungarian nuns, the Sisters of Divine Charity, the minders of St Joseph's Hill Academy on Staten Island, NY. We were taught that God gave us the freedom to choose and that our decisions in life would determine whether we walked the path of righteousness or not. We had to earn our way to everlasting joy in the hereafter by a stubborn will to do so. Temptations would be put into our path but we must remain strong and deny them. We were the masters of our destiny and our destiny was to know God. Pretty daunting stuff for a seven-year-old and it's stuck with me. The religious fervour has paled somewhat but I do believe that every action has a reaction. Our futures are the result of a myriad of decisions we have taken and deeds done, not always consciously but nevertheless bearing a consequence upon our tomorrows... and yet, it is tempting to believe that fate did have a hand in my discovering Bonneval.

If that day in June 1989 had not been brilliant with sunshine... if Jeremy Nicholas had not been part of the cast... if Bill had not been directing the third series of *Wish Me Luck* and not offered me the daytime role of 'Virginia' and the night-time part of 'director's perks'... if the municipal authorities of Le Puy-en-Velay had not allowed us to convert their city into a Nazi stronghold and to fly the swastika boldly from three large windows of their Hotel de Ville... if a certain architect had not looked down with curiosity from the terrace of his penthouse flat at our film unit's camp of caravans and lorries squatting on the 'parking' of Place Michelet below, and if the name 'Valentine' had not figured so strongly in Bill's family, perhaps none of the following would ever have happened.

Jeremy Nicholas and I were to enjoy a day off from acting as agents parachuted in from England to liaise with the French resistance during the Second World War. Bryan Pringle's priest's collar would rest in the wardrobe van that day, as would Sid Livingstone's Wehrmacht uniform. It was Jeremy's decision, and he was adamant that we visit La Chaise-Dieu. Jeremy was the sort of person you could grow to resent the longer and more intimately you became acquainted with him. He knew too much and could practise what he knew. He was a splendid actor, broadcaster, published writer, lyricist, composer, pianist, cook, driver, internet browser, married to a very pretty young woman (so I have to presume a good lover) and the only reason I liked him was that he couldn't ride a horse and knit at the same time.

The goal of our little outing which Jeremy insisted upon was a visit to a medieval abbey in La Chaise-Dieu which housed an ancient, magnificent organ still under repair. This intricate and expensive renovation was being funded from the proceeds of a classical music festival which takes place the latter two weeks in August of every year. This now famous event had been inspired by the Hungarian pianist, György Cziffra. György and I were fellow countrymen, different generations but same birthplace. I had never heard of him. Jeremy was aghast.

'What?! You don't know of one of your own country's most famous modern-day musicians?' he scolded, showing me his silver-haired, noble profile to its best advantage. 'Aren't you ashamed?' I was, but I wasn't going to let him know.

'Oh! You mean György *Tziffra*.' I leant heavily on the 'tz' as the name should be pronounced in Hungarian rather than as a 'ch'. 'Of course I know of him,' I lied. 'I didn't recognise the name the way you were saying it.' That's another reason I like Jeremy: he doesn't speak Hungarian.

We borrowed a car from the unit, a fact that was not advertised to Michael Chaplin, the producer. Four of his leading characters crammed into the same vehicle driving along French country roads could have caused him to worry to the point of cardiac arrest. Actors are, after all, quite integral to a drama production, and the absence of only one of them due to an unfortunate road accident could result in extremely expensive delays. The absence of all four didn't even bear thinking about so we thought it better not to worry Michael.

It was a glorious June day. Le Puy and all of the Haute-Loire was basking in a heatwave. Jeremy was driving. Sid was next to him, the map on his lap, taking his role as Nazi navigator extremely seriously, barking directions in a perfect, harsh Gestapo accent. It was an extraordinary contradiction as the voice was emitting from a sweet, gentle, cherubic face.

'I said, *RECHTS!* You *VERFLUCHTE BRATWURST!*' A buzzard was lazily circling in the sky above. 'Shtop this *PANZER!* We must give *ZIEG HEIL* to that brave *FOKKER* at one o'clock!'

Pringle and I were relaxing in the back, enjoying the performance as well as the view. We left Le Puy on the departmental road which winds its way to the foot of the ruined fortress of Polignac sitting high on a shelf on the remains of a volcanic peak. To either side of us, the verges, not yet mown, and the meadows beyond were gaudy with their abundant display of wild flowers. We were intrigued by the eerie jade-green rock which jutted mysteriously from the forested hills, and when we drove along the crest of the plateau between Saint-Paulien and Bellevue-la-Montagne we were humbled by the vastness of these horizons and marvelled at the strange blue volcanic shapes looming in the distance. Needless to say, upon finally arriving at La Chaise-Dieu we were exhausted from this relentless attack on our aesthetic senses and decided (well, it was Pringle, actually, who decided) we were in need of an imbibement of the alcoholic kind in order to re-energise our spent 'appreciation batteries'. Unfortunately, Pringle had chosen the bar immediately opposite the imposing edifice we were about to visit. The lengthy flight of steps which we would have to climb flowed like lava from its Gothic entrance; they were, to say the least, daunting. The more we studied them, the more sustenance we required, and so time passed before we found the will to accomplish what we had decided would be comparable to climbing the north face of the Eiger.

Between the abbey and the terrace of the café was a round stone fountain with three iron spouts out of which poured a steady stream of water. Two riders appeared, halted their horses and allowed them to drink. They dismounted and one held the reins while the other entered the bar and reappeared with two glasses of beer. The horses sucked from the fountain. The riders relaxed drinking their beers, a young man and woman in T-shirts, patting the necks of their mounts, shooing the flies away from their beautiful eyes. Having returned their empty glasses, they remounted and continued on their way, beating a metallic rhythm as they disappeared around the side of the café. Horses are my passion. I thought I was in heaven. Then Bryan lifted his tall, lank shape off the seat and said, 'Everybody up! We're going to climb that bloody mountain and have a look at Jeremy's organ.'

The midday sun had not yet cast its glow upon the western face of the abbey; only its jutting terraces halfway up the long reach of stairs and the steps themselves were highlighted in a brilliant glare. Our goal at the summit was a small dark rectangle, the threshold through which visitors passed, cut into an immense oak carved panel. As we were struggling up the steps people were exiting from the black hole into the light. We reached the terraces and I was amazed there weren't any benches for the unathletic to rest upon. Gulping for more breath we continued to climb. More people issued forth from the interior. At the very top we paused for breath and, during that moment, in front of our faces the entrance was abruptly plugged. The oak-panelled structure was complete. Upon the closed wooden door hung a notice: FERMÉ ENTRE 12:00 ET 14:00 H. Those of us with watches looked at our wrists. It was exactly noon and the bells began to chime. The vehemence of our blasphemies so close to a sacred place should have attracted lightning bolts to destroy us. If British football hooligans had been getting drunk at the bar across the square, our loud curses would have made them blush in shame.

I've heard it said the French claim God as one of their own and, as such, He obviously honours their sacred custom of the two-hour midday meal. We decided to do likewise, not in the town itself but to continue our explorations and find a little restaurant with a view somewhere in the glorious countryside, then return later when He would be picking His teeth. Once again the large Michelin map was studied and we found ourselves on a little road due east of La Chaise-Dieu. We drove under a narrow railway bridge and, fifty metres farther, came to a stop. The road forked. A decision had to be made; to the left, Malvières, to the right, Bonneval. A meaningless discussion ensued. After all, both were only tiny black dots on the map.

I shouted from the back, 'Take the right!'

Three inquisitive faces turned towards me. 'Why?'

With great determination, I answered, 'Because!'

Being gentlemen, they indulged my whim.

Jeremy steered to the right and we followed a serpentine route that took us into the shadows of forests, giving way to sunlit pastures with browsing brown-and-white patchwork cows, their heads nodding benignly as we passed. A glassy dark lake appeared on our left. Expanding shimmering circles on its surface marked where the fish had come up to grab lunch. We continued downhill, the road snaking its way through a fairy-tale landscape, expecting to spot a little girl wearing a bright red cloak and carrying a basket of fruit. Could we warn her in time of the big bad wolf waiting to pounce from the darkness of the woods beyond? Where were the babes, the wicked witch and the gingerbread cottage? Little did I know.

Civilisation accosted us around the next bend. Ahead was a small stone church dating surely from centuries before and carrying an ambitious steeple: the beacon of Bonneval. As the car approached we became convinced that this tiny hamlet could not host a restaurant as well as a church and so we continued, passing the church on the left, the obligatory war monument on the right with the names of the commune's glorious dead engraved on a stone plinth upon which a brave bronze soldier stood guard, and next to him a beautiful, delicately painted blue-and-white statue of the Virgin. In the absence of any living people to be seen, Pringle remarked dolefully from the back, 'That was the welcoming committee.'

I turned around to have another look at the disappearing church and suddenly spied through the obscuring foliage of the trees what looked like a colourful parasol, nay, *two* colourful parasols on what must be a terrace.

'Stop! There are umbrellas back there. It's got to be a restaurant!' I screamed.

'Don't be ridiculous,' they replied. 'It's probably a private house. This place is too small to have a restaurant.'

'No private person owns *two* parasols! I'll bet you anything.'

Once again, they indulged me. We turned around and headed back up towards the church. Now they could also see the splashes of colour through the trees and, with a little more confidence, we turned by the church.

'No arrow pointing to CENTRE VILLE,' Jeremy observed, drily.

He stopped the car against a narrow stone entrance, above and to the right of which hung a bracket with a discreet black metal sign reading AUBERGE DE LA DORETTE. Whoopee! It was exactly what we were searching for: a simple restaurant with a terrace from which we could admire the view. Paradise… and then the balding, bearded, gnome-like *aubergiste* arrived wearing khaki Bermuda-length shorts, ankle socks and sandals. He must have heard us talking because his very first words were spoken in English. Or so we presumed.

'Wailcome! You hare Eenglish?'

'Yes, that's right. We've come all the way from Le Puy. Could we have a spot of lunch? I take it you are the *patron*,' Pringle enunciated with his best stage voice.

'You hare Eenglish comedians?' he asked. We didn't realise that '*comédiens*' was the French word for 'actors'. I think it was Sid, who'd scored the most laughs up until then, who replied, 'How perceptive of you to have guessed.'

'You hare feelming in Le Puy?'

How on earth could he have known? It wasn't as if we were wearing make-up or in costume and this place was in the back of beyond.

'How very correct!' boomed Pringle from his full height, the heavy bags under his eyes wobbling.

'How the hell did you know?' asked Jeremy, flabbergasted.

'Hit 'as been in all of the noisepaypers, hand I can tell you hare not normal.'

We weren't quite sure how to accept this. He then made a knowing gesture, tapping his index finger against his nose. 'You 'ave the hair of making cinema about you.'

As entertaining as his attempts at using English vocabulary were, we were here for a purpose and so I conjured up what little I remembered from my French-Swiss summer-school days and asked, '*Pourrions-nous avoir un repas, Monsieur?*'

Perhaps my accent was as atrocious as his because he continued in English, 'You hare wonting to heat? We hare not yet preparing tourists. To be sure we hare feeding the locos. I will hask my waife.'

He ushered us to a table on the terrace under one of the parasols and disappeared into the interior. A few moments later he re-emerged. The bushy growth on his round face stretched to its horizontal limits depicting a smile. Following him was his 'waife', amply bosomed, curvaceous and, from what we could see from just above her knees to her ankles, possessing nicely shaped legs. To have called her pretty would have been from a subjective point of view but she did have a sultry sexiness about her, like a blonde version of the Italian actress, Anna Magnani, with the same lazy, insolent, swaying walk. She explained, using less vocabulary but infinitely better pronunciation, that as they themselves had only recently arrived to run the *auberge*, they were not yet fully prepared for tourists and had merely welcomed the locals till now. If we would like she could make us an omelette with cold meat to start and, to finish, some cheese. We were delighted! Fresh bread and a bottle of wine were placed on the table. The *charcuterie* arrived and we devoured it. If someone had told us the meat had been carved from a dried haunch of a donkey we'd still have found it wonderful. The omelette was deliciously runny and the dressing on the mixed salad was perfect. We savoured the different morsels of cheese with another bottle of wine, and then a basket was placed on the table containing shiny, dark, plump, succulent cherries. Sublime. Anna Magnani knew how to appease your appetite.

We were loath to leave this charming spot but Jeremy was anxious to set his eyes on God's great organ and so, reluctantly, we asked for *l'addition, s'il vous plait*. The *aubergiste* arrived carrying, in one hand, the bill and a bottle of twenty-year-old Macallan malt whisky. In the other, he held a basket containing four pairs of metal balls, each engraved with a different design, and a little wooden one.

'Do you know 'ow to play bowels?' he asked and immediately began to clear tables and chairs away from a sandy area of the terrace.

'Surely, he means *boules*?' I whispered to the fellows.

We were now in a quandary. Do we stay and play in the heavenly sunshine or do we satisfy Jeremy's desire and visit the cold gloom of the abbey's interior? It was no contest once Pringle had spotted the whisky.

'Jeremy, it won't take long,' I said.

'Won't take long?! We've watched those old buggers playing it in Le Puy from early morning until it gets dark *and* they're back the next day! It takes longer than a bloody cricket match!'

It was true. We had watched elderly men throwing their metal balls which, on landing, rolled to knock away their opponent's nearest to the jack with a pleasing *kathonk*. The game was played in the main square of Le Puy on a sandy stretch next to the magnificently sculpted fountain overlooked by the Prefecture. As a spectator, this gently hypnotic pastime is strongly recommended for those who suffer from high blood pressure or insomnia.

The *aubergiste* proceeded to explain the game, unaware that we already had some rudimentary knowledge of it. Even Jeremy was prepared to stay and listen to this blatant vandalism being committed upon the English language. As a writer he wanted to soak up whatever copy he could use for the future.

'This,' said our host, pointing to the jack (it was amazing: he could pronounce the *th* perfectly and yet would proceed to murder the vowels), 'his thrown, hand where hit lands you throw the bowls.' I was later to accept this anomaly as normal. When an 'h' is required the French cannot pronounce it; when not required, they aspirate with abandon.

'The bowl nairest to this woden one,' he explained as he threw the jack which landed and rolled to about ten yards away, 'is the wining bowl. I 'ave this,' he said, removing a measuring tape from his pocket, 'to be sure.'

'Well, I think that was clear enough,' said Pringle. 'Let the "bowels" commence!'

As a gesture of appeasement, we allowed Jeremy to begin; and for the next half hour the pleasant sounds of metal rolling on to metal and the dull thud as the heavy balls were dropped on to the sand were occasionally disturbed by our shrieks of, 'Bastard!' (or 'Bitch!') 'You've knocked my balls away!' I hasten to add, the effects of playing *boules* can be in direct contrast to simply watching it. The *aubergiste* performed like a demented ballerina, twirling, leaping between the rolling metal orbs and finally pointing his toes to the 'wining bowl'.

While waiting for one of my turns I wandered off to the edge of the terrace and gazed into the distance. I could see a little stone bridge under which flowed a sparkling stream. My eyes followed the silver ribbon as it meandered through the sweet valley below and then alighted on the terracotta roof of a building directly beneath where I was standing. It belonged to a little hovel attached to a barn and on its other side, slightly lower, clung another appendage. It all looked sadly neglected. The moss-covered roof was sagging. A smoky dark stain reached up the wall from the door to an opening just under the roof out of which drooped the remnants from a bale of straw. Paint was peeling on the closed shuttered windows either side of the door. The ancient rendering on its façade was crumbling. I pitied the poor thing. It seemed so abandoned and forlorn.

Can a house cry? Can it whimper like a lost puppy begging for a home? I was sure I heard a squeak. (Probably one of the fellows losing a round.) I was convinced this house was longing for a host.

And then I noticed it: a white piece of paper stuck to one of the shutters, its frayed corners slightly flapping in the gentle breeze. Straining my sight to read the handwritten notice, I finally discerned the message, MAISON À VENDRE.

'Hey, guys!' I called. 'Come and look at this! There's a house for sale.'

'Oh, God, what has she found now?' said Pringle, his face wincing and looking more than ever like a turtle's. His head bobbed up and down and from side to side, extending forward from his shoulders on his long thin neck as he slowly came to see. Curiosity got the better of the other two and they also joined me at the fence to have a look.

'It's a ruin,' remarked Jeremy with a little too much disdain.

'Oh, I don't know,' said Sid, the most practical of all of us. 'It's standing and it's got a roof.'

'Only just,' retorted Jeremy.

I pointed to some dark spaghetti-looped wires which entered the house via a hole above the front door.

'Is that for electricity?' I asked Sid. He spotted a cement pylon towards the right from which the cable had been suspended.

'Yes, that's definitely for a power supply,' he answered.

By this time we were joined by the *aubergiste*.

'It's for sale?' I enquired.

' Yes,' he replied. 'Hit 'as not been souled for a lowng time.' I just loved the way he said 'sold'.

'For how long?'

'Seven, maybe hate years.'

'Why?'

'Nowbody wonts hit.'

'Does it have running water?'

'Yes.'

'If you like rust-coloured water,' Jeremy interjected.

'Hit was the owld *auberge* of the village,' the *aubergiste* continued.

'It had rooms to let?' I was amazed. What I presumed was the habitable part of the house looked too small to offer rooms for passers-by.

'Well, it would have to, wouldn't it?' declared Pringle. 'If you found your way to the end of the world they'd have to offer you a meal and a room for the night before you left the next day to fall off.'

'Two rooms,' added the *aubergiste*.

Two rooms to let to the public gave rise to some hope of amenities for instant occupation.

' A bathroom or shower?' I asked.

The *aubergiste* just laughed.

'A toilet?'

He laughed even harder.

The three fellows and I looked at each other in horror, thinking of the consequence this lack of conveniences would have caused for the guests and their hosts.

'I can only imagine,' said Sid, ever practical, 'the rooms are on the other side of the house, that they look over the fields and have windows.'

I was still intrigued. 'Would you know how much it costs?'

'Thirty thousand francs,' replied the *aubergiste* and made a face implying it wasn't worth it.

'Thirty thousand francs!?' we all exclaimed, absolutely stunned.

'Yes,' the aubergiste confirmed. 'I ham knowing the family. They hare loco.'

In disbelief, Pringle pointed his finger to write into the air while voicing, 'Three, zero, comma, zero, zero, zero. Is that correct?' To which the *aubergiste* nodded so strongly, I thought his head would fall off.

At that time the currency exchange fluctuated between FF10.50 and FF11.00 to the pound. Even figuring at a pessimistic rate of ten to one, the house would only cost £3,000! I owned a second-hand car I'd bought four years earlier for £5,000 and that didn't have a toilet, either. It was a Ford.

Suddenly we were all very excited. 'Do you know what this means?' I asked them. 'Who's got their Visa cards on them? Between the four of us we could go to a hole in the wall and extract the cash to pay for it now!'

I hurried off the terrace and ran down the hill to make a closer inspection. The men followed. We rushed around the exterior and discovered the house had been constructed in granite stone and dug into the hillside. The southern face had ample windows and reached a height of four floors. Including the barns on either side, it was immense, not at all the little hovel it first presented to me. There was a nasty crack on the western wall leading from a massive oak lintel above the wide stable door all the way towards the apex of the roof.

'Is that serious?' I asked Sid.

'This building will have been around for over a century. I reckon the stone walls are about a metre thick.' He added knowingly, 'That doesn't look like recent subsidence. It could be filled in with a bit of cement. No problem.'

Jeremy and Pringle joined us. 'It's a bit glorious!' enthused Pringle. 'Look at that view! I wouldn't mind waking up to that.' The fields at the back of the house descended to the stream whose comforting gurglings we could now hear more clearly. Just beyond rose a hill covered with dark pines, interspersed with the brighter hues of deciduous trees. It was like a painter's palette of every green you could imagine.

Even Jeremy no longer remained aloof. 'I'd have to speak to Jilly-poo first… before making any commitments. But I think she'd enjoy spending some time here.' Pringle agreed. 'I'd have to speak to Annie. She's the commandant in such affairs.'

I turned to Sid. He was the only one of us who was unattached. 'I've got no money at all, but I could make this house habitable. You pay for the materials and whatever equipment I would need and I'd do the place up. Pay a little extra for my food and wine and I'd consider it a working holiday.'

'You could do all of this? Like a proper builder? Electrics? Plumbing? What about the roof?' Jeremy interrogated.

'Won't have been the first house. How else do you think I survive when I'm not acting?' he confessed.

'How's your French?' I asked.

'Buy me a dictionary.'

'Oh! Right!' said Pringle, never one to miss a cue. 'The price is bloody going up already!'

The *aubergiste* was hovering. By then we had discovered his name was Jean-Pierre. I was surprised that it was French. I'd expected him to be called something like 'Moredork' considering his very extraterrestrial accent.

'I don't suppose you'd have a key so we could have a look at the inside?' I asked him.

He didn't, of course, so we made arrangements that he would contact the owners after which I would phone and make a date to view the interior. It was explained to us that we would be dealing with a family of cousins. These individuals were the nearest blood relatives to the last occupant of the house. Due to the absence of a will, they all shared as its inheritors. The reason the house was on the market was that they had agreed to its sale and to place their required signatures to the necessary documents. The many skeletal ruins which sadly mar the French landscape are often due to members of feuding families who withdraw their signatures, preferring to see their ancestral home fall into a heap of rubble than for a hated relative to benefit from its eventual sale.

We forgot to finish our game of *boules*, leaving Jean-Pierre to gather up our steel balls scattered across the terrace, said our *au revoirs* and hurried back up to La Chaise-Dieu, all the way in animated conversation about our happy prospects of becoming property owners in *La Belle France*. We weren't only colleagues but also great friends. We knew each other's spouses and often socialised in London. It was not so impossible to contemplate sharing a house as well as some holidays together.

I was too excited and preoccupied to really appreciate the cultural wealth of the abbey's interior and hardly glanced at the beautiful and intricately woven sixteenth-century Flemish tapestries adorning its walls, depicting stories from the Bible. Passing by the faded fifteenth-century fresco of the famous *Danse Macabre*, I only noted they were very interesting squiggles, especially the skeletons.

As I approached him, Jeremy was gazing in utter admiration towards the gallery above at the huge medieval organ, its pipes reaching high into the vaulted ceiling. I heard him moan with longing, 'I'd love to get my hands on that.' But for the lack of a few million pounds, what a perfect present it would have made for him, albeit I doubted Jilly, his wife, could have ever organised their thatched cottage in Essex to house it. Although, flashing forward to the future, after much pleading with the monks who were the guardians of the abbey, we were able to offer him, as a birthday gift, permission for an afternoon to hammer away at its keys and pull out all of its stops while stomping to his heart's content on the pedals. The abbey literally trembled with delight at the sound of his playing.

Before I exited, after that first visit, I lit a candle in a red jar by a side altar and said a little prayer for my mother, the 'dragon lady', in gratitude for the week of conciliation and affection I had recently spent with her in Budapest. And then I lit another for the little house I had just seen and fallen madly in love with.

On the return route to Le Puy, I noticed a tangible cooling from my fellow participants towards the previous enthusiasm we had all shared when discovering the little treasure of Bonneval. Spouses loomed threateningly. They would have to come out and inspect the property. That would take time and money. Sid would hate to commit himself to undertake the vast amount of renovations needed. It would take months and he was waiting to hear about another acting job. They were making perfectly plausible excuses. I felt a cold shroud of reality descend and envelop our spontaneous dream.

The nearer we approached Le Puy the more silent we became. Only my thoughts screamed. *Three thousand pounds!!* Bill and I could afford that! We could find extra money to pay local builders. We're not talking London prices. Look around at all the sawmills. Wood must be cheap. There was a builder's yard five kilometres outside La Chaise-Dieu. At least builders wouldn't have to transport their materials from a hundred kilometres away. That must be a saving. Until the house was habitable we could live in the *auberge* just above. He's got a telephone if our agents needed to contact us. She's a great cook. We'll have some memorable meals. He could help us with the more difficult translations… no, maybe not. I'll just have to learn the language.

All the way back as the sun was lowering in the west, spilling dark pools of shadows across the road, my mind was buzzing with the possibilities.

Now I only had Bill to convince.

Chapter Two

'THIS IS THE ARSEHOLE OF FRANCE! Are you mad?!'

I could see convincing Bill was not going to be easy.

The conversation started pleasantly enough. Bill arrived back at the hotel at about 7:30, hot and sweaty after the shoot and production meeting that followed. He made his usual detour to the bar to order a scotch. He normally took it to the room where he would shower and change before the evening meal. I was already gracing a bar stool when he entered. We'd only been separated for half a day but it always struck me on seeing him anew that, if I'd placed on his head a blonde, shoulder-length wig to cover his dark hair, plucked out some of the bushiness of his perfectly arched eyebrows, added some mascara to thicken the already ample eyelashes which shielded his olive-green eyes, darkened the mole on his left cheek and painted his lips a sumptuous red, he'd look exactly like Marilyn Monroe.

'Hello, darling,' I said.

'Hello, darling,' he answered.

'Did you have a good day?' I asked him.

'Yes.' He ordered his scotch which arrived immediately. 'We finished all the shots. Bloody struggle, though, in this heat.'

'Yes, poor baby, it's been extremely hot.'

'Did you go to La Chaise-Dieu?'

'Yes. It was a very interesting outing.'

'Did you go anywhere else?'

'Yes. I found the time to do some shopping.'

'Really? Did you buy anything?'

'I think I bought a house.'

'What?!!' Quick as a flash, his arm stretched out to the bartender, holding what had suddenly become an empty glass. Perhaps the bartender had understood what I had said because he now refilled it with a much more generous portion from the bottle.

The conversation was going to deteriorate into a fracas and in order not to embarrass any witnesses we decided to retire to our adjoining rooms where I continued my pleadings that at least he should view the house before categorically dismissing it. I excitedly described the circumstances of its discovery, the setting, the scenery, the little stream at the bottom of the hill; the enthusiasm of my three companions, his very dear friends; even the weird *aubergiste* and the marvellous food Anna Magnani had served. He was so anxious to escape my enthusings, I had to remind him to take his clothes off as he hurried into the shower.

While the water was running, I quickly sped off to the bar for another top-up in his glass in the hope of the mellower mood this usually produced. I was back in the room when he reappeared, wet but a little more refreshed, and handed him the drink. As he took a sip I helped to pat him dry with his towel, taking extra special care with the 'dangly bits'. Whether it was the attention he was receiving, the scotch or the effects of the cleansing shower, he began in a more reasonable tone: 'If…' he said, looking down at me, 'and that's an enormous *if*, I go out to the house and like it, then we buy it on our own. I don't like the idea of committee decisions.'

Well, he wouldn't, would he? That's why he's a director and I'm an actress.

'I don't think that will be a problem.' I changed tack. 'I have a feeling the boys were only humouring me, anyway. I'm sure they were suffering from very cold feet on the way home. Let's just go, have a wonderful lunch and look at the house. If you like it, we'll buy it and if you don't, we won't but at least we'll have spent a very pleasant afternoon.' And if you don't like it, I thought, I will *hate* you for the rest of my life.

Bill usually dined with various members of the cast during which the following day's shots would be discussed over a civilised meal accompanied with copious amounts of red wine. Our gathering place was the bar, and as we entered Jeremy and Sid were already waiting for us. They had both taken it for granted that Bill would have been informed.

'I've spoken to Jilly,' Jeremy began. 'She sends her love. But I'm afraid the house is a no-no. She thinks we should spend any spare money doing up the kitchen back home.' While speaking Jeremy was staring into his first scotch of the evening. He took a deep gulp and then muttered something about priorities. I was surprised to feel that he was disappointed after all but understood entirely. They had only just moved to a cottage in the country and it, too, was in dire need of renovations.

Sid had had a conversation with his agent and was even more optimistic about the job he was hoping for; and then Bryan arrived. 'I've just got off the phone with Annie,' he said. 'Not that we can afford it, but if you're short of cash, she's willing to put up a thousand. We could become very minor partners in this enterprise. At least it would pay for a toilet.'

Bill thanked him and then explained that if he ever even considered buying the house it could not be as a joint venture. We would have to do it on our own but, of course, everyone present would be most welcome to spend holidays there. I have to say, Bryan looked relieved which made me appreciate his offer even more.

The following Sunday was to be the unit's rest day. I phoned Jean-Pierre to reserve for lunch and for him to organise whatever was necessary for us to be able to visit the house. He told me that he had already contacted most of the relatives concerned but that he had given us false information as to the price. The family were willing to part with the house for FF40,000. Instant 33% inflation but it still cost less than my car. I decided, for the time being, to keep this information from Bill.

Glyn Grain who was playing my handsome, gallant French lover in the series was being visited by his real lover, the alluring actress Sara Kestelman. For the duration of her stay, they had rented a car and out of curiosity offered to drive us to Bonneval. She was an excellent photographer, in possession of a rather impressive-looking camera and searching for interesting subjects to snap. He would be delighted to while away an afternoon, eating a meal on a terrace in glorious sunshine. Unfortunately, that Sunday was the first dismally grey day we had experienced in Le Puy. The stunning scenery along the way that I had so raved about was blurred behind a wet veil of mist. But Bill didn't seem to mind. His eyes were happily lowered to a map from which he expertly guided us, avoiding La Chaise-Dieu to approach Bonneval by another route.

We descended from Sembadel-Gare and wound our way through different forests. With the lack of any sunlight these sombre, dripping woods seemed more foreboding. Whereas during the previous journey thoughts of children's fairy tales came to mind and were noisily commented upon, on this occasion a pregnant, diplomatic silence prevailed, almost reproachful, as if I were leading my fellow passengers to their doom. These were more like the forests of Transylvania, reminding one of other tales: werewolves and vampires. I felt forced to explain, 'You have to imagine all this with a clear blue sky like we had the other day and daggers of sunbeams piercing through the trees, lighting up the forest floor. It's magical.'

Bill continued to stare silently out of the window.

'I'm sure it would be,' Sara said kindly.

'So, how much further to Dracula's castle?' asked Glyn from the driver's seat, catching my eyes in the rear-view mirror. But he did wink.

'You're being very quiet, Mr Hays,' I said to Bill anxiously. He had been concentrating far too long for my liking on the dense, dark accumulation of trees.

'It's a pity I hadn't been shown these forests before. They would have made the perfect location for the scenes when the *Maquis* were hiding from the Germans,' he mused. I needn't have worried. He was more preoccupied with the filming than the object of this excursion: ever professional, studying the setting as through a viewfinder.

We finally exited the tunnel of branches and I felt vindicated when the undulating landscape of the valley opened before us. Although painted today with a duller brush it was still beautiful. The green meadows glistened in the drizzle and distant copses appeared silhouetted, criss-crossing the brume. Pockets of mist hovered over the orange roofs of the small settlements nestling within the valley's dips and swayed gently around others perching on its heights. Little branch-roads led from ours with a signpost identifying the settlements with poetically evocative names: L'ABRY, LE CHALAT, TARTARY. Why does everything sound more romantic when pronounced in French?

It took a few more bends in the road to arrive at the little bridge I had spotted from the terrace. Bonneval appeared above us, clinging to the hillside.

'We're here!' I shouted from the back. 'That's the church, and next to it the Auberge; and just under its terrace,' I pointed to the lowest collection of connected buildings which were doing most of the clinging, 'that's the house!'

Glyn slowed the car; and, from this vantage point, the 'hovel' looked very imposing, dominating the fields which swept away down to the rushing stream.

'It's vast,' said Sara, obviously impressed.

'But for the missing towers it could be a chateau,' Glyn added.

I was waiting for a positive reaction from Bill.

'I thought I was coming to see a *little* ruin,' was what he said, stressing the 'little'. Meaning, of course, it was a huge ruin.

'The house, itself, is really quite small,' I said reassuringly. 'It's tucked in between those two great big barns. We'll only have to renovate what we're going to use.' I have to admit, though, I was already imagining the advantages of all that available space: pool table, ping-pong, horse boxes, indoor swimming pool... He must have been reading my thoughts because he turned to me and said, 'Exactly!'

We arrived at our destination and Glyn parked the rented car against one of those strange, small, French vans that look as if they are made of recycled corrugated iron (usually painted mustard yellow) and propped up by four splayed, skinny wheels. The only concession to modernity was the addition of that fourth wheel.

As the terrace was too damp, we made our way through the entrance of the restaurant and were welcomed there. Jean-Pierre introduced us to two men who were already waiting, presumably the owners of the vehicle outside. The elder was small, dark and wizened, wearing the conventional French blue overalls. He proffered a bony hand in greeting. The other was younger, fairer and in identical garb. The hand he extended was digitally challenged with only three remaining fingers. We stood there, grinning at each other. It was obvious they spoke no English and when they opened their mouths to speak their own language, it could have been Greek. This was my first experience of hearing true *Auvergnat*. It didn't matter to Bill. He had no illusions: he neither spoke nor understood French. But I had thought I'd been getting along reasonably well. This was a serious blow to my confidence.

'The 'ouse, she 'as been hopened,' pronounced Jean-Pierre.

It was eleven o'clock which would give us a good hour to explore the depths of the property.

'Good. Shall we go, then?' Bill said quite eagerly. Was he anxious to get this tour over with because he was looking forward to lunch, I wondered, and the red wine it would accompany?

Jean-Pierre turned to the elder of the two men who had been studying the four of us as if we were wax effigies at Madame Tussaud's. I had the feeling that we were the very first foreigners he had ever encountered. Jean-Pierre translated to him in French that we were prepared to visit the house.

The old man smiled, revealing numerous dark gaps where teeth should have been. Ah, dentist, I thought; if we bought the house, we must make regular visits to our dentist before holidaying here. He made a gesture and said something to Jean-Pierre, the only words of which I thought I caught were '*petit canon*'. Why was he talking about light artillery? Jean-Pierre laughed merrily while agreeing. Were we here to be shot? The infamous '*auberge rouge*' was not that very far away on a lonely cross-road south of Le Puy, where, we had been told with relish by members of the French crew, a hundred-odd years ago travellers were murdered and then served up in a tasty *ragoût*. The distinct lack of tourism hereabouts was beginning to make me suspicious. But while I was thinking these faint-hearted thoughts, Jean-Pierre had placed six small bevelled glasses on the bar and was filling them with dark red wine. Our would-be guides through the house lifted theirs, saluted us with a '*Santé!*' and downed them in one go. We lifted ours, said, 'Cheers!' and took a tentative sip.

'Cheese?' asked Jean-Pierre; but, before we could correct him, he held forth to the Frenchmen about the unusual English custom of wishing cheese to their drinking companions. The word *fromage* figured largely in his banter.

He tipped the remains of the bottle into what we learned were their *canons* and without a moment's hesitation, once again saluting us but not daring to pronounce it in English, they politely said, '*Fromage!*' before emptying the contents down past their bobbing Adam's apples.

It would take too long to explain and we were all very impatient to tour the house. If, in the future, other English people would be toasted by the locals with '*Fromage!*', so be it.

At 11:30 the half-hour bell must have rung in their stomachs heralding the midday meal. Their watches were examined and suddenly they, too, were eager to lead us to the property.

Before walking down the little hill, I showed Bill the exact spot on the terrace from where I discovered the house. I was trying to interest him in the scenery, excusing the miserable weather, explaining the effects in glorious sunshine, pitying the dullness of the little stream which had glinted with crystals when I'd last seen it, extolling its situation, anything… anything to distract his attention from the horrible condition of the roof. Throughout my continuous babbling he remained silent, eyes fixed on the façade of the house, and then left me to join the others who were waiting at the entrance. I followed him meekly.

The shutters had been unfastened and were hugging the walls, exposing the windows on both sides of the now opened door. We entered into a dungeon-like darkness, a narrow gloomy hallway from which three rooms led off. Remembering that this was the original *auberge*, we were not surprised to find a kitchen to the left, its walls smeared black, bearing the evidence of decades of smoke. An ancient wood-burning stove, its oven door hanging off, was placed in the alcove of what was the huge, wide open fireplace. The pipe that led from its back, instead of reaching up into the chimney, mysteriously angled its way to disappear through a round hole cut into a wooden dividing wall. The one concession towards hygiene was a shallow, stained, white sink tucked into a corner near to the stove. Dark greasy pots and dented aluminium ones littered the floor and window sill. A three-legged table, having lost its battle to balance, lay tipped on its side in the middle of the room.

A space not larger than a comfortably sized cupboard which had served as the *tabac* and grocery store was to the right. Directly in front of us, we were told, was the *café*. It had obviously been turned into a dormitory at some time as there were rusting single metal beds placed haphazardly around the room with fungus-marked and rodent-chewed mattresses falling off them. The floor was carpeted with eight years of the rodents' droppings. They had found the perfect 'squat'. The mystery of the stovepipe was revealed as it entered from the kitchen, bending its way diagonally and upwards to return through another hole into the actual chimney breast. Central heating, we presumed. Over our heads was a false slatted ceiling, painted khaki, which bulged ominously towards us. The boards beneath our feet groaned, exhausted from the effort of carrying our weight. Sara pointed her camera, busily snapping as if she were recording a crime scene.

We were led through a door in the right-hand corner of the *café* and took two steps down into a room built within what we rightly presumed was the adjoining barn. A window had been knocked out of the exterior stone wall for light. Tongue-and-groove covered the walls; and here, the slatted wooden ceiling gleamed with brilliant varnish. A psychedelic floral-patterned carpet was stretched into the four corners. It may not have been vacuumed for years but the colours were still bravely fighting through the accumulated layers of debris. Except for a picture of Christ hanging on a wall, the room was bare; but even considering the cobwebs which had replaced the curtains, it was the most civilised space we had seen so far.

We were able to understand enough from our guides who told us proudly that this was the bedroom of Rosalie, built into the barn by her son with help from the two standing before us. They continued a lively discourse, no doubt describing her in detail but incomprehensible to us. We nodded appreciatively, though, to the few words we did recognise, such as: *mère... enfants... tante... patronne... aimer.* Our expressions changed to a more sympathetic one when we heard the words, *âgée... malade... morte.* Having completed the account of the life and death of Rosalie, they beckoned us through another more narrow door which led from the bedroom into the vast volume of the barn.

All the openings to the outside were firmly closed and the only light which entered came from a small triangle pierced through the wall near to the apex of the roof. In this dim light we discerned the magnificent shapes of a bygone age and carefully squeezed through and between a huge hay-wagon with wooden ribs to contain its load, a smaller cart with the spokes of its large wheels painted blue, a pot-bellied butter churn, little wooden chairs with ragged straw seats piled precariously one on the other, chaffing machines with iron turning-handles, scythes, ploughs, wooden and metal hay-forks and, amongst all this jumble, an old church pulpit, seriously infested with woodworm.

The breeze-block box which had been built into the barn and contained the bedroom had yet another door. When it was opened I was relieved to see, within this narrow cubicle, a toilet. At least the ageing Rosalie had somewhere nearby when nature called, but I hated to think of the obstacle course she had to traverse to get there on a cold, dark winter's night.

They removed a ladder which had been leaning against the great barn door and placed it against a wall. The ladder reached a rectangular opening about 1m by 1.5m. We were invited to scale it but warned to avoid placing our feet on certain rotten rungs. The younger Frenchman climbed first with Bill following. I waited until they both disappeared safely into the hole before having the courage to do the same. The older man beckoned to Glyn and Sara; they demurred the invitation, considering that the sudden weight of so many people in such a short space of time may have finished the ladder off (after all, we were all going to have to use it on our way back down), but the old man decided to risk it.

Walking through so many doors had confused my geography of the house. It wasn't until I'd crawled through the opening, straightened up and saw the three windows at floor level, the central one being slightly larger and hanging out of which I had seen the remnants of the bale of straw, that I realised we were directly above the kitchen/*tabac*/*café*. This was the attic under the gabled roof, but I could have been excused for thinking it was the higher level of the further barn. The floor was deep with straw and chicken feathers camouflaging the precarious floorboards. I remembered the ominously bulging ceilings below and trod very carefully.

Bill remarked on this fusty-smelling cover underfoot: 'Insulation for the downstairs,' he said. Of course, none of this evidence of a former way of life came as a surprise to him. While searching all over France for locations for the filming, he had come across far worse sights: farmhouses with earth floors where inhabitants lived side by side with their animals, profiting from their body heat, cooking from a cauldron suspended from inside the chimney over an open fire, an outdoor wooden shack containing a bench with a round hole cut into it and a bucket directly underneath serving as a modern convenience. (The primitive version was just the bucket placed in a convenient corner.) And in almost every muddy yard, there would be a painfully thin, ferocious dog chained to a wall, its narrow metal collar embedded into the skin of its scrawny neck. These were some of the descriptions he related to me, having returned to London, while settled on a comfortable sofa with the cat wrapped across his lap and the music of Bizet's *L'Arlésienne Suite* floating through our beautiful, centrally heated, modernised flat.

Therefore, when we thought we understood that the wooden structure built into one corner of the attic housed the *cochon,* the pig, we were not overly shocked; disturbed at the miserable short life it would have led being fattened in a space it could hardly have turned around in, but not shocked. I imagined the daily swills being carried up the rickety ladder, the mucking out of what was expelled from the other end lest it seep through the ceiling of the *café*, and marvelled at the commitment to eating pork all these duties would have involved.

Strange wooden cages with wire-mesh fronts, some containing shelves, their roofs spotted with bird droppings, were littered around in the straw. A few were hanging from rusty hooks pierced into the great trusses holding up the roof. Being so near, it became obvious that everything of timber would have to be replaced. Insects, here, had had a veritable feast.

Thinking they may have kept rabbits I pointed to the cages and asked, '*Pour les lapins?*'

'*Non, non,*' they replied. '*Pour le fromage et du lard!*' They opened the door to the wooden hut and gestured, '*Le cochon,*' and then towards the cages, '*Fromage et lard. Pour secher.*'

I was comforted to see when they opened the door that at least the pig had a window, albeit small but with a striking view on to a verdant hillside. I hoped the window had served as a pleasure and not a torture.

So, I understood, while the pig was kept in the hut, the cages were for drying cheese and bacon, and shared this information with Bill.

'No wonder French cheese is so pungent,' he remarked.

Picking one of the smaller cages up from the straw, the older man began to explain something excitedly. As his thick Auvergnat accent was difficult to understand, I translated as best I could.

'Cheese… drying… crust… grow craftsman,' was all I comprehended.

'Craftsman?' Bill asked doubtfully.

'Well, he said the word *artisan,* you know, like in English, artisan,' I interpreted, struggling.

Having heard us, the younger of the two interjected, '*Non, non, artisons!*' putting a strong emphasis on the 'o'.

'Oh, *artison* with an "o". What's that?' I asked in French and continued translating his reply. 'Little beasts… little… microscopic…'

'Beasts?' Bill asked. 'Are you sure you're getting this right?'

'The French use *bête* for any animal, large or small,' I explained and then added much more quietly, 'It can also mean stupid.' I was getting very confused.

'*Quelles bêtes?*' I asked in desperation.

'*Tout, tout petit.*' They looked at me, willing me to understand; and one of them held up his hand, squeezing his thumb and forefinger together, and tried to squint through the unavailable space.

'A tiny something,' I said to Bill and then suddenly thought of yoghurt. 'You mean, like bacteria?' again I asked in French using the word, *bactéries.*

The word is pronounced very similarly in both languages and so Bill, wrongly concluding, turned to me amazed and said, 'They grow listeria on purpose in their cheese?'

Now they understood because, again, 'listeria' has virtually the same pronunciation in their language.

'*Non, non, non!*' they said emphatically. '*Pas listeria!*' We had insulted them. At that point, the older man made an open fist and curled his fingers towards his palm, wriggling them about. The other tapped his tummy and beamed a broad smile as if to say it was delicious; and then I understood and shared with Bill: '… Millions… and… millions… like… dust… microscopic … *spiders?!*'

I remembered then, one of the cheeses we had tasted the other day was covered with dark brown powder. Anna Magnani had pointed to it and said, '*Artisons, tres bon, speciale.*' We had assumed she meant handcrafted, not factory made. It was the one we ate the most of.

In a state of shock, we carefully descended the ladder where Glyn and Sara were still waiting.

'Are you all right, Catherine?' they asked, concerned. 'You look a bit green.'

'You won't believe what used to go on up there,' I replied, weakly.

'Never order cheese unless you're carrying a magnifying glass,' warned Bill.

We returned via the doors we had come through and were led back into the *tabac*. After some strained heaving, the younger and stronger of the two managed to lift a trapdoor from the floor. We were beckoned to follow him down another dilapidated ladder. If the upstairs was consumed by a dungeon-like darkness, the area into which we were stepping was more of a tomb. Being deprived of our sense of sight, the four of us huddled together, afraid to move over the uneven floor we felt beneath our feet. A strong smell of coal permeated the damp air, mingled with stale, acrid smoke. Slivers of light peeked through the cracks from a large wooden door, telling us we were not entirely underground.

The vague shape of our leader moved slowly away. He opened a door and suddenly light from a far window dispersed the gloom. We realised we were standing in a forge. A pile of coal was heaped into the corner behind the ladder against the massive granite rock face uncovered from the hillside and forming the building's northern foundation. An enormous pair of bellows with a large leather bag and two wooden handles was suspended from the low ceiling, its metal nozzle aimed at a waist-high stone fireplace. All manner of tools hung from hooks or nails hammered into a long breeze-block wall. Another door opened next to the first and we established these were the bedrooms that accommodated the paying guests. Both shared the separating breeze-block wall of the forge, and Sid had been correct: they had windows and they overlooked the fields. Being caught short at night, aiming 'little jobs' out of the window would not have been a problem… for a man, and rather beneficial if the compost heap were situated within aiming distance below. I sincerely hoped there had been a receptacle of some kind to facilitate the needs of ladies. Guests would not have been cold in such close proximity to the working forge but, from the state of the darkened walls, the word 'kippered' did come to mind.

While Bill and Glyn stood gazing in awe at the magnificent ancient bellows, Sara and I admired the only piece of furniture we had seen so far that had not been destroyed by insects, damp or just carelessness. One of the bedrooms contained an antique, solid, knotted pine wardrobe. Age and perhaps the smoke had turned its colour to a warm amber, and the simplicity of the naive carvings in its panelled doors made me desire it desperately. It had probably been an heirloom or part of a dowry transferred from one generation to the next. We wondered why this proudly rustic closet, which said so much about its owners, had been allowed to stay neglected here.

Bending low in order not to knock our heads on a wooden lintel, we hopped down through a small door from the forge into a stable. It may not have sheltered an animal for years but the associated smells lingered on. Running the length of the northern stone wall was a wooden manger from whose ragged edges cobwebs drooped like muslin. Here, too, the remains of defunct farming paraphernalia lay abandoned, gathering dust on the dirt floor. The ceiling, though, looked reassuringly solid. It consisted of massive round timbers which carried the thick boarding that took the weight of the heavy wagons we had seen on the upper floor.

Upon exiting the stables, Bill turned round and looked up at the western façade. The crack separating the stones and leading up to the barn above towards the roof began to look very intimidating to me, but he made no comment.

We were shown the *cave* directly under the forge where shiny rivulets of water ran down within the crevices of the excavated boulders from the hill, forming deep dark pools in which tadpoles could have spawned. Next to the *cave* and attached at a slight angle to the house was the eastern barn. The wide doorway to the lower part gaped open to the elements. We peered into the darkness. It was a vast area, which we were not prepared to enter as the floor was literally knee-deep in dung and we didn't want to risk our shoes sinking into its still-moist depths. Except for this accumulation, the area was completely empty. When the doors had existed, it would have sheltered the cattle overnight to be freed the following morning for grazing on the surrounding fields. The evidence of previous 'muckings out' was heaped high against the corner of the building with squadrons of interested flies buzzing its summit.

With their stomachs audibly grumbling, our guides hurried us around the circumference of the building to visit the upper floor of the eastern barn. Along the way, a stretch of wooded land separating the structure from the road above was pointed out to us which, we were told, belonged to the property. It was through those trees that I had glimpsed the colourful umbrellas that had brought us to the terrace of the restaurant the other day. In all, we would inherit 2,500 square metres of land.

The barn above the cows' dormitory was comparatively bright, the reason being the amount of daylight shining through the roof. It augured badly for the state of the timbers holding it up. Bales of musty hay and straw were stacked against the walls, their residue carpeting the spongy floorboards. More mysterious farming equipment remained stored here. Our curiosity was especially aroused by a cart which consisted of a 1.5m by 0.75m plank attached at its midsection to two wheels on either side. It stood not much higher than a sleigh and had a single shaft jutting from the front into which an iron rod had been bored with two metal rings hanging from its ends. Logically, we presumed, it was to transport the bales of hay to the lower barns.

'But there's a hay door,' said Bill. It was true. In the southern wall a boarded-up opening was plainly visible. 'They'd have dropped the bales through that.'

There were other objects within this barn far more worthy of our observations, but for some strange reason we became fascinated with this low-slung, sled-like vehicle lifted off the ground by iron wheels sprouting pimples of rust. The Auvergnats noticed our curiosity and so Sara asked, '*Qu'est-ce que c'est?*' A great deal of information came our way, none of which we understood, except for a word we took to be *coucher* which was repeated several times. Sara and I agreed: *coucher* means to lie down.

'It was for lying down,' I enlightened our Englishmen.

'What? For a midget? And why on a wagon? Didn't they deserve beds?' asked Bill with a hint of sarcasm.

Then Sara, drawing from the recesses of her mind the remnants of her French education, said, '*Coucher* can also mean to give birth.'

'Ah! A birthing board? On two wheels? That can rock up and down like a see-saw. Interesting,' said Glyn sardonically; and then I remarked on some dark stains which had seeped into the wood.

'That could be blood,' I said, pointing to them.

'Or spilt red wine,' deduced Glyn.

'As a coffee table, it's a bit low,' reasoned Bill, 'even for a midget.'

We were now in the midst of a puzzle that needed lateral thinking or a rural ancestry to resolve. Our Frenchmen lifted the shaft and, pointing to the rings, began to explain at speed again something about, *cochon... attacher... la tête... coucher... jambs.*

'Darling, they've mentioned pigs again,' I whispered to Bill. 'I think they attach its head to those rings...' He didn't allow me to finish.

'They train pigs to pull carts?!' he asked incredulously.

'What? For a circus act?' added Glyn.

We looked at the French with a mixture of astonishment and respect, to which they shrugged their shoulders and said, simply, '*Ici, c'était fait comme ca.*' (That's how it was done here.) The gruesome truth we later learned about the cart would test our English sensitivities.

The tour was over. We had inspected all there was to see and my heart was heavy with disappointment. Including the two levels of the vast barns and from the *cave* to the attic of the house itself, our eyes had examined at least 1,500 cubic metres of volume. I imagined packing crates 1m by 1m by 1m placed side to side along a straight road 1.5 kilometres long. That's almost a mile, and just about everything contained in that space had to be renewed or repaired.

No wonder the house had remained on the market. No one could be so daft as to take on that kind of financial responsibility. The house could be renovated, but the barns on both sides would crumble with time. That's not how I imagined my 'chateau'. I had desperately hoped there would have been more of the interior to salvage, and with the absence of any encouraging remarks from Bill I had to remain realistic.

Well, at least we'd had a guided tour through the Middle Ages and we could look forward to a good meal. Glyn and Sara walked up the hill to the restaurant a little ahead of us. Her camera, replaced in its case, was hanging from her shoulder and they were conversing quietly. Bill held my hand as we followed a little slower in the company of the two Frenchmen. From their expressions I assumed they expected a comment relating to our intentions.

What could we say? My French was not fluent enough to express, 'Thank you for taking the trouble and time to show us around but our finances could never afford the complete rehabilitation the property would require.' So, I just smiled politely and waited for Jean-Pierre to convey the bad news.

Halfway up the hill, Bill stopped and took one more look back at the house. I couldn't believe how deceivingly insignificant it appeared from this side. The phrase 'biting off more than you could chew' came to mind.

Then Bill squeezed my hand, faced me with his cheeky smile and said calmly, 'We'll buy it. I want it.' Just like that.

'What!?' I had prepared myself to acquiesce to reason and depended on his superior experience in such matters.

'Why?' I couldn't believe it. 'When? You haven't said anything throughout. When did you decide?'

'When I first saw it from the terrace. It was obvious.' Ooooh! How my husband could speak in riddles.

'What was obvious?' I asked, pressing him.

'You of all people should know. Look at what's on the façade,' he said to me, amazed I hadn't noticed.

I had seen it in sunshine and, today, in the rain. I had acknowledged the state of the roof, the walls, the timbers. I had considered the practicalities of water, electricity, and the neighbouring *auberge* with its telephone. I had fallen in love with the view, the position and its promise of *Gemütlichkeit*. But I had not paid attention to a most important detail.

It was staring at me, begging to be noticed. Above the door and its adjacent windows, across the entire frontage, the fading *art deco* letters of VALENTIN AUBERGISTE had been painted. The fact that an artisan would have been employed more than half a century ago, would have travelled down through the forests on a dirt path and then emblazoned this publicity on the wall of a house in the back of beyond, was remarkable. But even more noteworthy was the name itself.

'Valentine' was an heirloom in Bill's maternal family, proudly borne by a great grandfather, grandfather, uncle and Bill's younger brother. Somehow his mother had neglected to bestow this name on her firstborn son and thus he was called just 'William' which was shortened to 'Bill'.

After leaving art college, his intention was to do theatre design. He once confided to me that, had he become successful as a designer, he would have adopted the name 'William Valentine Hays' because of its more decorative appearance on a theatrical poster. At that time, I teased him mercilessly for desiring such an ostentatious name.

Armed with this confession, during a play we did together for the BBC, I secretly cajoled the graphics department who were responsible for the titles to furnish a card for the 'directed by' credit with the full name of 'William Valentine Hays' to replace his more humble one. They gleefully complied.

Once the taping of a television play has been completed, the director, unlike the actors, cannot leave the studio immediately. One camera will continue to record the credits for the end of the programme with all the participants' names and billings, usually ending second before last with PRODUCED BY and finally DIRECTED BY. The procedure is finely timed and, more often than not, accompanied with the theme music of the play, to correspond to the exact second for which the production slot will have been designated. The director watches the monitor in the gallery and assures the process runs smoothly. I confided the joke to some of my fellow actors and we eagerly huddled, still in our Victorian costumes, around the last remaining monitor to be working on the studio floor. But when his credit, DIRECTED BY, appeared it was followed with the usual BILL HAYS. We felt cheated of a well-deserved giggle.

A little later that night, the producer held a small farewell and thank-you party in his office to which we were all invited. My co-conspirator from graphics handed me the card, explaining that the recording had gone into overtime. As every extra minute in a studio cost thousands of pounds, he couldn't risk his future employment on such an expensive joke. We commiserated together and then showed the plaque to Bill informing him of our unaccomplished scheme. He reacted with delighted surprise and peals of laughter but then admonished my accomplice for his lack of nerve, affirming he would have paid whatever it cost to have seen just once his alter ego's name flaunted on a television screen. We kept the plaque and discreetly displayed it above the door of the 'snoring' room.

How can you deny something to someone who says, 'I have to have it,' when they can honestly add, '… it has my name all over it'?

'Are you really, really sure?' I asked Bill, secretly thrilled, loving the adrenalin rush but needing to know he was totally convinced.

'Is the Pope a Catholic?' he replied.

'We can celebrate, then?' I asked, hoping Jean-Pierre had a bottle of champagne in stock.

'Yes. Twice,' said Bill. 'Now and...' He whispered in my ear, 'at about eleven o'clock tonight.'

It was the perfect time to tell him the price had gone up by a thousand pounds.

Chapter Three

T HE SMOOTH, ROUNDED SHAPES OF WET COBBLESTONES reflect the light of the lanterns which hang from arched brackets attached to the façades of medieval townhouses. Their irregular forms cling to each other, wall to wall, and line both sides of the narrow rue Meymard.

Suddenly two long shadows are cast on to the pavement, creeping from around the bend at the very top of the lane. The shadows intermingle as the dark figures move furtively, making their way to the point where the street enters the Place du Martouret. Armoured cars and personnel carriers painted with German insignia crowd the square in front of the Hotel de Ville in the city of Le Puy.

An armed guard stands on the stairs at the entrance surveying the scene. He takes a cigarette from his lips and exhales. The white smoke is quickly dispersed by the falling rain.

The two dark shapes duck between the empty vehicles, approaching until they are near enough to take aim. They are both carrying single-bore hunting rifles. It will be a futile gesture, but they have revenge in their hearts.

The father and son lift the rifles to their shoulders and the solid silence is pierced by gunshots. The shocked guard is killed and crumbles to the floor. His fingers open and a tiny red glow from the cigarette rolls down to be extinguished in a puddle at the foot of the steps.

Loud German voices are heard from within, followed by the thunder of heavy boots on stone floors. The door is flung open and soldiers pour out, their repeating fire flashing in the darkness.

The son is hit and the power of the bullets throws him backwards to lie splayed on the bonnet of a personnel carrier. Silence.

On the first floor, a French window is opened and a blonde-haired officer with steely blue eyes and a chiselled face steps on to a balcony. He is holding a Luger in his right hand. His tall figure is silhouetted against the light from the room behind. Beneath him the soldiers stand like statues, staring at the dead body on the bonnet.

Slowly, the father emerges from the sheltering shadow of an armoured car. The barrel of his rifle points to the ground. No one moves as he walks haltingly towards the corpse of his son.

He drops his useless gun which clatters on to the cobblestones and, with both hands, drags his son off the bonnet and holds the limp body in his arms.

The father looks up to face the silhouette of the officer and emits an anguished howl.

'Shit!' he yells. 'Bloody bumholes! I can't remember his name.'

Bill leaps out of the scanning van where he's been glued to his TV monitors and screams, 'Cut!', whereupon the entire area echoes with the French crew's hollers of, '*Coupez! Coupez!*' as they scuttle out of their hidden positions and rush around the square. The 'corpse' comes giggling back to life and slides out of his 'father's' arms to stand upright. The poor actor who fluffed is blushing with remorse. When Bill arrives, closely followed by his PA holding the script, he is full of apologies.

'Sorry, Guv. What can I say? I blew it. It's that German name I had to learn… Couldn't remember.'

The PA prompts him from the script. 'Von Klementz,' she pronounces.

'Just think of the bells, you old bugger,' says the younger actor, 'and stick Von in front of it.'

The older man looks down at his shoes in shame. 'It's the Von I couldn't remember.'

'No matter,' Bill says. 'We'll just pick it up from when you take the body off the bonnet.' He looks up to one of the darkened windows where it seems a sniper is located and shouts, 'Camera four! We'll take it from you! Okay love?' and rushes back to disappear into the van. Everyone takes their positions and the night's recording continues.

While this drama was taking place outside, I was shrouded in a blue fug of Gauloises emissions in a little bar around the corner experiencing another drama. Bill's driver, Gerard, who also sometimes doubled as second assistant to the French crew, was with me. The *patron* had kindly allowed us the use of his telephone which he'd placed on the counter. We were both perched on bar stools. I was dressed in a charcoal-grey skirt which came discreetly below my knees, a short-sleeved white cotton blouse buttoned up to my neck with a drab brown knitted sweater to cover this ensemble. A pair of sensible laced-up shoes and ankle socks adorned my feet. The hideous little hat I would have to wear was tucked away for the very last moment. Wartime fashion, even in France, was not exactly glamorous and the wardrobe designer was committed to the 'authentic look', despite my pleadings to put me in a more appealing costume. The make-up and hair departments conspired to do likewise. I studiously avoided the mirror, which was facing me and ran the length of the entire wall, lest my confidence drained for the scene I would be shooting later during that night. Two men in their sixties, both with ravaged faces and deep furrows ploughed into their foreheads, were eyeing me. I couldn't imagine it was from lust. They turned away to face each other and continued a mumbled conversation.

Gerard held the receiver to his ear and was holding a hectic dialogue with Jean-Pierre who was acting as the contact between the family and ourselves. I had spoken to him earlier but did not trust the sounds I heard to correlate with the information he was trying to convey. To be certain, I handed the phone to Gerard in the hopes of receiving an intelligent interpretation. Very tall, broad-shouldered and Nordic-looking, Gerard belied the preconception that all Frenchmen were short and dark like Napoleon who, of course, wasn't French at all. He spoke English reasonably well, was devoted to Bill and would make the perfect ally in our endeavours to buy the house.

Scribbling some numbers on the back of my script which lay across my lap, he hung up and said to me, 'We have a problem,' and then pointing to the numbers he'd written down, continued, 'There is a woman who is also an inheritor. She has taken it upon herself to do the negotiations for the family. We are supposed to phone her. She has raised the price to 60,000 francs.'

I was astonished. France was not awash with English imports but it seemed *gazumping* had been readily adopted from across the Channel.

'We shook hands with those two men on 40,000,' I assured Gerard.

'Yes, I know. I feel ashamed. This should not happen. She thinks she is more clever than her cousins and you are English which means you are rich.' He was obviously disturbed at this turn of events.

Of course we could afford another 20,000, but the situation didn't feel correct. If we gave in to her, what was the assurance the price wouldn't go

35

up again? And how much more would we have to pay the builders? They could rightly take advantage of our naive free-spending ways.

I followed his eyes as he glanced up to the clock above the entrance. It was almost eleven p.m.

'She was expecting us to phone at eight o'clock tonight,' he said. 'Now it is too late. We will talk to her tomorrow.'

'I wouldn't dream of calling her now,' I said angrily; and then calming down, 'Anyway, I'll have to speak to Bill and I don't think he'll be most pleased. We'll let her stew for a while.'

'Stew?' he asked.

'It's an expression,' I explained. 'To stew in your own juice. To allow someone time to worry in the hopes it will soften them up.'

'But stew is a *ragoût,* no?'

'Yes,' I replied, 'but it can also be used as a verb.'

He looked at me pensively while nodding.

The two sexagenarians had their glasses refilled. Their discourse had taken on another mood. I didn't have to know the language to realise a certain amount of abuse was being interchanged. The bar was fairly crowded and I noticed I was not the only one paying them attention.

'What's happening?' I asked Gerard. 'What are they shouting at each other?'

'They must be drunk. You do not want to know those words. They are very bad,' he said, protectively.

One of the men slammed down his glass angrily. It shattered, spilling the red wine which flowed over the edges of the table, staining both of their trousers. For elderly men, they were certainly agile as they both leapt to their feet and glared at one another. I was glad they were nowhere near me. Wardrobe would not have been happy if I'd appeared for my scene with dark red blotches on my clothes. The *patron* shouted something and hurried in their direction with a cloth.

At that moment the door opened and a French 3rd assistant called me for my scene. As I left, Gerard whispered, 'It is good you go now. That will turn into a *bagarre.* I will follow with some coffee and "brown milk" for Bill.'

'Go easy on the brown milk,' I told him, aware of the euphemism they both shared for cognac. 'He's got a long night's work to get through.'

Outside in the square, I asked the 3rd, 'What does *bagarre* mean?'

He gave me a strange look. 'Why do you ask?'

'Because two men are going to have a *bagarre* in the bar,' I said.

'It means a big fight,' he answered.

It was difficult to contemplate two granddads having a brawl. Over what? A paternity suit?

While I was bumping over the cobblestones trying to master the 1940s bicycle the props department had furnished for my scene in which I must deliver a secret message, I noticed Gerard stepping into the scanning van. He was holding Bill's coffee.

I had not mentioned the further inflation to the price of the house, considering it wiser to allow him full concentration on his job. Frankly, I was not looking forward to his reaction.

Everyone is silent, waiting in their positions. I am astride the bicycle which has been behaving like a rogue supermarket trolley. Bill calls 'Action!' and in a second, he can see on his monitors the dim light of a bicycle appear, coming down a cobbled street. It wobbles precariously from side to side. The bike slides to a stop in front of a house and a woman dismounts. She corrects the position of her hat, lifts the bicycle on to the pavement and moves to the entrance. Her hand taps three times on a dark door. In a moment a muffled question is heard from within to which she gives a whispered reply. The door opens slightly to reveal the shape of a man in a lighted hallway. They have a brief conversation. She turns to look up and down the street. The coast is clear and she unwinds the grip of the handlebar, retrieving from its hollow tube a rolled piece of paper which she hands to him. The door is closed, she gets on the bicycle and wobbles away.

An English 1st assistant who had been hiding out of shot in a doorway called, 'Cut!'

'We'll have to go again,' I moaned, embarrassed. 'I'm sorry. I couldn't control this thing.' I was feeling guilty as I should have spent more time practising on the clumsy bicycle rather than making phone calls and being fascinated with would-be brawls in a bar.

The assistant was in contact with Bill via a radio phone and transmitted my message. Hearing Bill's reply, he said to me, 'It's a print. He liked it.' Then listening some more, he continued, 'He thought it was a brilliant touch… pretending to be drunk… Good undercover disguise.'

A woman drunk on a bike is not going to attract attention? But who was I to question the director? I was only too happy not to have to remount the two-wheeled beast and couldn't wait to be introduced to the horse I would be riding to deliver my messages and rally the troops at the next location. Far more dignified mode of transport, I thought.

The scene was finished. I needn't have worried how I looked as most of it was shot on the back of my head.

On my way to the wardrobe van to get out of costume, I stopped to say goodnight to Bill.

'What's this I hear about a woman who wants more money for the house?' he asked, but the tone of his question was not as forbidding as I'd expected.

'Gerard told you? I was going to wait until tomorrow,' I said.

'It was a lot funnier coming from Gerard.'

'What do you mean? I didn't find it funny. She's a bloody cow!'

'Well, according to him, when you ring her tomorrow she will agree to the original price because she will have been boiled in a stew until she is only juice.' He continued in mock sternness, 'Catherine, I don't think a Hungarian should teach the French English expressions.'

Gerard and I were back in the same bar the following night. Not having to work, I was in my own clothes. We sat on the same stools with the phone back on the counter. I looked around me and noticed that most of the faces from the previous night were also present except for the two sixty-year-olds. The clock said 8:30. We had decided to wait until nine before ringing. To fill in some time and because I was curious, I asked Gerard, 'Did those men have a fight after I left?'

'If they did,' he said, 'I did not see them. The *patron* threw them out.'

'And you don't know why they were arguing?' I was goading him for information.

'I was not paying much attention but I think I heard something about the war. One was earning more money and then they said to each other very bad words.' Part of the reason Gerard was such enjoyable company was that he loved a good gossip; but on this occasion his reticence on the topic was tangible, so I politely pressed him no further and was surprised when he continued. 'You know, this was a part of Vichy France. Many things have happened and for generations they will not be forgotten. There were people who collaborated with the Germans against their fellow Frenchmen.' Then he quickly picked up the receiver: 'We will call her now,' ending the subject.

Bill had worked the previous night into the wee hours of the morning and hadn't gone to bed until dawn. He had slept almost until noon and would be working again that night. Instead of breakfasting, we had decided to have lunch. It was Gerard's suggestion that he drive us to a place the French crew had discovered outside of Le Puy. Over lunch the three of us had discussed our tactics: what our approach to the woman would be. Bill and I were agreed that out of principle we would not pay the further 20,000.

'But if she went down to 50,000?' I asked.

Bill was adamant. 'Not another centime! We don't need the house.' He was right, of course. It would break my heart but with time I'd get over it, whereas being taken advantage of could have future implications.

'Now, rehearse your answer, Catherine. Say no!'

'No,' I muttered.

'Once more with feeling.'

'No,' I said, a little louder.

'Move your head from side to side as you say it,' he directed. 'I want to feel your conviction.'

I looked to Gerard for sympathy but he was in total accord with Bill. So as my head moved from left to right practising *no*, his was moving up and down in agreement.

Thus primed, later that evening back in the bar, Gerard dialled the telephone number he had been given. It was answered almost immediately. That was a good sign. She had been waiting impatiently.

There are some French women who do not speak but shriek. They don't need a telephone to communicate short distances; they only need to open a window to be heard within a radius of five kilometres. She was one of those!

Gerard separated the receiver from his ear every time she spoke, allowing the entire bar to partake in the conversation. He introduced himself as our translator, and I could hear a tirade emanating from her side. She was obviously not into polite preliminaries. The present audience understood better than I, but the gist was that she was in total disagreement with the price of the house and the two who had shaken our hands had had no right to do so.

Gerard, while remaining calm and polite, nevertheless went straight for her jugular. He knew French law and asked if the new price had been lodged with the *notaire*, or was she expecting the English couple to pay the extra amount under the table in cash?

The atmosphere in the bar was electric. She screamed some more, stating that on no account would the house be sold for less. Gerard replied that as a

Frenchman, he found her behaviour a disgrace. Everyone in the bar, including the *patron*, mumbled in agreement. Never budging from the 60,000, she didn't even give me the opportunity to be tempted into negotiating a compromise. Her stubbornness provided me with resolve.

The discussion had ended and Gerard was about to hang up when, suddenly, she shouted, 'Ring me back tomorrow!'

'Why?' he asked her. 'Will you be more reasonable tomorrow?'

She continued like a harridan, 'You must ring me back but the price will be the same!!'

Gerard looked towards me for a reaction and so did the rest of the bar. As rehearsed, I turned my head from east to west and he nodded his in approval from north to south.

'It will not be necessary to call back,' he said, firmly, into the receiver.

'But you will…'

He hung up the phone, cutting her off in mid-scream. The whole bar erupted with, 'Bravo!'

I was desolate. We were leaving Le Puy the next day to travel to our new location in the Vercors from where I would ring Jean-Pierre to tell him the sad news.

Not accepting a lift back to the hotel, I took what I thought would be my last walk through the streets. I'd become very fond of Le Puy, nestling in a crater, surrounded by the domes of ancient volcanos. It is an extraordinary little city with a generous heart. The medieval architecture is carefully maintained, and everything built thereafter either complemented it or showed such bravado that you had to admire the imagination of those responsible. Standing high on a rock overlooking the tiled roofs of the city was the enormous statue of the red Virgin. She had been cast from the melted-down cannons captured from the Russians in the battle of Sevastopol. At night the statue was brilliantly lit, as was, in the distance, the little chapel of Saint Michel, perched on top of a needle-like, eroded volcanic chimney. If there was a peak jutting from the city, something religious was built on it. The people of Le Puy felt no shame in vaunting their faith and were used to welcoming strangers as its Place du Plot remains one of the major gathering points for those who have come from afar to journey on the pilgrimage of Saint Jacques de Compostelle. I passed the Pagès building with its gorgeous *art nouveau* roof, reminding me of an outsized jewelled bauble, worthy of use as an extravagant Christmas decoration. All the lanterns along my route dripped with colourful baskets containing trailing geraniums and every traffic island was planted with a dazzling display of flowers.

The unit hotel was directly opposite Le Puy station. Each night we admired a tractor disguised as a toy locomotive, painted white with its little open carriages trailing behind it for the tourists to effortlessly view the city. We laughed at the irony of parking it to sleep off its day's work directly next to where the serious trains did their job. Before negotiating the revolving doors of the hotel, I gave the cute little thing one last glance and blew it a kiss goodbye.

During the next day, the unit would decamp and head to the village of Villard-de-Lans high in the alpine beauty of the Vercors. Being married to the director had its perks: I could share the comfort of his chauffeur-driven car. Cases packed, we were waiting in the lobby when Gerard arrived, punctually but looking somewhat hung-over.

I had told Bill of last night's developments but he didn't seem too disappointed. As we travelled out of Le Puy I couldn't help but be possessed by the remarkable coincidence; what would be the chances of someone from England finding, by accident, in the heart of a wilderness in the centre of France, a house with their name painted on it? Impossible odds. It had to be meant and I was not giving up hope.

En route, Gerard mentioned something interesting. 'There was an article in a local paper this morning,' he said. 'All the French crew are talking about it.'

Not being able to receive BBC Radio 4 and the lack of English papers had kept us all in ignorance of current affairs. Naturally, we were curious whether a monumental event had taken place which could have had a drastic effect on our lives.

'What?' Bill asked. 'The French have finally invaded Guernsey?'

Gerard laughed. 'No, not yet.'

'Pity,' I said from the back. 'The food there would be so much better.'

'Something happened in Le Puy,' Gerard continued, giving me an intriguing look in the mirror. 'Two men had a fight. One man stabbed the other, causing very grave injuries. He was taken to the hospital. It happened very late the night before last.'

I caught his blue (though somewhat bloodshot) eyes again in the mirror. 'It couldn't have been those two. They'd be too old to fight with knives,' I told him.

'Many men here have a knife in their pocket,' he informed us.

Bill looked at him, astonished, 'What? On the off-chance of a rumble?'

'Rumble?' Gerard asked, not knowing the word.

'*Bagarre,*' I said, proudly remembering this addition to my French vocabulary.

'It is to cut the meat. They have their own knife and, even in a restaurant or at friends', they will use their knife to cut the meat,' he said.

I wondered how, all of my life, I had managed to trust other people's cutlery to do the job expected of it and never had a problem.

'Do women carry knives as well?' I asked.

'No. It is a male thing. A man is given a knife as a present,' he replied.

'And then he cuts up his wife's meat and fork-feeds her,' Bill added.

'Strange,' I mused. 'I've never seen it happen in a restaurant.' But I had seen many four-to-six-inch blades which folded into beautifully carved handles in the souvenir shops.

'The fight was to do with the filming,' Gerard continued. 'All of the German vehicles, uniforms and the flags, people dressed in wartime clothes… it brought back bad memories. I think one was a collaborator and perhaps the other has been holding a grudge. Anyway, that's what the French crew were saying.'

Film units are notorious breeding grounds for rumours and so I asked, 'Did you see the paper?'

'No. I was wanting to buy one for you to show but it was too late. After twelve o'clock all of the *presses* are closed.'

Bill was quite happy to believe this revelation because he would have taken pride in the credence that his efforts for authenticity had been so convincing. Personally, I had my suspicions that the departments of make-up, wardrobe and props had conspired to instigate this fantastic tale.

'So, you missed the *presses,*' Bill said to Gerard. 'Late night, was it?' We were all aware of his reputation as a naughty boy. Many of the unit's females had succumbed to his charms. He remained discreet about his adventures; it was the ladies who weren't.

'I was saying goodbye to a friend.'

'Must have taken long, saying goodbye,' Bill added. 'You look awful. What time did you get back to bed?'

'Six o'clock in the morning.'

Bill turned to me and ordered, 'Say goodbye, Catherine.'

As directed, I said, 'Goodbye, Catherine.'

'That didn't take long.' Bill was in his teasing mode and Gerard was the perfect victim. 'I suppose you said it in French.'

'Yes, of course. She is being French. I was saying, *au revoir*.'

'What was her name?' Bill asked.

'Juliette… but you do not know her.'

He ordered me again, 'Say "*au revoir*, Juliette"!'

I complied, '*Au revoir*, Juliette.'

'That took a little longer… but not a lot.'

'Yes,' Gerard said in all innocence, 'but I had to do it many times.' And thus, another euphemism was created between them.

Instead of playing 'I spy' for the remaining time the journey would take, we all came up with the longest goodbyes in different languages followed by names with the most amount of syllables. French hyphenated ones didn't count. I think I won with the Hungarian, '*Viszontlátásra*, Nebuchadnezzar'.

Gerard was speeding us down the autoroute in his powerful turbo-boosted Saab. I had every confidence that his 35-year-old body could withstand the strains of his nocturnal exertions but didn't like the way his head periodically nodded towards his chest. For his benefit and our security, we stopped for coffee breaks en route, thus arriving incident-free at our hotel where we sent Gerard off to sleep. Supplied with my key, I hurried up to the room to phone Jean-Pierre and transmit our disappointment regarding the purchase of the house.

'Dough nut worry,' he began. 'Leaf hit to me. I will coil the concerned peepoles. Wring me back in two dies. To be sure, you will be 'aving a sufferactory conclusion.' My communication skills were being stretched but I was pretty sure he meant 'satisfactory conclusion'. I also noticed, beyond his peculiar pronunciation, a certain speech pattern which hinted that he may have been tasting a little too much of his own alcoholic stock. Future conversations had better take place a little earlier in the day; but I was, nevertheless, grateful for his enthusiastic involvement.

During the two days that followed, Bill seemed almost to lose interest in the house. For my part, those forty-eight hours of suspense were alleviated only by my encounter with the dappled iron-grey gelding I was to ride for many of my scenes. In order not to repeat making a fool of myself astride another saddle, I had the perfect excuse to spend hours hacking on its back through the stunningly beautiful countryside. As it turned out, the horse was obsessively ambitious, far too handsome, outrageously vain and managed to steal every scene we shared together. Even while I was on top of it! It's true what they say about working with children and animals, but at least you can discreetly elbow a child out of shot. Try doing that to a horse whose agenda is eclipsing 'Trigger' as a Hollywood legend.

When I rang back as agreed, Jean-Pierre gave me the good news. 'The relations 'oo hare loco, hare completely embare-assed. The hother woeman his beehiving badly. To be sure, the price his wot you were shaking your 'ands for.'

To be absolutely certain, I repeated the price we had shaken hands on and was reassured that it remained as such.

'What happens now?' I asked him, elated with the news.

'You will be making a special date to be singing at the *Mairie* in front of a *notaire* with the relations.' I sincerely hoped he meant signing, as my singing is notoriously off-key. On the other hand, they might give us the house just to make me stop.

With the little French I had and many English words thrown in, I explained that we would have to consult the schedule to find a time to return to Bonneval. He would, of course, contact the *notaire*. I was also made to understand that this signing process was called the '*compromis*'. We would be handing over 10% of the asking price which was irretrievable should we renege on the actual purchase. It was, in effect, the same transaction as when contracts are exchanged in England between the seller and prospective buyer.

Sid's role had been shot and he had returned to England, as had Sara, but Jeremy, Pringle and Glyn were still with us. I ordered a bottle of the local bubbly, Clairette de Die, in celebration which we savoured together that evening on the poolside terrace of the hotel. Then Jeremy, carried along with my euphoria, ordered another, as did, in turn, Pringle and Glyn. By the time Bill returned from a production meeting we were almost too sozzled to explain the reason for our revelry.

'Gesh what?' I began, not in complete control of my tongue.

'You're drunk?' Bill surmised with a hint of envy. He was looking down on the four of us stretched out on our deckchairs. Besides the wine, we had been enjoying the last rays of sunshine the early July evening had to offer. Our fluted glasses and the ice bucket containing the last bottle were delicately perched on little round tables beside us.

'Yesh, but why?' I knew I should try to stand up and embrace him but I was afraid my legs would behave the same as my tongue.

'You've had too much to drink,' he answered, curtly.

Then, without meaning to, I did something very cruel to my friends. I said, 'All those present who are not prospective own homers in France, stand up!' The fools not only understood, but obeyed me!

Pringle made a huge effort to become vertical. Bending his long legs at the knees, he straddled the low lounger, feet firmly planted on either side. His head moved forward on his outstretched neck as he lifted his backside off the canvas, but the manoeuvre was not to be completed. He fell backwards, collapsing the front supports of the chair with his arms slipping through the canvas and the wooden arm rests. No further movement was possible. He was like a turtle on its back, struggling to become upright. Jeremy fared slightly better but he used a round table for leverage upon which a glass and the ice bucket were poised. It was the table nearest to me and performed according to the laws of physics: too much weight on one side made it begin to topple over. By a miracle, I managed to rescue the glass which was sliding towards the edge but the bottle, tumbling out of the bucket, was in dire jeopardy of shattering on the tiled floor surface. With surprising coordination, Jeremy swung his arm skywards, grabbing the neck of the bottle with his hand; but the movement was too quick and his grip too feeble. The bottle slid through his hand, projecting upwards. Glyn, who had made it most gracefully to a standing position, was near enough behind Jeremy to make a rugby lunge in order to catch it. Alas, the bottle had been nestling in a generous amount of crushed ice and was wet and slippery. His fingers lost hold but instinctively hoisted it into the air where it made one large loop and then nose-dived straight into the pool, righting itself immediately.

Bryan arduously rid himself of the canvas carapace to become finally upright, if swaying slightly. I was the only one who remained lounging in my deck chair. Bill had been watching on in fascination at the dramatic bottle trick.

'Well?' The trio were facing Bill. 'What do you say?'

'Smashing act... but what do you do for an encore?' He was being deliberately obtuse.

'Bill!' I shouted. 'What does it tell you? They're on their feet and I am not; and you should be...' (I didn't dare say the word 'sitting' as I was having pronunciation problems) '... down on your bum!'

He gave me one of those 'are you teaching your grandmother to suck eggs' looks and said, 'Good girl. At what price?'

'As agreed,' I answered proudly, still recumbent. 'We'll have to make a date to go back to sign.'

'It's already done,' he smiled slyly.

'What? How?' I was beginning to sober up.

Still smiling, he told me. 'Gerard couldn't sleep. He phoned the *aubergiste* soon after you'd spoken to him and received the same news. I was told when he came to pick me up at the production office. We had a look at the schedule and rang back.'

'You rotter!' I exclaimed. 'Why didn't you say?'

Bryan's neck elongated forwards until it was almost perpendicular to his chest. His chin jutted out as he said, 'You should have stopped us. We could have had a naxy asstident obeying Madame's orders.'

Jeremy was looking at the pool. The floating bottle was no longer bobbing on the surface. It must have tipped over, filled with the chlorinated water and sunk to the bottom. 'The bottle was half full,' he bemoaned.

'Yes… and it was bloody good stuff,' added Glyn.

'It's not my fault,' Bill said. 'Blame it on her.'

The four men turned to face me and for a terrible moment I thought I was going to take the same flight through the air as the bottle had.

'I'll buy another!' I said quickly.

The celebration continued. We enjoyed a wonderful meal at the hotel and that night, Bill told me, I fell asleep with a broad smile on my face.

The next morning, though, I awoke with three hatchets piercing my cranium, two rows of drawing pins pricked into my forehead just above my eyebrows, and a colony of bluebottle flies buzzing in my stomach. But with the aid of a viciously foaming concoction (two parts Alka-Seltzer to one part vitamin C) tactfully prepared by my make-up girl, these painful appendages were removed, my appearance repaired and my spirits renewed. Bill and I had so much to look forward to.

Chapter Four

WHILE MAKING THE DATE FOR THE SIGNING, Bill had spotted in the schedule the possibility for a further bonus. He knew the production would have moved to Grenoble by then, which meant an hour cut off the journey back to Bonneval; and figured that Friday, the twelfth of July, we could leave the location with Gerard after the 'wrap' and get there around nine at night. We'd have dinner and sleep at the *auberge*. The following Saturday morning, immediately after the meeting at the *Mairie,* we'd travel down to the South of France, where we had been invited by a close Danish friend called Lotti to partake in the weekend's special festivities, if we could manage it.

I had met Lotti in a previous life, which I refer to as my 'rich bitch' days. It was during a time when Bill and I had put a stop to our clandestine affair. In consolation, I allowed myself to be wooed by a certain chairman at Lloyd's of London, who was an acquaintance of hers. I was flown around in an eight-seater private jet and played his hostess while cruising the Mediterranean on a marble yacht. He bought expensive clothes and golden gewgaws to adorn me. It didn't last long. I didn't like myself in the part and I couldn't stop loving Bill. I left that scene but Lotti remained a friend; and when eventually Bill and I renewed our relationship, she met and immediately adored him.

This was the year, on the fourteenth of July, when the French would commemorate the bicentenary of the storming of the Bastille which had led to the birth of the republic. Lotti had booked a table on the pier of the Carlton Hotel in Cannes where we would dine and witness a spectacular firework display honouring this unique event. The thirteenth and fourteenth had already been designated as unit rest days but Monday, the fifteenth, could pose a problem. It would be impossible to contemplate Gerard driving through the night to deliver Bill on the set early in the morning to resume work. It was an ambitious plan and depended entirely on whether or not he could remain ahead of schedule, thereby winning three consecutive days off. As much as we would have liked to participate in those celebrations, we did realise it was an indulgence and if necessary would have to cancel the invitation, but there was no way I would cancel the *Compromis* unless, of course, by *force majeure* or if the producer demanded it.

We must have pleased the sun god of some denomination because the sky remained brilliantly clear. Not a single moment was lost due to bad weather. I had threatened the cast with extended torture leading to a painful death if they fluffed their lines. To keep me on my toes, they promised to do likewise should I not deliver mine. I managed to finish an exterior scene in which Glyn and I met secretly in a wood and had an intimate dialogue, with the crushing hoof of my upstaging horse planted firmly on my foot while he, with pricked ears, glinting dark eyes and toothy smile stared straight into the camera. (The horse, I mean, not Glyn.) I didn't cry until I heard Bill say, 'Cut! Let's move to the next shot.'

The French army had kindly agreed to cooperate with the filming by lending us a number of their paratroopers. These ten days would see some of Bill's most complicated action scenes, most of which would have to succeed in the first take, as setting up again would take too long or in some cases be impossible. He was going to have to record *Maquis* fighters, some on horses, charging German machine-gun positions while our French paras, dressed as Germans leaping out of aeroplanes, slowly descended with open 'chutes from the sky. Immediately on landing they would have to engage the waiting *Maquis* in a firefight. Special effects were kept busy planting explosives for all manner of battle scenes.

The production had been given permission to build a fountain in the central square of a village. The mayor was ecstatic. He remembered from his childhood that there had been a fountain in the very same place which had been destroyed by the invading German army. The fountain had never been rebuilt. He helpfully produced photographs of that period and the art department faithfully replicated the structure. It was filled and, with the use of a pump, the water flowed continuously from its spouts. The entire village feted its completion.

In the grey dawn of the following morning before the villagers were awake, special effects set their charges. The locals had been invited to watch the scene if they remained hidden behind net curtains in the bar which overlooked the square. Jeremy and I were not required for that particular scene, so we stayed concealed amongst them. There was a noisy buzz of excitement as they saw the German tanks rolling slowly up their main street. The borrowed paras, dressed in Wehrmacht uniforms, trotted alongside the lumbering vehicles, darting in and out of doorways, returning the gunfire from the resisting *Maquis* who were shooting from windows or other covering positions. It all looked and sounded frighteningly realistic; and then the lead Panzer's turret with its cannon turned and took aim. It blasted a blank charge and, in that instant, the fountain exploded into the sky. The effect was startling. Water rained down and bits of polystyrene 'stone' fell, littering the square. The bar was gripped in a shocked hush. The villagers couldn't believe it. Their darling fountain around which they had danced the night before had once again been destroyed.

I'm not sure the mayor had been fully informed as to the purpose behind the building of the fountain. Filming is a ruthless business. The only friendly face to bid us goodbye was the bartender's who had made an exceptional profit that morning, as we quickly retreated and headed towards the next place that had been scheduled to be blown up.

Bill's luck seemed to be holding. Every day he gained precious minutes of screen time. During the nightly production meetings, he added more scenes to the following day's schedule; but they had to be completed at their chosen locations, otherwise the unit couldn't move to the next. The crew were very willing to cooperate. They, too, were happily anticipating three consecutive rest days. Some of them were hoping their wives or sweethearts could come to join them. The French crew could go home during the break.

Even the *gendarmes* were amenable. Traffic was stopped on major roads to allow our tanks to go by. People waited in their cars showing amazing restraint. They had been told filming was in progress, and in France it is considered an art form and worthy of respect. On one occasion, the unit cavalcade had to be moved to another site. Precious time could be saved by taking the shortest route but that would entail driving the wrong way up a motorway. The French location manager negotiated this possibility with the responsible *gendarmerie*. 'No problem,' he was told. 'We will close the autoroute between the two exits required.' Thirty kilometres of the two southern lanes on the busy A49 were barred to allow our vehicles free passage to travel north. This would have been unheard of back in England. Closing a section of the M1 in consideration for a film crew? Are you mad?

The Friday came and we were well within our schedule. Our cases were packed and placed into the boot of Gerard's car. I could see Bill and me in Bonneval, pens poised for the signing. The banker's draft I'd organised for the 10% to be handed to the *notaire* had arrived and was safely tucked away. We'd kept in contact with Lotti and she was thrilled that we'd be able to join her.

At the previous evening's production meeting, Bill had had to accede to a proposal set by the producer. If, unfortunately, the scenes were not completed at Friday's location, Saturday the thirteenth would be designated a working day. It was considered more appropriate to ensure Monday as a rest day in order that the French crew could sleep off their hangovers from Sunday's bicentenary celebrations, but the workload was uncomplicated and he was fairly sure we could make our planned getaway. If not, it meant the entire weekend would have to be cancelled, including the *Compromis*. I trusted utterly in Bill's competence and that our good fortune hitherto enjoyed would continue.

Then suddenly, in the mid-afternoon, disaster loomed in the guise of an enormous milk tanker. We were filming in a courtyard and the surrounding fields of a farmhouse. The crew was rushing about setting up for the next shot. While waiting to be called on the set, Glyn was giving a nature tour for those who were interested through some nearby pastures, counting and identifying over forty varieties of wild flowers. We were surprised to discover that, in his spare time, Glyn amused himself by behaving as an amateur botanist.

The huge white tanker insinuated itself into the courtyard and hissed to a halt. The throaty sound of its diesel engine continued to chug. The driver leapt out of the cab and entered the house, quickly followed by several irate French assistants.

The farmer had cows. They were in an adjacent barn being milked. None of the unit, least of all Bill, had any experience of dairy farming. How the herd's produce would enter the tanker, be it pouring the milk churns by hand or via a hose, nobody knew. But it would obviously take time during which filming could not proceed as the tanker had assumed the central position on the set.

The driver reappeared with the farmer and they made their way to the barn. The assistants approached Bill with worried faces. 'It must be done now,' they said seriously. 'The milk must be delivered to Sassenage by this afternoon.'

'That bloody great tanker has to be filled?' Bill was furious. 'Why weren't we warned? There are a lot of shots we still have to get through! Who's responsible for this?'

'I am sorry,' apologised the 1st assistant. 'Milk is the farmer's main income. We were not told it would be picked up today.'

'Where's Gerard?' Bill demanded, looking around him. 'He can take me to the nearest bar. That's where you'll find me when we're ready to shoot.'

At that precise moment, the driver came out of the barn holding a small test tube containing a white liquid. Bill watched him in horror, wondering if the entire tanker was going to be filled vial by vial, imagining the time that would take; but before Gerard could be found, the driver fitted a cork to the top of the tube and placed it into the breast pocket of his jacket, climbed back in his cab and drove the huge tanker away.

Bill looked at his assistants in confusion. 'That was it? That's all his herd produced?' He looked towards the farmhouse, which he had chosen exactly for its dilapidated aspect, and said, 'No wonder the poor bugger has no money.'

The assistants, who had been informed a few minutes earlier by the farmer as to the purpose of the tanker's visit, could now have a hearty laugh at Bill's expense. 'They are having to test in the laboratories to see if the cows have been eating enough flowers. It is for the famous local blue cheese of Sassenage,' they informed him merrily. 'They do not make the cheese until the milk is absolutely correct. It is that which gives it the special flavour.' How true it was. We had all tasted copious amounts of the delicious *Bleu de Sassenage* and much preferred the inclusion of nectar and pollen to microscopic spiders.

The rest of the day, we suffered no more disturbances and finished the filming as planned. Relaxing in the back of Gerard's car, I gratefully thanked the gods for any interventions they may have made on our behalf for what promised to be a wonderful weekend.

Speeding downwards through the tunnels and along the curves of the Gorges de la Bourne to reach the autoroute, we were surprised to arrive at the tail end of a traffic jam. Our lane was inching forward while the opposing one was travelling only slightly faster. There was a bridge ahead and to the left of us which crossed the river Bourne. There, too, traffic was creeping across it. We assumed it was the cars filtering from the bridge into our lanes that were causing the hold-up.

It was only five in the afternoon and the temperature outside was still fairly hot. I had lowered my window, feeling unperturbed, indulging in my daytime reveries, picturing myself as the *châtelaine* of Bonneval, when, suddenly, through the open window we heard the most blood-curdling scream. And then we heard another, and then another. The frightening sounds suggested a horrible accident up ahead with the victims being painfully extracted from the wreckage. I had never heard such excruciating pain and fear of death so vocalised in my life. Hearing it in reality, I realised that even in the most terrifying of horror films the actors had not been able to imitate it. That feeling had to be experienced for it to be convincingly performed. We felt completely useless, stuck in our car as the screams continued, sometimes from a woman, sometimes from a man.

As we crawled past the bridge and could see through the windows of the slow oncoming cars, the reason for the screaming became evident. A group of suicidal maniacs were *bungee jumping off the bridge!!* They were hurling themselves down, deep into the gorge, missing literally by inches the rocks which jutted out of the river below, and then being hoisted up at tremendous speed to once again barely miss smashing their heads against the underside of the stone bridge. One after the other, they leapt into the air to be swallowed, screaming, into the abyss, only to be spat back up again. They bobbed up and down, hanging from the bridge like demented, screeching yo-yos. I couldn't believe that such a death-tempting activity was allowed to be performed in public. They may see the morrow to buy new underwear but what about the innocent passer-by who suffers from heart disease or tends towards a nervous disposition? What about depressives?

The traffic in the two opposing lanes moved slowly as everyone gawked at the spectacle. When eventually it speeded up and the bridge was out of sight, Bill turned around to me and said, 'It's a pity you had to see that.'

'I agree,' I answered. 'It will give me those awful nightmares, when you wake up with a jolt because you feel you're falling.'

'Shame,' he said, sadly. 'It was going to be a surprise.'

'What?' I asked.

'I bought you five sessions for your birthday. Bungee jumping with an expert. Hundred francs a go.'

'You have to pay to do that?!'

But, thank God, I knew he was joking. Settling once again comfortably in the back of the Saab, I continued my daydreaming, grateful not to have to jump off bridges to get a thrill. The anticipation of owning a house, sweetly called 'Valentin', was enough. Maybe a miracle would happen and the forgotten wardrobe would be thrown in.

That evening in Bonneval we dined *en famille* with Jean-Pierre, his 'waife' and three 'doubters', as he pronounced it. The young girls were delightful. I didn't know then that this introduction to French children would be followed by many more and I would notice a distinct difference in their upbringing as opposed to their counterparts back in England. Smiling, polite and unafraid to show affection, they were in happy expectation of having an English couple at such close proximity. The eldest, who had already been studying English, was eager to practise what she had learned.

''Owe... are... you?' she asked, slowly enunciating each word.

'Very well, thank you,' I replied, noting she had fortunately not inherited her father's extraterrestrial accent, but was not yet able to aspirate.

Before retiring without arguments, the children gave us the three Haute-Loire obligatory kisses (the number varies from department to department) on our cheeks; and then Jean-Pierre proudly invited us to have a game on his 'doart bard' which he had hung on a wall between two windows. During the meal, he made blatant his partiality towards the restaurant's liquid assets. Drinking as someone who had just been rescued from the Sahara, he emptied, in seconds, large glasses of wine in thirsty gulps. This exaggerated consumption made our drinking look like a dainty debutante's. So, when he suggested throwing darts, I perceived them as dangerous weapons in his hands and sought the security of our room and its very narrow double bed. While Anna Magnani also made a discreet exit, Bill and Gerard remained, more to ensure he did not do himself an injury than for the sport.

The excitement of meeting Madame 'Screecher' and her relations woke me early the following morning. I quietly left the room with Bill still sound asleep. Over a disgusting, lukewarm brew which I was assured by Jean-Pierre was tea and which had been placed rattling in front of me by his trembling hands, I gazed out of the window to the right of the dartboard and noticed a tiny hole in a pane of glass from which hairline cracks diffused. I didn't become aware of Bill's limp until we later walked together to the *Mairie*. Horrific images of darts sticking out of his thigh prompted my concern.

'What's the matter with your leg?' I asked him. But we had reached the other signatories and became too busy being introduced and shaking hands for him to reply.

The woman who had pounded Gerard's ears was not immediately recognisable. I only assumed it was the diminutive Margaret Thatcher look-alike and not the gentle brunette or the tall shy blonde, and was correct. It was she, when shaking Gerard's hand, who admitted with a coquettish smile that they had already spoken. From her flirtatious manner, the company could have assumed he had asked her out for a date.

A young and surprisingly trendy *notaire* arrived, sporting the stubble of a designer beard and carrying a heavy briefcase. We were all ushered into the back room of the *Mairie* to take our positions around a long conference table. The meeting commenced. There were six of them: the two who had shown us around originally, the three women and the husband of the brunette. Our need for Gerard's presence became painfully evident as I could not understand a word during the proceedings.

Before our signatures were assigned to the contract, certain information was asked of us: address, place of birth, my maiden name. When it came to our date of birth, Bill offered his effortlessly. When it came to mine and being faced by so many comparative strangers with whom I would have to share such intimate information, I baulked.

'Why? I asked Gerard as if the *notaire* had prescribed extracting a completely healthy molar without novocaine.

'Because the *notaire* needs to know,' he answered perfectly normally.

'Can't you just tell him, I'm old enough to buy a house?' I pleaded.

Bill was enjoying my discomfort. As a man and a director, he didn't suffer from such complexes. I was a woman and an actress. We only admit to our age when we're young enough or too old that it should matter. I was thirty when I met Bill and had nothing to hide. Fifteen years on, though, I wished to plead amnesia.

Every face around the table stared at me in expectation. They looked benign enough but I felt like an actress on stage who had dried. I was dying. Could I ad-lib?

'Go on,' Bill encouraged me. He was unable to proffer the information as he'd always forgotten my birthdays. Thank God.

'Do I have to tell the truth?' I asked, anticipating the agony. The dental extracting tool was nearing my mouth.

'I'm afraid you do,' said Gerard. 'It is a means of identification.'

'Do you mean, there could possibly be another Catherine Hays, née Schell, born in Budapest, Hungary, married to William Hays, born in Wingate, England and living at my address who would impersonate me and steal the house?' I asked, incredulously. 'I'd rather show some identifying marks,' I added in a more reasonable tone.

Poor Gerard, coming from a French culture which looked more kindly upon a woman's maturity, misunderstood my adopted Anglo-Saxon reluctance to confess my age and simply asked, 'What?'

'I have a rather attractive constellation of little moles just around my belly button,' I admitted.

The *notaire*, who didn't understand a word of English, was watching me, bored and scratching his manicured stubble.

'Get on with it,' said Bill. 'They're not interested in your moles.'

And so for the first time, at my delicate age and in front of so many witnesses, I gave the date of my birth – very quickly.

'*Pardon?*' asked the *notaire*, absolutely unimpressed. What did I expect? A compliment?

'Once again, Catherine,' Bill tiredly directed me, 'only slower.'

With all the courage I could muster, I repeated in French, 'July the seventeenth, 1944' and hoped for an immediate earthquake.

'But that is the year of my birth!!' screeched Margaret Thatcher; and continued as if we'd become bosom companions, 'We have the same age!'

Notwithstanding the loss of my birth certificate due to the many moves my family had made, this convinced me of the importance of their destruction after having reached a certain age. How dared she!

The banker's draft was handed into the *notaire*'s safekeeping. We then made a date, September the first, for the completion. Gerard translated that from now until then, the relatives could remove any objects from the property, but on the first of September, when it legally became ours, anything contained therein would be considered part of the sale. My hopes rose for the wardrobe, and it was then that the gentle brunette turned to me and, with an apologetic smile, said that, of course, it would be removed; and I, of course, completely understood.

The proceedings were finished. Smiles and handshakes were exchanged as we moved towards the car to make our departure. Bill was still slightly limping.

'You weren't hit by a dart last night?' I asked him anxiously.

'No,' he answered while opening the rear door for me. 'But I think you must have dreamt you were a kangaroo. My leg got a real pummelling from your leg during the night.'

The threatened dreams from the bungee jumping did occur. I was woken up several times with a start and a sensation of falling. The fact was, what the French call a double bed is often only four feet wide. I had jerked violently awake with a kick of my leg prior to nearly falling off the mattress. What a brave darling that he had not complained.

Turning around in the back of the Saab to wave another farewell to the vendors, I was happy to note that the natives were friendly but had a slight reservation concerning Mme Thatcher. Her smile seemed a little different as she returned our waves, almost defiant. I had an eerie premonition that we would hear her voice raised in dispute again.

'Tee-hee,' I heard Bill titter from the front of the car as we rolled away.

'What are you tee-heeing about?' I asked him.

'Nobody mentioned the bellows,' he said, extremely satisfied. I had completely forgotten his fascination for them.

Gerard dropped us off at Lotti's villa later that day. He lived not far away in Nice and was happy for the opportunity to make an appearance at his home. Even though various ladies had experienced his frequent 'goodbyes', he did have a loving wife to whom he would now say 'hello!' We set an hour for Monday's pick-up and wished him a *bon week-end*.

Lotti's two Viking sons were staying with her. They were huge, bearded, long-haired and but for their gentle natures would have put the fear of annihilation into anyone whose path they crossed. The Vikings didn't have to conquer Britain in battle. A gentle knock on a door, the opening of that door and the vision of these enormous, fierce-looking beings would have made the population swoon. Village captured. They were probably only asking for a cup of tea.

As there was no room at her house, Lotti was putting us up in a neighbouring chateau which had been converted into an exclusive hotel. A few days before our arrival, she had given a ball, reserving the entire chateau for the affair. The who's who of Europe had been invited. Her generosity was renowned.

'Now, you are not to pay for anything,' she commanded in her delightful Danish accent while accompanying us to our room. It was magnificent.

Looking around her, she nodded in approval and then tipped the bell-boy who had placed our very common luggage on a rack.

'One of the boys will pick you up at 7:30,' she said in the doorway before leaving. 'We will have a cosy evening at my place with a simple dinner. I hope you like *langouste*. We bought some fresh from the market this morning.' Tucking her high-cheekboned, pretty face back through the door, she added, 'Oh and, Catherine, there is lots of caviar left over from the ball. What is it that you like saying? We'll "pig out" tonight?' The smile widened her face, made square by the surgically straight cut of her fringe. A soft click and the door closed. We were left with the gentle patter of her elegantly shod feet disappearing down the hallway.

That weekend would forever remain one of the highlights of our lives. A tiny parcel of France had been promised to become ours; pigging out on *langouste* and caviar; gossiping in Lotti's garden until dawn while Bill was laid out snoring on a sofa; sitting at the farthest table on the Carlton's pier, the Mediterranean gently lapping against the wooden piles beneath our feet and watching a fireworks display, orchestrated from barges well out to sea, that I can only describe as awesome – and we did 'awe', loudly and a lot, when the rockets exploded far above our heads, erupting into brilliant, intricate designs. They were choreographed exactly to the music which was blaring from several loudspeakers positioned along the sea front. We 'awed' some more when the showers of their multi-coloured sparks floated down towards us like raining stars. All at our table rose to their feet for the finale, when *La Marseillaise* resounded across the coastline with red, white and blue rockets bursting against the black sky in perfect rhythm to the anthem. Tears of emotion stained my cheeks. As a Hungarian, I was used to being moved to cry but was surprised to see that Bill's eyes were also shiny and liquid.

The music ended. The sparks slowly faded and, as the crowd's jubilation roared across the beach, Bill quietly said to me, 'I never want to see another fireworks display again. Nothing can ever top this experience.'

When we were standing in respect for the song and the spectacle, I glanced behind me towards the other tables. Except for some waiters, not one other person was upright. They had remained seated. As we were leaving and walked the length of the pier I heard the other diners conversing in French. Strange that they had not stood. Perhaps they were Belgians.

Lotti's elder son who had been appointed driver for the evening had dropped us earlier in front of the Carlton and then searched for a good half hour through the backstreets of Cannes to legally park the car. He now led the way with his forefathers' navigational talents to retrieve it. We followed in a happy mood, profusely thanking Lotti for that night's enjoyments. There had been twelve other guests around the table. Champagne had flowed and she had chosen the most expensive menu to delight us. As we meandered through dimly lit streets still echoing with the sounds of laughter and celebrations, she in her turn thanked Bill for being the only man at the table who had shown the colour of his credit card and had offered to, at least, pay a share of the bill.

'Noo, Beel,' she had said, 'I told you. You are my guests.' Lotti had given him the honour of sitting at the head of the table with herself and me flanking either side. When the bill arrived, it had been placed in front of him. He had caught a glimpse of the amount. Our episodic fees combined would not have covered it. Instinctively, he reached for his wallet and withdrew his card which was neither silver, nor gold but a very ordinary blue.

Her soft and beautifully manicured hand discreetly covered the plastic card and gently pushed it back towards him.

'Lotti, at least let me pay for something,' Bill had insisted. The exchange between them was obvious but the other diners at our table chose to ignore it.

On our walk, she admitted to having invited only three couples. The rest, having heard of her plans, simply invited themselves.

It was well beyond midnight. We were deliciously tired and longing for our comfortable beds but, upon finally arriving at the car, we were confronted with a problem. A Volkswagen Golf with Parisian plates was double-parked against ours. My French experience had only just begun; Bill and I were not yet educated in the anarchic disregard for the rules of the road, habitually practised in our would-be adopted country.

Our flat in London was near to Baron's Court where, every year, the Stella Artois tennis tournament took place. During those two weeks an impossible influx of visiting cars invaded our area and imposed themselves on to our parking spaces. It was extremely annoying and I dealt with those weeks by leaving my car and using the Tube. Not once in the seventeen years we lived there, when I needed my car, was it ever blocked except by a neighbour's, who had asked my permission to do so.

For a while, we waited patiently in the expectation that the owners were aware of the inconvenience they would have caused and were keeping a look-out in order to move it when we had arrived. After twenty minutes and several hootings of our horn, causing irate heads to pop out from overlooking windows, like disturbed occupants of cuckoo-clocks, I angrily decided to scour the nearby restaurants and bars. Having had enough to drink to give me courage, I brazenly entered these establishments shouting in Franglais, '*Une Golf est double parkée against notre voiture! Movez-la vite!*' The only reactions this caused were peculiar stares and my instant removal by head waiters or tenders of bars. Unsuccessful and somewhat humiliated, I made my way back to the car.

An immensely tall, long-haired silhouette was lurking at the top of an alley. 'Come quickly!' it shouted. 'We have managed to move.' I was relieved the voice belonged to one of Lotti's sons. He hurried me to the car which was unblocked in the street with its engine running. Bill and Lotti were in the back and her other son was at the wheel. They were anxious for a fast getaway. During my absence, they too had lost their cool. With Bill's minor help and Lotti's encouragement the two Vikings had managed to bounce the Golf backwards, but were incapable of correcting the steering; the car ended up denting the street-side front door of the Peugeot which had been parked immediately behind ours. Lotti had quickly scribbled down the offending vehicle's licence number on the back of the second page of that night's dinner bill and attached it to the damaged Peugeot's windscreen. Luckily, the note was not traceable.

Then I, before taking my place in the waiting car, committed my first and, as of this writing, last act of criminal vandalism. With the motivation of a woman scorned, I pounced upon the Golf's windscreen and bent its two wipers into perfect V's, disabling them of their intended use, and hoped for a deluge.

Naturally, I was caught *in flagrante delicto*. Two men in their late thirties were running up the street. Not unreasonably, they both wore angry faces. They had witnessed the elegant figure of a female form, dressed impeccably in silk trousers and a colourful chiffon blouse, light and floating as her perfume, wreaking havoc upon the windscreen of their car.

'Hey, lady! Whaddya think you're doin'?'

Oh, dear. They were American. I quickly pretended to be French but the only thing I could think of to say with convincing *panache* was, stupidly, '*C'est la vie!*' They stared at me with gobsmacked expressions and then turned to examine the damage I had caused.

'It's a rented car,' whined one of them, tragically.

'How could you do such a thing?' said the other; and then, louder, 'Are you nuts?!'

Viking son No. 1, who had been standing a little aloof, disturbed by my behaviour, now approached protectively towards me. The two Americans had to lift their chins considerably to look him in the eyes. His height alone struck them dumb.

Shedding my French pretence, I then said in a crisp, clear English accent, 'That's what you get for bloody well double-parking. It was an asshole thing to do!' I turned my back on them and was escorted majestically by my Viking to our car. Son No. 2 had been gunning the motor, anxious to disappear, lest the damage to the Peugeot's door be also discovered.

The last words I heard from behind us, before closing the door and speeding away, were uttered with a mixture of shock and admiration.

'Son of a bitch,' drawled an American voice.

The evening had been sublime and then descended into the ridiculous. To this day, I am ashamed of those actions. Lotti leant forward in the back of the car to see me more clearly. Bill was sitting between us, studying me. I had shown a side to my nature not even I knew existed and I don't think he liked it.

'Cathween,' Lotti said in her child-like Danish accent. 'You supwise me!'

Even her sons commented on the way home: 'That was a wild thing to do.'

I put that night's hooligan behaviour down to a rogue Tartar gene which had, to that point, lain dormant amongst the more genteel ones I had inherited from my parents. It was a stranger to me. I didn't realise then that, if disciplined, it could be useful in the future.

Gerard drove us back to Grenoble where we completed the French locations and thereafter returned to England. On the first of September, as promised, we were back at Bonneval in the *Mairie* and our ears were being punished.

'The bellows are mine!' She was screeching again in her high-pitched French voice. We were sitting around the same conference table as before. The door of the house had been opened earlier for us and we'd made a cursory inspection. The walls were still standing and the roof had not collapsed in our absence. The farming paraphernalia including the large wagons were still cluttering the barns. A rectangle, comparatively free of dust, marked the spot on the floor of the bedroom where the rustic wardrobe had stood. To Bill's delight, though, the bellows remained hanging from the forge ceiling.

We had finished the last scenes of the series back in the London studios. Gerard's contract had run its course but we'd negotiated with him to fetch us at Lyon airport and stay the planned three days in Bonneval to once again act as our interpreter.

The proceedings had been running smoothly until the diminutive Margaret Thatcher stubbornly refused to sign the final contract unless we handed her FF3,000 for the bellows. Without her signature, the sale could not go through.

'They were left to me in the will!' she insisted loudly.

'And the wagons were left to me,' said the shy blonde, trying to reason with her. 'They are of no use to me. I wouldn't dream of asking money for them.'

'But I am! I'm not signing unless I am paid!!' The pitch of her voice was making a banshee's howl sound like a soothing lullaby.

'You are being ridiculous,' said another relative seated at the table in fear of the proceedings collapsing.

'Tell her, Gerard,' Bill interjected, 'I'm not buying the house unless the bellows are included.'

An embarrassed shuffling of feet became audible from under the table as most of the relatives began fidgeting. The *notaire* left his seat and made a discreet exit from the room. It was quite common that during these dealings a certain amount of cash was secretly handed over, of which he would have preferred to remain ignorant.

The argument continued, with Gerard's translation, during which some relatives also left the room in frustration. She remained adamant, as did Bill. If our British Prime Minister at that time was known as the Iron Lady because of her resolve, this little doppelganger was made of reinforced tungsten.

Through Gerard I asked, if she had wanted the bellows, why had they not been removed? That had been the understanding. She had had six weeks to do so. 'What would I do with them?' she cackled.

So, what it came down to was this: Bill wanted the bellows but didn't think he should pay, she didn't want the bellows but wanted to be paid for them. I didn't give a damn. I just wanted the house and when Bill threatened to walk out and forget about the purchase, my little dream was in danger of being shattered.

'What do you want them for?' I questioned Bill during a heated exchange Gerard was having with her on our behalf. 'We're surely not going to open a smithy?' I asked in horror.

'They're magnificent! I can't expect you to understand, but they're important to me,' he answered and then whispered, 'Besides, they're probably worth more than the house.'

'Then let's pay for them,' I suggested to him quietly. 'You'll have the bellows. I'll have the house and she'll have the money. Everyone will be happy. Only promise me, they will never be made into a coffee table.'

'I promise,' he smiled. 'But one day I shall paint a beautiful design on them and they will be hung outside as a decoration.' True to his word, in years to come, when we opened the B&B, they were hung under the eaves, against a stone wall, and his artwork much complimented by our guests.

The dispute was settled. The *notaire* repositioned himself at the head of the table. The bill of sale was signed by everyone present and the house became ours.

'Madame Bellows', as she would forever after be known, smiled smugly, FF3,000 richer than her fellow inheritors. To this day, I'm not sure where the legalities had lain; had we called her bluff and insisted upon their removal, she would hardly have had the strength to do so. Therefore, according to the original contract they should have made part of the purchase. In the *notaire*'s deliberate absence, we were bereft of the necessary arbitration.

Nevertheless, we returned as a large and happy group to the *auberge*, where Jean-Pierre had generously uncorked some champagne, and were made to feel welcome as Bonneval's newest arrivals. The relatives who were local would become our neighbours. They kindly extended their hands in friendship. We were assured of their help and their relief that the house they had known as children would not be allowed to crumble. The reception was warm and gave us confidence. These first impressions never altered.

I even managed a smile when, a few years later, Mme Bellows made an appearance (she lived farther away) and we showed her the renovations we had accomplished. As we passed the bellows which were hanging on the exterior wall, I stopped and asked, 'Do you remember these?'

'How could I forget?' she answered coyly. Too many wonderful things had happened since then for me to hold a grudge.

Chapter Five

'IT IS VERY IMPORTANT THAT ALL OF THE PENISES ARE HIDDEN.' I was speaking on the telephone in French to our architect, having scoured Cassell's French-English dictionary for the building terms I would need. I had written a script for myself with the necessary words for this conversation. Unfortunately, I hadn't looked up the word for pipes, assuming it would be the same, only with the French pronunciation, as 'peeps'.

There was a slight intake of breath coming from his end of the line.

'In England,' I continued, blithely, 'we try to hide our penises, especially the big ones. I noticed, in France, they are very evident.'

'No, Catherine, it's...' he began to say. By this time, we had dropped the *monsieur* and *madame* and were calling each other by our first names. Before he could carry on, I cut him off.

'Yes, Patrick. Even in the restaurant of the *auberge* and in their bathroom, they are climbing up walls and hanging from ceilings. Bill and I were very shocked.'

The intake of breaths became heavier and I realised he was laughing.

'Why are you laughing?' I asked, confused. 'For Bill it is a matter of aesthetics. They are ugly to look at.'

'Catherine, you are not using the correct word. You are meaning, *les tuyaux.*'

'Then what is "peeps"?' There was an embarrassing pause. He didn't need to explain. With a little imagination its meaning dawned on me and I was grateful we were separated by the telephone, as the red heat of a blush was crawling up my face.

It would not be the last time I would take for granted that the casual French pronunciation of an English word would share the same meaning. It was my first of many introductions to what the French call *les faux amis* (false friends).

While we were in Bonneval to buy the house, it had been advised that we meet an architect. Our massive amount of planned renovations, we were told, would require professional drawings and local permissions.

Thus, Gerard, Bill and I were waiting in the restaurant part of the *auberge* for the meeting which had been arranged by the mayor to take place in the mid-afternoon on the day after the purchase. The architect had been informed that we were an English couple who had discovered the house during filming which had occurred in Le Puy. At the appointed hour, a tall, dark, slender man quietly entered. He was dapperly dressed in a camel-coloured sports jacket, dark trousers and elegantly comfortable soft leather tan shoes. A cravat was tied around his neck and neatly tucked into the collar of his cream silk shirt. The accessory of an expensive attaché case finished his fashionable attire. He glanced timidly around him. Within the simple decor of his surroundings, he looked completely out of place.

'That could only be the architect,' observed Bill. Gerard caught his eye and bade him to come over. After the introductions, he sat down at our table. We discussed the project, but not before he admitted to having watched us with intense curiosity from the height of his penthouse terrace in Le Puy when the production's vehicles were camped on the spacious parking of the square immediately below him.

Through Gerard's translations, we were told he was able to discern which were the vans containing wardrobe and make-up by simply noting the transformations of the people who entered and then exited them. What intrigued him most of all, though, was the converted lorry with windows framed by red-and-white gingham curtains, which he recognised as our restaurant car, the ingenious asset of our French caterers.

'I thought I was having problems with my sight,' he said to us. 'One day, I saw it swelling. It looked normal and then, suddenly, it began to expand. Both sides were moving outwards to become almost twice its size. It was very impressive.'

'Yes!' Bill answered, 'but a little disconcerting when you're sitting inside it and the tables and chairs begin to move mysteriously away from you. Especially before you've even had a drink.'

'It's a marvel,' added the architect in admiration. 'I wish I could do that with my buildings. But, tell me,' he asked in all earnestness, 'why was it parked in such close proximity to the *pissoires*?'

'Yes! We found that strange, as well,' Bill and I admitted.

He then added with an air of mischief, 'Did it have anything to do with the food?'

We both wondered what he had intended by making this connection and thought the worst. Even Gerard hesitantly translated, 'No, we don't think so. Why?'

'English food,' the architect replied. 'French flies would not have been attracted.'

We informed him that the food was French and that it must have been marvellous because the thousands of native bluebottles who competed with us to eat it couldn't all have been wrong. And so began a deep and lasting – though sometimes challenging – friendship.

Bill was going to be in the editing suites in London cutting the eight episodes together for the following two months. We arranged with Patrick that he would send us the plans. Bill would make sense of them and suggest alterations which I would translate and send back to him. Lesser details would be handled via the telephone.

Back in London and jobless or, as actors prefer to say, 'resting', I immersed myself in the effort of trying to recapture some of the French I had spoken as a teenager. Strangely, the exercise books which had been used for my curriculum were still in my possession, cluttering up a bookshelf. My birth certificate had disappeared, but two French-Canadian editions of *Français: Vocabulaire et Grammaire* (Levels 2 and 3) had always been scrupulously packed to follow me as part of my effects.

Bill, too, was determined to learn the language. Having spotted an ad in a newspaper, he sent off a cheque and received by return of post an audio-visual kit containing tapes of French conversation and a book illustrating the vocabulary. Instead of his usual quiet pursuit of struggling with the *Guardian*'s cryptic crossword puzzle in the hour before setting off to work, he was now mimicking the sentences he'd been hearing on the tapes. The flat had no particular acoustic insulation and so I was often woken up to the monotonous repetition of certain phrases he was memorising, such as, '*Voudriez-vous quelque chose à boire?*' (Would you like something to drink?) and the response, '*Oui, volontiers, un verre de vin rouge.*' (Yes, gladly, a glass of red wine.) He concentrated mainly on the vocabulary he would regularly use, ignoring words related to bureaucracy and, not being a driver, anything to do with cars. Household goods and appliances, numbers, banking terminology, phrases needed for visits to doctors, dentists, the post office, train stations, all these were designated as a low priority. He focused primarily on words relating to food and drink, but it took him ages to learn how to say 'Water, please.'

To be fair, though, Bill suffered from the handicap of never having learned another language in his youth. Having missed the eleven-plus exams due to an operation, he didn't sit them until the age of thirteen. He made excellent marks and was then found a place in a grammar school. As he was two years behind the other students of his age, the headmaster of that establishment very wisely set him a curriculum which was adapted to his particular talents. It was decided to drop maths and all foreign languages and to concentrate on history, geography, English, art and music. The brain cells which are used in learning a second language were never exercised in his case and so he found it difficult in later life. It would have demanded a tremendous effort for which he had very little time. On the other hand, why bark if you have a dog?

Both of my parents were quadrilingual. My father spoke Hungarian, French, German and English as a native. Just for fun, with some of his friends, he corresponded in Latin. My mother also spoke, besides Hungarian, the other three modern languages mentioned: only she uttered them with a weirdly charismatic accent, somewhere between Bela Lugosi's Dracula and Zsa Zsa Gabor.

I was forced to learn languages in school. The fact that, by the age of fourteen, I had lived in four different countries made it imperative. Re-learning French after you've spotted your first grey hair (and immediately plucked it out) was going to be a challenge but I had a better chance than Bill of becoming fluent. My mother kindly offered to help by suggesting that, henceforth, we would only converse in French together. I turned her down. I didn't want to pick up her accent and be known in France as Dracula's daughter. I'd experienced that already in Germany.

The phone calls and correspondence with Patrick were beneficial for my learning process, obliging me to regularly search for words in the French-English dictionary, some of which I'd never even used in English. My vocabulary in building terminology grew simultaneously in both languages.

Words I had heard but never needed suddenly became clear to me, such as *screed, lintel, truss* (which I'd thought was something men wrapped around their middles to avoid hernias), *ridge tiles, flaunching, flashing* (which I'd only ever associated with men in dirty macs), *joist, hardcore* (underground blue movies?) *newel post, riser, anti-syphon bottle trap…* The list could go on but I won't bore you. To think I'd lived in ignorant bliss of such terminology. Well, I had never been cast as a builder. But these words were not going to help me in my personal life. I needed the vocabulary for such phrases as:

'The waistband in this skirt is too tight. Do you have an elasticated one?'

'My hair is very curly. Can you straighten it with a blow-dryer?'

'These shoes pinch my feet. I must consider my bunions.'

'My husband prefers his wine in a larger glass. May I borrow your bucket?'

Patrick gave us the impressive news that the construction of the roof would be completed by Christmas. Bill and I were amazed that such an enormous job could be done so quickly. But we had been warned that all depended on the weather, which prompted me to make frantic phone-calls to Jean-Pierre enquiring what the long-range forecast predicted.

'I ham not wotching the *Meteo* to know that. I ham hasking the loco paysants, who know butter. To be sure, hit will be sweet.' (The French define mild as *doux*, which means sweet.)

Having bought the house, it was difficult to stay away and so we decided to spend Christmas at the *auberge* in Bonneval to inspect our new roof. Our friends, the actor Bill Simons and his bubbly red-headed wife Janie, had a house in the Lot, a department of France due west from the Haute-Loire. They invited us to drive across to them for the New Year.

We regularly received photos from Jean-Pierre keeping us informed as to the progress of the roof. A huge crane had been brought in to lift off the old timbers and replace them with new ones. Entire trees of the local firs were put into place without the aid of calculating instruments. It was a complicated structure as the house and the immediately adjoining barn were at a slight angle to each other. The men, who looked like dwarfs in the pictures, stood on top of the stone walls and helped gently to lower the heavy logs into place, depending only on the accuracy of their instincts and the measuring skills of their experienced eyes. Fascinated as we were when the photos arrived, we were also happy to note that the sky in the background remained a cloudless, brilliant blue, which augured well for our intended trip.

Deciding that the Portsmouth-Le Havre overnight ferry would suit us best, on the twenty-second of December we set off on a path which would be repeated many times in the future.

All things French seemed attractive and so I had traded the Ford for a Peugeot, although the steering was still on the right. The car had been serviced, the tyres checked and what I had deemed an electrical malfunction was examined. The car was a frisky, fuel-injected model, but I was horrified at the amount of petrol it consumed. Winston, who had been the nurse to my previous car, said when I picked it up from his garage/hospital, 'Hey, Cath. You ain't never driven such a powerful automobile. It takes a lot of juice to make this baby perform. Just ease up on that pedal which says "go".' His dreadlocks bounced merrily around his shoulders as he spoke. The car was approved and given Winston's clean bill of health.

It was loaded full of presents for the *aubergiste*, his family, and Bill and Janie. My Bill's son, Daniel, was going to join us in the Lot for New Year's Eve. There was a cache of assorted fireworks secreted in the boot for that occasion.

A small zipped bag contained the tapes Bill, in his role as disc jockey, had chosen to entertain us along the route: a little Elgar to serenade us as far as Portsmouth, and then, in France, Berlioz and Saint-Saens, interspersed (to fulfil my need to hear vocabulary) with Edith Piaf and Charles Trenet, which Jeremy had kindly recorded for me from his vast musical library. For the final hour, when we would ascend into the mountains of the Haute-Loire, he had chosen César Franck's Symphony to accompany us, mindful of its dramatic climax.

We were not even three blocks away from our address when Bill turned to me with a smile, poised his index finger and, with an Oliver-Hardy-like twirling gesture, depressed the radio-cassette's 'on' button. The digital read-out screen lit up and blinked: CODE... CODE... CODE.

'What's that supposed to mean?' he asked, trying to feed the Elgar tape into the machine. I had just joined the Fulham Palace Road and was busy paying attention to the traffic and the pedestrians who were assuming their right to traverse the zebra crossings, regardless of the speed of the approaching cars.

'What does what mean?' I replied, my eyes remaining on the road.

'Code. It keeps repeating, code.'

I darted a glance to the little screen. 'Oh, shit. It means it won't work without the code,' I said with an inkling of looming disaster.

'Well, what's the code, then?' Desperation coloured his question.

'I haven't got the slightest idea,' I admitted. 'Look in the glove compartment. There should be a radio manual. Maybe it's written on it.'

The manual was there but, naturally, without the number.

'I'm not going to France unless I have my music!' he declared. 'Turn the car around! I want to go home.'

We'd arrived in Putney High Street. Doing a U-turn would have been impossible; but then he wouldn't know, never having driven a car.

'How can you not know the code!?' he demanded rather angrily.

'I forgot to ask. It was working when I bought it. I didn't even realise it needed a code,' I answered defensively as the four letters continued to flash accusingly on the screen.

'Why has it been lost? Who lost it? I'd planned what to play every single stage of the way. I want my music or the trip's off!'

We had just left Robin Hood Roundabout behind and were now on the A3, wedged into the remnants of London's south-west-flowing rush-hour traffic. I blamed his upbringing for this petulant behaviour. His parents must have spoiled him rotten.

'They would have removed the battery at the garage while the motor was connected to the computer that was checking for the fault which was making the fuel consumption so exorbitant,' I explained. 'And while so doing, the radio lost its memory for the code.'

'That's a load of gobbledygook,' he muttered and slumped deeper into the passenger seat.

Bereft of his music, his mood grew darker the nearer we came to Portsmouth. I'd so looked forward to this trip and now I had a bundle of gloom sitting beside me.

'We'll make a stop tomorrow morning in France and I'll ring the dealers who I bought the car from. They'll be able to get the code for me,' I said to placate him.

'The ferry doesn't dock until seven. France is an hour ahead, so we'll be driving in silence for over two hours before you can even make the call and hope for a reply. Then it will take another two hours before they'll get the code.' He was almost in tears.

I had an inspiration. Every piece of paper to do with the buying of the car was tucked into a folder and travelling with us. Perhaps the name of the previous owner would be amongst them. That person would have been the one who'd inserted the code. I mentioned this to Bill who immediately fished out the plastic folder from the glove compartment, switched on the reading light and rifled through the documents. He found a man's name with an address in Surrey.

Most of the traffic had cleared. I put my foot down on the 'go' pedal and promised him to ring directory enquiries for the man's phone number the moment we arrived at the boarding terminal. His mood immediately lifted and he began to hum some of the Elgar he had intended to play.

We arrived at the docks, did the necessaries at the ticket booth, parked the car in our allotted lane and hurried to the terminal with twenty minutes to spare before the 10:30 boarding time. Bill spotted the bar and I spotted the two public phones. They were both occupied. I listened to the conversations to decide which of the two would hang up first to wait behind that person, and guessed wrongly. The other phone became free but not before someone else had queued in order to grab it, so I stood glaring at the dandruff on the back of a stranger's shoulder, willing him to say 'goodbye'. Eventually, he replaced the receiver and I rushed to pick it up. Armed with the name and address, I called directory enquiries and prayed the number would be listed. It was. Bill had bought the drinks and found a table. I caught his eyes, gave him the thumbs up and dialled the number I'd been given. There was an indistinct announcement on the tannoy which I ignored. Now I prayed not to hear a recorded voice on an answering machine. After two rings, there was a response.

'Hello!' said a man sounding quite chipper.

'Hello! You don't know me...' I began hectically, 'but I just bought your car.'

'Really?' he said, bemused. 'My car's parked in the garage.'

'No, no. I mean the red Peugeot. I've only had it for a couple of weeks.'

'Nothing wrong, I hope. It was perfectly fine when the dealers took it off my hands,' he said defensively.

'No, I'm not complaining. It's a wonderful car. I'm ringing you from the Portsmouth ferry docks and we're just about to board...'

'I know it well!' he interrupted. 'Going to France, are you?'

'Yes! That's right.' I was trying to speak as rapidly as I could. 'I don't have the time to explain. You'll have to trust me but I've lost the code to make the radio-cassette work. We're taking a long journey through France and my husband will divorce me if he can't listen to his music.'

Another announcement was made over the tannoy and I noticed people were gathering their belongings to leave the terminal and return to their cars.

He must have decided a thief couldn't possibly have invented such a story and said with some concern, 'I see. But it wasn't my car. It belonged to my wife and I don't know the number.'

'Is she there? Can I speak to her?' I asked urgently.

'No, I'm afraid she's in Portugal and I have no way of contacting her.'

'Oh, no!' I howled.

'Listen,' he continued quickly, 'she's supposed to ring me any moment now. I thought it was her when I picked up the phone. Hang up and ring me back in ten minutes. I should have it for you then.'

I joined Bill at the table and told him of the conversation. By now the terminal had considerably emptied. Only a few stragglers, possibly foot passengers, were left behind finishing their drinks. I noticed some of the lanes in the huge car park outside were vacated, the drivers having been signalled to board.

The ferry was leaving at 11:00. It was now 10:45. I stared at the clock, frustrated at how slowly the ten minutes were passing. More vehicles were making their way to board; and then the headlights of the cars in our lane were being put on. Their exhausts belched white clouds in the cold night air as they, too, began to move. I ran to the phone and dialled the number. Short frequent beeps announced that it was busy.

Calling over to Bill, I said, 'He's talking to her now. Go to the car!' Ours was the only one left standing.

'What am I supposed to do? I can't drive!' he shouted across the now empty space. The only people remaining were the ones closing the shutters of the bar.

'Someone has to be with the car! They might think there's a bomb on board.' I crossed over to him and handed him the piece of paper I'd written the number down on. 'You phone him, then,' I said.

'But you know I'm hopeless with numbers. I'll never remember the code!'

'Try! There are only four digits. Write them down on the paper!' I gave him a pen and ran out to our lane where a boarding official was circling the car while speaking on a walkie-talkie.

'I'm here!' I screamed. 'It's all right,' and quickly opened the door to get in.

'You're late!' he admonished me. 'Board immediately!'

'I can't. I'm waiting for my husband. He's still inside.'

71

'If you don't move now, you won't board at all!' he shouted angrily.

Bill just being on the phone, other than calling in instructions for remote brain surgery, was not going to be a good enough excuse, so I thought of the next best thing; something this angry official might empathise with.

'We stopped at an Indian restaurant on our way here and had a vindaloo,' I lied to him. 'And now my husband has diarrhoea!' I said, begging for understanding. That stopped his scowling. I turned the engine on and Bill emerged from the terminal, running towards me.

'Thank God you gave me that paper,' he said as he reached the car and opened the passenger door. And then remarked, 'I'd have never managed without it,' still within hearing distance of the now sympathetic official, who once again lifted the walkie-talkie to his mouth.

Bill entered the code he'd written down and within seconds, Elgar blared through our speakers. The car was quickly waved through passport control and then up the steep ramp to be the last vehicle swallowed into the belly of our ferry, the *Pride of Hampshire.*

"He was a very nice man,' Bill was saying while we climbed the steps in the narrow staircase to achieve the upper decks of the ship. 'I explained I was the husband of the woman who had called, and he told me not to divorce you and then spouted the number very quickly. He even wished us *bon voyage.*'

We were met on every level that we reached by a steward who welcomed us aboard and discreetly pointed out to Bill the whereabouts of the lavatories. By the third time, as we continued mounting the stairs, Bill turned to me and whispered, 'Why are they so obsessed with showing us the loos? I only want to find the bar.'

I didn't dare tell him.

It was not yet daylight when we disembarked to the sound of Bill's chosen music. Many times during that first journey, I was grateful to that stranger and his wife's prompt phone call with the information of her previous code. In France with a right-hand drive Bill was put, as it were, in the driver's seat. It was up to his judgement whether or not I could pass the many articulated lorries directly in front of us. If he'd been sitting in a brooding silence, he may have nurtured suicidal thoughts. As it was, the predicament for a passenger in an English car was already nerve-wracking enough, especially one who has no experience of the speed of acceleration the driver is capable of. Whenever we arrived after that seven-hour drive, Bill was in a far more delicate state than I. No wonder he opened his cooled thermos flask as we neared Clermont-Ferrand and enjoyed the pre-mixed vodka and tonic prepared therein.

After six hours of driving with only short petrol and coffee stops along the way, one would think I should have been tired; but the last hour of the journey, as we climbed into the Massif Central from Issoire and headed towards La Chaise-Dieu, the scenery was so utterly magnificent, it literally made my heart beat faster. Those views, even today, work as an amphetamine on my system. Henri Pourrat, the author of *Gaspard des Montagnes* who walked the route before it was properly modernised for the automobile, has definitively immortalised the beauty of those landscapes in his literary works. I wouldn't dare describe them.

Bill's timing was perfect. César Franck's Symphony climaxed exactly as we rounded a bend and the majesty of La Chaise-Dieu's abbey came into view. Dominating the plateau, from a distance it appeared like a throne and all the town's medieval buildings were closely gathered beneath it, as if worshipping at its feet. The music quietened and the image before me blurred. I instinctively turned the windscreen wipers on.

'It's not raining,' said Bill, softly. We both had tears in our eyes.

The weather was sweet as promised. We sat that afternoon in soft sunlight on the terrace in front of the *auberge* watching little men like Snow White's seven dwarfs scampering about on our roof, clipping the last tiles into place. Then, a belly was pushed through the narrow gateway. It was closely followed by its owner. He was the chief of the little men whose finishing touches we were admiring.

'*Monsieur Bill!*' he called out in a castrato voice. '*Et c'est la Marie!*' he added as he saw us and approached with an outstretched hand. It was the first time we had met 'Roger Rabbit', master carpenter, roof builder and a notorious tweaker of female buttocks. Patrick had put all our works out to tender and sent the estimates to us in London. He could vouch for all of the builders concerned and so we obviously chose the cheapest amongst them. Roger's estimate seemed the most reasonable and we were already pleased with what he had achieved.

I corrected him as to my name, saying that it was Catherine.

'*Non, non,*' he replied, '*c'est toujours, La Marie!*'

We later learned that in order not to confuse the names of his numerous women, he simply called each 'Marie'. And every woman he met was a

73

prospective partner to cavort with in a bed, on some straw, in the woods, or whilst twirling her on a dance floor. His brilliant blue eyes were set in a face as round and red as an apple. The Buddah-like swelling he carried above his belted trousers was the result of forty years of indulgence where wine and food were concerned, the weight of which had caused a noticeable bowing of his legs. But the local ladies loved him, as Bill and I did in an instant.

Having finished, his workers scuttled down their ladders. One by one he introduced them. As we shook their hands, I had the feeling they were slightly in awe of us. Roger had obviously been told by Patrick what our professions were, and he then exaggerated in his high-pitched voice. I heard him describe Bill as a famous English director, equating him with Truffaut, while I was compared to the film star Catherine Deneuve. Who were we to disillusion them?

I can't remember how many bottles of wine Jean-Pierre opened on that occasion, as most of them were not on our bill. Roger built a good roof. He was also extremely generous. No wonder the ladies liked him. We were all in a mood to celebrate. The roof had been beautifully completed and in a comparatively short time, which, as Roger added, was due to the unusually clement weather. In between calling out, '*Patron,* open another bottle, we're still thirsty!' he made promises to maintain his excellent standards when building our bedroom floor, staircases, windows, doors, everything that was made of wood. It was dark by the time he and his gang climbed into their vans to drive home. I wished them a safe arrival and was glad not to be on a winding road with the possibility of meeting them in my path.

The day before leaving to drive to the Lot, we woke up to a Christmas-card scene. The temperature had dropped dramatically and heavy clouds had gathered in ambush during the night. Snow is silent. With stealth, while one sleeps, it lays siege to your house. Our car was unrecognisable under a foot of snow, and the powdery flakes were still falling. By the afternoon it seemed I'd parked an igloo in front of the terrace gate.

The *aubergiste*'s three daughters were having a wonderful time. They had been given a sleigh for Christmas, which should have forewarned me, and were taking it in turns to drag it up the hill to the church, from whence they'd merrily slide back down towards the terrace, exactly where my igloo stood. Noticing the speed of their descent, I began to have doubts as to the incline of this hill. My car was going to have to climb it in order to begin our journey to Bill and Janie's the next morning. Mr Hays (I had too many Bills in my life) was happily unaware of our predicament, sleeping soundly after the food and wine he'd consumed at the previous day's lunch.

It was the first time I had heard the question, 'You mean, you are not equipped?' It was posed with a hint of panic. 'You 'ave no shaines?' Jean-Pierre asked in amazement. I'd swept the snow from the car and, with his help, and two shovels, we'd dug out a path for the rediscovered wheels to glide over. It was then Jean-Pierre noticed I was driving on summer tyres; useless for negotiating the hill and necessitating the use of chains, which had somehow been omitted from my Christmas shopping list.

'I thought I wouldn't need them,' I said weakly. 'I was depending on the peasant forecast.'

'Nowbody's perfect,' he replied, quoting the final line from *Some Like it Hot*.

I learned a few things that afternoon. At three thousand feet altitude, during the winter, even in southern France, blizzards were likely to blow; a front-wheel-drive car has to be backed up a slippery slope; and help in Bonneval is only a phone call away. It arrived in the stocky form of Jacqui.

Somewhere in the recesses of my mind I remembered an image when I was a small child in Salzburg. In similar snowy conditions, the pavements were strewn with straw, enabling pedestrians to walk without slipping. The eastern barn contained plenty of that.

After the children's tobogganing and my trying to drive the car up the hill several times, only to slide back down again, sometimes even sideways, we had between us created a smooth, packed surface not even a tractor could have negotiated. That was when I remembered the straw. I borrowed the sleigh, dragged it to the barn, piled a couple of bales upon it and with the help of the two eldest girls pulled it like a *troika* to where my car was stuck. We carpeted the treacherous surface with the straw. Jean-Pierre and Anna Magnani looked on in disbelief. I tried to explain that this was how as a child I had seen it done. There was something else I learned that day: it is very difficult to convince the French to adopt a foreign solution. They could not imagine my way would work. I got back in the car but my failure at the next attempt only added credence to their misgivings.

Then Jacqui came on the scene. He was a true Auvergnat, lived in a nearby hamlet, was well acquainted with the vagaries of the local winter weather and knew how to deal with them. Anna Magnani had phoned him to come to my aid.

Seeing the animal bedding covering the snow, he asked, 'What's this?' I thought it was blatantly obvious and tried once again to explain. He gave me a look which conveyed his sympathy for my utter ignorance.

'I need a broom and a shovel,' he said like a surgeon to a nurse in an operating theatre. He was given both and proceeded to sweep away the straw as he climbed towards the summit. There, unbeknownst to Jean-Pierre and myself, was a mound set back from the road. With the shovel, he uncovered it from its casing of snow to reveal a pyramid of grit. He filled the shovel and, waving it from side to side, covered generously the path I would have to climb.

'Get the back of the car to face the hill,' he told me. 'It cannot pull itself up. The engine has to push.' With the two men's help, I manoeuvred the car into position and, in reverse gear, managed the steep ascent. I'll admit: grit is better than straw, when you know where to find it.

With the car safely parked at the top and facing the direction we would have to take the following morning, we retired to the *auberge* with Jacqui to drink to this minor success. During that animated hour I learned something else: there was more than just neighbourly friendship developing between Jacqui and the *aubergiste*'s wife.

It was a terrifying drive to reach Bill and Janie. We'd made a date to meet at a restaurant in their nearest town, Bretenoux, at noon. They'd begun to worry seriously when at two p.m. we had not yet arrived. An hour later, they were relieved to see our car creeping into the parking directly opposite to where they were sitting. I had driven over snow and the wheels had skated on ice. Several times we had barely missed slipping into deep ravines as the car skidded round the tortuous hairpin bends on the narrow mountain passes we had to cross.

All the tension of the past few hours had gone directly to my legs. Bill had to support me as I walked on shaking knees to the restaurant entrance. Janie and her Bill noticed my distress and rushed out to join us. With everyone's help I was led to a chair. A glass of wine was put into my hand. Unfortunately, the nerves had got there first. Most of the content was spilt on the tablecloth before it reached my lips. Never again would I attempt that drive in the winter without being 'equipped'.

But it was worth it. During that lunch Janie told us a story which I'd have skied from the Haute-Loire to hear (and I'm a dangerously incompetent skier).

They had owned their house for several years but, lacking the finances, were forced to do the renovations themselves. During the early stages, their French was rudimentary. They did as I was doing now: searching in a dictionary for the words they would need, sometimes assuming, as I had, that the English one would mean the same in French. But simply reading a word from a page, even with phonetic symbols, can lead to mispronunciations.

While on a visit to the house and doing the work around them, Janie's husband Bill had gone up to the attic to examine the roof timbers. He discovered that the ridge pole was in need of attention, but not seriously enough to require replacing. He sent Janie off to the local *bricolage* (DIY store) to buy a large quantity of wood preservative. She didn't know her way around the shop and accosted an assistant to guide her to the correct aisle. Having informed him of her needs, she was amazed that he burst out laughing.

In her best French but mispronouncing *poutre* (beam) and also using a *faux ami*, she had told him, '*Nous avons une très grande pute dans notre grenier. Elle est énorme. Mon mari a besoin de beaucoup, beaucoup des préservatifs.*'

Translated into English what she had said to a French ear was: 'We have a very big whore in our attic. She is enormous. My husband needs many, many condoms.'

When, in years to come, I was serving breakfast to my French guests and had placed my home-made jams on the table, I liked to assure them they contained absolutely no preservatives, and used that *faux ami* on purpose. I knew I'd get a giggle. Well, I was still an actress at heart.

Bill's son, Daniel, arrived the day before New Year's Eve. Between us we had convinced Bill to forgo his oath of never wanting to see another firework display again. It could not be as spectacular as the one we'd witnessed in Cannes, but at least this one he would be directing. All afternoon they worked, planting the fireworks into their positions from whence they would be ignited to illuminate the sky above the Simons' hilltop house at exactly midnight.

We sat around a large kitchen table amongst other friends of Bill and Janie's enjoying a sumptuous meal. The programme on the black-and-white television set in a corner of the room announced the appointed hour and we all headed with excitement through the door to watch the display. While we had been eating, however, the clear black sky in which we'd earlier seen the twinklings of tiny stars had been displaced by a cover of clouds. We decided to ignore them, hoping they were high enough, and proceeded with the show.

Father and son set about lighting the cheaper ones which exploded to our delight just above our heads. We could only afford the one spectacular rocket which I'd been promised would take off high into the sky and explode into a myriad of multi-coloured sparks. Bill had saved that one for last.

It shot up into the darkness. We waited for the explosion. Nothing happened. The rocket had streaked into the dense clouds to display its burst of sparks beyond our sight. We knew it had exploded because a momentary, teasing light brightened the covering above. Our expectations for the rocket had led to disappointment and then, inadvertently, to laughter.

I often think of that night with the rocket and compare it with hindsight to what was happening to our lives at that time. The act of buying the house was the lighting of a fuse. We were being projected towards a particular future, the destination of which was beyond our perception. But we were being taken there, nevertheless.

Chapter Six

I T WOULD TAKE EIGHTEEN MONTHS FOR THE HOUSE to become habitable. The express completion of the roof deceived us into believing we could live in it by the following spring or summer at the latest. In fact, it was not until March 1991 that we took possession and spent our first night within its walls. The length of time the building works took was mainly due to our absence. We had not set a date in a contract for their completion. There was no penalty clause. Patrick advised us to make more appearances, to warn the builders of our imminent arrival and our expectations of finding another stage completed. I sent postcards to Roger from London with pictures of the Queen's Guards and threatened a British invasion if he didn't complete his jobs so that the mason, plumbers and electricians could get on to do theirs. I phoned the wives of the builders who understood our longing to take possession of the house, but they told me of the many other sites their husbands were employed on. It was a matter of time and priority. We'd evidently chosen the most popular builders.

Once the roof was in place the house was completely gutted. We had decided on concrete flooring except for the bedroom and bathroom which would be of wood. They were planned in the attic where we could admire our enormous round timbers holding up the gabled roof, and the pine slats that made up the underside of the very expensive insulation Patrick had insisted we needed to survive the severe winters the region could experience. I had argued at the time that the extra cost would be unnecessary as the house would only serve as a holiday home and we would avoid spending time there during the coldest seasons. In the future I was grateful to him for my having lost the argument.

During the initial renovations, Bill and Patrick only had minor disputes. The more major ones would come later, when the eastern barn would be converted to house the four rooms for the bed-and-breakfast venture. Patrick was an architect; Bill was a director. I became a diplomat bringing the two temperamental personalities back on speaking terms.

We had bought the house for four thousand pounds and were going to spend at least another forty making it habitable. I was wrong about French building prices; they compared equally with English ones, mainly due to the elevated VAT of 20.6%. By chance, I'd spotted an ad in an English paper from a French bank offering mortgages at an interest rate of 10.5%. At that time, our home-grown rate was nearer to 14%. We decided we would have to borrow some money towards the rebuilding costs. This became our first introduction to French bureaucracy.

As a single actress, I'd managed twice in the past to obtain a mortgage. If the building society was willing to lend money to someone who fell into the high-risk category, described vaguely between 'gypsy and female vagabond', the paperwork was not too strenuous. We approached the French bank as a couple and were informed of the *dossier* we would have to supply before a favourable decision could be given. We had to produce every page of our passports, including the visas; our company's last half-yearly statements; a letter from the company secretary; another from our accountant; a letter from our agents prognosticating our future prospects; telephone, electricity, water and rate bills and service charges of our London address; a letter from our existing mortgagee confirming our prompt payments; life insurance policies; tax statements; the architect's plans; builders' estimates; all required construction permissions; deeds to the house; marriage certificate; and divorce certificates from previous marriages. They could not have been keen on bigamy. We were amazed they didn't ask for a certified shoe size. All this documentation would already make a hefty bundle. But wait for it... we needed to submit *seven* photocopies of each! When the *dossier* was complete, we dragged it to the bank in a suitcase which, fortunately, had wheels.

Unknown to us, when we had bought the house, if we had needed a French mortgage we would only have had six months from the date of purchase to apply. French law did not permit the exploitation of turning the value of a property into a liquid asset. It was a major reason why their prices, as opposed to English ones, remained comparatively low. A house could only be mortgaged once.

We had tendered our application just in time. The helpful young French woman we were dealing with announced that she would be taking the papers in person to the bank's branch in Le Puy. I had a sneaking suspicion her air fare with the *dossier* checked in as luggage would have cost less than if they sent it unaccompanied via the post. We received a letter shortly afterwards granting our request, and repaid £13,000 at a fixed rate of 10.5% over the next ten years. Needless to say, with our luck in financial matters, the borrowing rates in England not long thereafter dropped well below that figure.

Whenever we could, we hopped on the ferry and sped to the house, still paying for a room above the restaurant of the *auberge* and sharing the family's bathroom. At the end of our stay, we were usually given an imaginative bill which, when studied on the homeward-bound ferry, often made us laugh. Bill and I both liked a drink, but I don't think either of us could have survived sharing eleven litres of wine during dinner. The price of the room began ridiculously low but that was corrected every time we returned. Within a year, a certain small hamlet in France suffered over 200% inflation. Thank God, it didn't affect the rest of the country. We forgave Jean-Pierre his creative calculations, considering it the price to pay for the nightly perform-ances he inadvertently acted for us. For a man who played the buffoon, he was surprisingly cultured. He had an impressive knowledge of classical music, as well as jazz. He devoured books, and his interest in the cinema, opera and theatre was more than shallow. His appreciation for Bill's many humorous theatrical stories was not pretended. Uprooting his family from Paris to run a small *auberge* in the wilderness of the Haute-Loire seemed an incongruous choice for him to have made, we thought. And I sometimes wondered, had he noticed his wife was wearing higher heels and shorter skirts, more make-up and a new very becoming hairstyle? Bonneval was far away from the Champs-Élysées but not too far from Jacqui.

Word had got around that an English couple had bought the old Auberge Valentin. We received a letter addressed to us in London offering the sale of two fields directly below the eastern barn. They were joined to its walls and led down to the river. The prospect of owning those fields teased my desire of one day looking through our living-room windows and watching a horse grazing on them. The handwriting in the letter was difficult to discern, as if the claws of a very small chicken had been dipped into ink and then allowed to run amok on a piece of paper. I replied, tentatively admitting to the logic of buying the land but adding that, of course, it would depend on the price;

and contacted Jean-Pierre to arrange a meeting with the owner concerned for our next visit to Bonneval.

It took place during a very cold and wet month. We had no idea of the price of land but assumed, as the top field consisted mainly of rock face and only the lower one, whose edge included a part of the river, was good for grazing, that they would not be prohibitive to buy. Jean-Pierre offered to accompany us, considering we were too innocent to deal with the wily Auvergnats. The owner was a farmer who lived in the rugged countryside a little distance from the trotting course just outside Jullianges, a village seven kilometres from us. This official racetrack boasts being at the highest altitude of any in Europe; it meets only twice a year.

Dusk was already falling when we found ourselves rattling over a dirt path towards a walled settlement perched on a hill. I was glad that Jean-Pierre was driving as I wouldn't have wanted to test my car's suspension on this bone-jolting track. We entered through an open gateway and stopped the car in a messy courtyard where the tyres immediately sank into a dark muck. A typical stone farmhouse attached to a huge barn was a short distance from the car. There were other outbuildings (which the French call *hangars*) scattered within the walls. All manner of farm animals were at liberty to roam about. It took some courage to get out of the car, as the dogs, pigs, goats and cows were beginning to pay undue interest to our presence, approaching us with barks, grunts, bahs and moos. This was free-range farming taken to extremes. The most frightening, though, were the feathered species, most of which I hardly recognised, only knowing them from super-markets where I'd bought them plucked and labelled.

Birds are vicious. No wonder Alfred Hitchcock could terrify us with his film. Every leg that was outstretched in order to get out of the car was attacked by a beak of one variety or another. We closed the car doors and waited to be rescued by the farmer. Alerted by the commotion outside, he eventually appeared and led us to his door, shooing the animals away from our path. The three of us followed behind him grouped tightly together, but our legs still made easy targets for the crazed peckings of the noisy fowl. Herding us from behind was a goat with very lethal-looking horns. I had taken him earlier for a lactating nanny until I realised the two heavy gourds hanging between his hind legs were actually his testicles.

We were ushered through the doorway which opened directly into a dimly lit kitchen and beckoned to sit around a large, rectangular table. A wood-burning stove, which was used for cooking, squatted in the fireplace giving off a pleasant heat. The bare lightbulb above the table, the ugly plastic cloth which covered it, and the rusting taps that provided water for the shallow enamel sink were the only visible evidence the old man lived in the twentieth century.

The farmer had an unmistakable Auvergnat look. Lines had gouged their way into his face, the result, no doubt, of working outdoors in severe conditions. Bill and I had marvelled at some of the faces we had seen in the local bars. The region was a paradise for casting sessions if you were looking for characters whose histories were evident in the hieroglyphics etched across their brows, around their eyes, down their cheeks. There was no such thing as an unobtrusive nose. Every nose we saw had attitude. And their eyes were usually set very wide apart, as if a greater field of vision was required amongst these vast horizons.

Glasses were placed in front of us and filled with red wine which he poured from a small plastic barrel. The bargaining process began. Bill and I could never have done the negotiations on our own. The farmer's accent was entirely incomprehensible, even sometimes to Jean-Pierre, as he later admitted. I understood the figure of five hundred thousand but only after Jean-Pierre repeated it in shocked amazement. Then we realised the old man was still counting in old French francs, from the time before de Gaulle's cunning solution in 1956 to the country's mounting inflation by simply ignoring the last two zeroes from the digits on the existing printed notes. Even so, we were not prepared to pay five thousand modern francs for the two parcels of land, which I would later discover only a mountain goat or a sure-footed donkey could graze. He was very generous, though, with his wine, refilling our glasses the second they were empty.

Jean-Pierre haggled on our behalf. We had told him on no account to go beyond three thousand francs. The atmosphere was friendly and I had the distinct feeling the farmer was enjoying this transaction. But he was not going to budge from his demand of five thousand. Slowly Jean-Pierre raised our original offer of one thousand by doubling it. The farmer grinned, inhaling a whistle while shaking his head from side to side, meaning no; and offered us more wine which we, of course, dutifully accepted. During what seemed this impasse, Bill became fascinated with the surface our elbows were leaning on. Lifting a corner of the plastic cover revealed the soft ochre colours of a thick, antique pine table. It was the sort of possession a devotee of *Country Life* would have drooled over.

'To hell with the fields,' Bill said. 'I'll give him five thousand for this table.'

'You cain not do that!' Jean-Pierre quickly interjected. 'That is an hinsult!'

'Five thousand francs isn't enough?' Bill asked while his hand caressed the smooth grain of the wood. 'This would be perfect in the house,' he said, turning to me. I have to admit I was extremely tempted; but there was a feeling of political incorrectness to the situation. After all, we'd come to buy fields, not the man's furniture.

The farmer noticed our interest and amiably showed us, at the head of the table, a deep, wide drawer. It opened, gliding smoothly; and sequestered therein was a dark round loaf, like a bloated cowpat.

'*Pour le pain*,' he said proudly. It was the first time I had seen this rich, dark, rye bread which, unlike the baguette, kept moist for several days.

'Practical, too,' observed Bill. 'Go on,' he demanded of Jean-Pierre again. 'Ask him if he wants to sell it.'

'It is an hinsult, I tell you!' Jean-Pierre said indignantly.

'It is an insult to cover this table with this disgusting plastic sheet,' responded Bill almost angrily. 'He obviously can't appreciate it.'

This was a hint of what would later become an obsession with Bill, when he longed to enforce on the local population his conceptions of taste and beauty. In the future, I would call him the 'aesthetics Gestapo'. When the commune, ecologically motivated, set up three large recycling bins near to the bridge at the bottom of our fields, Bill cried out in horror, 'How can they desecrate that site!'

'They have to go somewhere,' I'd reason with him.

'Why there? In full view!' he'd shout.

'So people can find them,' I'd answer logically.

'I'd blow them sky high,' he'd grumble.

There was a modern house being built with breeze blocks in a picturesque landscape. 'Look at that abomination!' he complained.

'They can't afford to build it with stone,' I argued.

'Then let them buy ruins! There are plenty of them around.'

'They're too expensive to renovate.'

'Look at that debris all over the place!'

'That's building material. They haven't finished yet.'

'That mess will never be cleared. And the house will never be rendered. We'll always have that ugly grey brick to look at.' Unfortunately, he was only too often correct.

'I'd shoot them. And the people who allowed them to build it,' was usually his final decree.

In the farmer's kitchen Jean-Pierre squirmed with embarrassment and refused to translate Bill's comments relating to the table.

'You cain not wok in somebody's 'ouse and hoffer to buy what they heat from,' he reprimanded Bill.

Blissfully unaware of Bill's intentions for the table, the farmer poured more wine. Whether he would have felt insulted or not, never became an issue. We continued to debate the price of the fields. Jean-Pierre offered our limit of three thousand. That too was calmly refused.

I'd had a little too much liquid during the last hour and needed urgently to relieve my bladder, and asked politely where a toilet could be found. The farmer pointed to the door we'd entered through. Presuming there was a shack outside, I asked directions. He lifted his arm and made a waving gesture with his hand which Jean-Pierre translated as, 'Wherever you want,' smirking ever so slightly.

'Can't you wait?' asked Bill sympathetically.

'No,' was my definite reply. Not wanting the farmer to know that I was shocked, I assumed a gracious, diplomatic smile and exited into the night. The kitchen windows cast a meagre glow, and that only for a few metres from the building. Feeling it impolite to squat so near to his house, I ventured further away into the darkness. Moving carefully, as my wellingtons were sticking into the mud, I reached a grassy area which felt more solid under my feet. I quickly unfastened my jeans and lowered them along with the woolly tights I was wearing underneath, squatted and began to pee.

The relief was divine but I had forgotten the animals. The feathered demons had spotted me. I had a feeling they had been lying in wait for just this sort of opportunity. Those with white feathers glowed in the dark. I knew they were geese and they'd surrounded me. As my eyes grew more accustomed to the darkness, I realised their four-legged friends had also come for the show. I felt I was starring in a sequel to Orwell's *Animal Farm*. This one was called *The Revenge* in which the birds dealt out a dubious justice. In the middle of a pee, my bare buttocks were at the optimum pecking height for a goose. They nipped my defenceless behind, no doubt in punishment for Christmases past. I was grateful the goat with its dagger-like horns, the pig and the cow were keeping a discreet distance, allowing the geese to do their dirty work for them.

There was nothing I could do but giggle hysterically in order to survive this humiliation. I was the daughter of a baron. My mother was a countess. I had starred in films and even had a fan club. And here I was peeing on a stranger's plot of land with his geese assaulting my naked posterior. If I'd ever had pretensions, this was the ultimate equalising experience.

Finished, I pulled up my clothes and headed quickly towards the lighted windows. The flock followed, pecking at my boots but with a little less appetite. Now that they had discovered a taste for flesh, rubber obviously didn't compare. Before I opened the door, I turned around. They had formed a semicircle behind me. Beady black eyes glared at me and their beaks smiled in triumph. I vowed never to become a vegetarian.

Back inside, I took my place around the table but sat down a little more gingerly than before.

'Does that feel better now?' Bill asked innocently.

'Not necessarily,' I answered through gritted teeth. 'Wait till you see my bum.' He gave me an enquiring look to which I responded, 'If you have to go outside to wee, do it from a ladder. Geese have long necks.' He understood.

During my humiliating absence, the price the farmer wanted for the fields had remained the same. It seemed useless to continue bargaining and so we decided to take our leave.

'Don't you want the land?' the old man asked anxiously, as if he didn't want his evening's entertainment to end.

'Tell him,' Bill asked Jean-Pierre to translate, 'he approached us about the land. It's of no significance to us.'

And I added, 'We're not going to climb down the cliff face to create a vegetable garden.'

The farmer gave a short laugh, and we were told that nothing was allowed to be grown on it anyway.

This was even more reason for the land to be sold cheaply. Much later, I discovered from a *notaire* while helping an English couple to negotiate for fields that the average price of fallow land was one franc a square metre. We were discussing buying one thousand square metres for which the farmer was expecting us to pay five times the going rate.

The matter depended on for whom the land was more important. As a result of the Napoleonic code which makes it impossible to disinherit your children and which is still practised to this day, the farmer would have inherited from previous generations these puny parcels of land twenty kilometres from his home. They were useless to him, and certainly not worth five thousand francs to us.

'There is wood on the land,' he mentioned as if this was of great consequence.

'Wood? Where?' Bill and I asked.

'I think 'e means the poles which 'old up the barbed woire,' Jean-Pierre said dismissively.

It was time to go. We'd not achieved what we had gone there for. The evening, except for the incident outside, had been convivial. We thanked the farmer for his hospitality and invited him to drop in on us should he ever need to visit his fields. With his help, we managed to walk to the car without being molested unduly by his animals and said our final farewells. Jean-Pierre started the motor and turned on the lights. At that moment the farmer stepped forward and tapped on the window. Jean-Pierre opened it.

'Very well,' said the farmer, leaning into the car. 'Three thousand francs. But the wood remains mine.' He grinned and extended his hand which we all shook. A date with a *notaire* for the signatures would be arranged. We said another farewell and Jean-Pierre put the car into gear. The wheels spun in the mud until they finally gripped and we drove away. The farmer's final compromise was so matter-of-fact that I suspected he would immediately have parted with his fields at that price; only, once agreed, what would there have been left to talk about? He had thoroughly enjoyed the past two hours. Perhaps he didn't like to drink alone.

The next day we examined our purchase. There was indeed barbed-wire fencing which necessitated wooden pickets, but on the very edge of the river stood three tall and splendid ash trees which we had assumed were part of the general wilderness. This was the wood that did not belong to us. Never mind, because the land abutted on to a fifty-metre stretch of the river. We had fishing rights. So there.

Little by little we learned more about our surroundings and about our house. The new *auberge* was housed in what used to be the presbytery. There was a time when the commune of Bonneval, which consisted of several hamlets dotted about in a large area, had a population exceeding 250 inhabitants. There had been a priest who tended their spiritual needs. His presbytery was a grand house and attached by a secret passage to the little church whose origins dated back to the thirteenth century. In time, when the population shrank, the youth disappeared to find employment in the larger towns and there were fewer weddings and christenings to occupy him. He packed his cassock and went in search of a bigger flock. In the late seventies, the empty residence converted perfectly into a communal *auberge*.

Across from the church, and set back a little from the road, was a large stone structure originally built as a convent. Presumably, the good sisters tended to the priest's more mundane necessities. Upon the demise of the last nun in 1919, the convent was sold to another religious order from further afield and became what the French call a *colonie*: a supervised retreat for children to spend their summer holidays in the open countryside. During the Second World War, it was used as a refuge for young Frenchmen escaping transportation to Germany to work as forced labour in their factories, while the attic of the presbytery sheltered the Jewish refugees. The old convent survived its many functions and is today a rest home for the elderly.

Visitors often comment on their surprise at finding a town hall and a church in such a tiny village. We reply that the *Mairie* serves the larger commune, as does the church.

'But how many people actually live in the village itself?' we are asked.

'The number can fluctuate,' is our answer. 'Including the residents in the old people's home, we can have a population of twelve when we go to sleep at night. The head count varies, depending on how many of us last through till the morning.'

The back room of the *Mairie*, where we had sat around the large table during the purchase, had served as a schoolroom for the children of the commune. They walked on dirt roads from kilometres away, through all weathers, to obtain their education. The teacher, usually a young woman, lived in a little apartment directly above. What an isolated life to lead for someone in their youth, I thought; and then people shared with us their memories of Rosalie, the woman whose bedroom had been built for her by the younger men in her family and proudly shown to us in the western barn. Born locally, she married the Valentin who had established our house as an *auberge*. After bearing four children, she became widowed but continued to run the *auberge* and brought up her three sons and a daughter alone.

It was Rosalie who employed the painter to emblazon VALENTIN AUBERGISTE across the house's façade, and it was she who encouraged the dancing. The property's floorboards, which we would eventually demolish and burn in our fireplace, were sound enough then to hold the weight of prancing feet. The dances mainly took place in the eastern barn. Bales of straw were pushed aside and men and women, having come by foot or ox-cart from as far away as La Chaise-Dieu or Sembadel, bounced joyously about to the happy sounds of an accordion or sometimes even two. Dancing partners became lovers and those lovers became husbands and brides. We've met some of these couples and they are still together today, thanks to the giddy music in Bonneval. I don't think the young teacher would have been bored.

Perhaps it was just my imagination but, later, when certain circumstances led me into deep despair, and I lay awake at night alone, I thought I heard sounds seeping from the walls, as if this atmosphere of laughter, gaiety and music had been captured by the stone. Oddly enough, it comforted me.

In 1995 Bill repainted the façade of the house. The rendering had been repaired and a scaffold built for his endeavours. We had many photographs from which he worked. With his designer's skills he achieved a precise replica of how the house would have looked in the 1940s, even distressing some of the paintwork to make it look aged. We managed to find the same burgundy colour to paint the *art deco* letters of VALENTIN AUBERGISTE across the entire frontage exactly as they had been.

An identical grey was used for the shutters which hung from the windows on either side of the door. Above the door was a skylight which contained four carved wooden numbers, depicting the date of the house: 1814. The figure 4 was mysteriously inverted. He copied the numbers exactly as the originals on to the shutters.

People watched his progression from the restaurant terrace above. They were convinced this Englishman was mad. Having seen a pristinely painted new façade, they witnessed a man daubing mud-coloured paint across it to make it look old and weathered. When he painted the shutters, though, they called out in alarm, '*Non, non! Pas le quatre comme ça! Ca n'est pas Français!*'

Bill was often forced to point to the figures above the door. They would notice the inverted 4 and mutter such phrases as, '*Dis donc... mais, c'est bizarre.*'

When he finished his work of art, he signed his name at the bottom left corner of the house. He dated it 1995. The 5 was also inverted.

Not long after, two men walked down the path to our house. One was elderly, perhaps in his early eighties. He was tall but with a delicate frame and was leaning on the arm of the younger man, whom I reckoned to be in his late forties. It was a warm day and the door was open. I could see them through its empty frame. They stood silently gazing at the front of the house. Then suddenly the old man heaved his shoulders and let out a sob. The younger put an arm around his back to comfort and support him. I went outside to ask if there was something I could do.

'No, no, it's fine,' said the younger man in French. 'But may we have your permission to take a photograph of the house?'

'Of course,' I replied, and saw the tears welling in the old man's eyes and couldn't help but wonder why the image of this building should create such emotion.

'This is my father,' the younger man informed me. 'He was hidden here in Bonneval for several months during the war.'

'In our house?' I asked.

'No. In the presbytery,' the son told me. 'There was a very kind priest. We are Jewish and he was hiding to not be deported. We have just come from there. He says it looks different now, as a restaurant.'

The old man smiled at me and nodded. His throat was too constricted to speak. Then the son continued: 'My father was made welcome in your house. He would drink his coffee and speak to the woman.' At that point the son turned to his father and asked, 'What was her name?'

'Rosalie,' replied the old man softly.

'He has never forgotten the good memories of this place. I promised that one day before he died, I would bring him back.'

The father managed then to ask, 'Are you English?'

'Yes,' I answered. I'd only spoken a few words but my accent must have given me away. Intrigued to know who these people were that I was speaking to, Bill came out to join us. 'We both are,' I went on to say. 'And it was my husband who repainted the façade as it used to be.'

'Thank you,' the old man said to Bill. 'Thank you for not changing it. It is exactly as I remembered.' He extended a hand which Bill proudly shook.

'We are no longer an *auberge* but we'd love to offer you a coffee.' I was sure he had some interesting tales to tell.

'Thank you, but no. My father is very weak. I must get him back to the car,' the son said. Bill and I stood aside while he took the photograph, after which he slowly began to walk his father back up the path.

After they had taken just a few paces, I felt I had to ask. 'Did you dance here?' I needed to know.

The old man turned slowly around. He looked again at the house, his eyes glowing with an inner memory. It took him a moment to reply. 'Yes; somehow, someone always found an accordion and you cannot sit still to that music.' They continued on their way while Bill and I watched them sadly disappear.

This was not the only incident when people returned after decades. For some it was a pilgrimage and finding the old *auberge* still standing, still alive, would speak to us of the happy times that they had spent there. They talked fondly of Rosalie, of her cooking, her charm and her kindness. All of these tributes she earned brought to mind a theatrical expression: she was not going to be an easy act to follow. But we would try.

When finally the workmen had completed their jobs, Bill and I commenced the decorating. We were horrified to see the price of paint in France. The brand name 'Valentin' which, for obvious reasons, we would have preferred and which was actually licensed by Dulux, cost twice as much to buy locally. We ended up weighing down the car, transporting gallons of paint from England to cover our vast acreage of walls. The living room was painted a sunflower yellow and darkened in places to evoke warmth and the smoke which would have emanated from the open fireplace. The angular wooden staircase which floated to the upper floor was coated with a blue glaze, thin enough to allow the grain to show through. Furniture and knick-knacks were in place. Pictures hung on the walls. The house was ready to receive.

We invited the builders, their wives, and Patrick and his wife Marie-Christine, for a party. Half an hour before their arrival, Bill painted what could have been a poster on the elbow-high wall of the bar, behind which the open-plan kitchen was placed. On the yellow background, in very large blue letters, he inscribed his name in French, GUILLAUME VALENTIN and then added, AUBERGISTE. Underneath, to the builders' and Patrick's delight, were all their names painted slightly smaller and the jobs for which they had been responsible. On either side of the writing was a design of branches with leaves. It was a perfect theatrical bill advertising their names for posterity.

Having finished, he proudly showed me his work. It was very attractive, but I noticed one tiny omission. He had failed to include me anywhere in its design.

'Where am I?' I asked, feeling truly hurt.

A genuine, 'Oops, I forgot,' was his guilty reply.

Have you ever seen a woman flounce? I flounced about the large living room in textbook, drama-school fashion. If it had been recorded on camera, my flouncing would have earned an Oscar.

A rather insignificant '*et femme*' (and wife) was hastily joined after his huge name. There was very little space left, so the letters vied with the foliage. They lost. This was not good psychology if you were married to an actress. I'd been used to better billing than that.

But I danced with Roger that night. He'd brought some records of accordion music which we played after the meal. Infected by the happy tunes and the rhythms, everyone rose to their feet to have a go.

It was the first time we witnessed the French in their pursuit of this uninhibited pleasure. It would not be the last. They adored dancing. Almost every party we attended ended with sofas, tables and chairs being pushed up against walls to liberate an area for the mad cavorting which would take place to music. It was a classless, ageless ritual practised in the most simple, as well as *bourgeois*, homes.

In fact, in the latter, the dancing was often even wilder. In a particularly beautiful country house which belonged to a very elite Lyonais family, Bill and I experienced the most bizarre form of dancing. While he was being belly-butted perfectly in rhythm to the music by the ballooned stomach belonging to a well-respected psychiatrist, I found myself with a different group of venerables following the steps of another dance. At some point the music stopped and all of the women had to collapse on the floor. The men then fell on top of them. The women were not allowed to get up unless they kissed the man who was holding them down. Unlike musical chairs, there were no winners or losers. It was just an excuse to kiss someone who was not your wife or your husband. I don't know if such dances have ever been cited as a cause for divorce, but I have been told of irate partners driving their cars into ditches on their way home after witnessing these activities.

Our evening was spent with more propriety. A close competition arose between the smooth *Come Dancing* movements of the plumber and his wife and Roger's and my frenzied twirlings. The plumber won. Roger and I were too dizzy and exhausted to contest the decision. Revenging Bill, though, I allowed Roger to tweak a buttock. Quite overtly.

I think Rosalie would have approved.

Chapter Seven

'**N**APOLEON – ASSASSIN! JEANNE D'ARC – CONNE!'

It was just as well Bill hadn't uttered these words. As an Englishman, he could have been shot on the spot. They were said, during an animated conversation after a few bottles of excellent wine, by a French Huguenot who was a neighbour and became a very dear friend. Because of his uncanny likeness to Jacques Tati, Bill affectionately called him '*mon oncle*'. There are some people you meet which make you curse circumstance. Jacques was already in his early seventies when we were introduced. I had never known Bill to immediately become so fond and respectful of someone before. Jacques' wife, Claudine, was twenty years his junior and loved him beyond passion. We regretted not having met this couple earlier in our lives.

They had bought a farmhouse with a mill on the edge of a river twenty-five years before we had found ours. At the end of a dirt track, surrounded by pines, it lay a mile from us and was their holiday home, now only visited in the summer. When Jacques was younger, though, he thought nothing of driving from Le Havre, where they lived, to enjoy the cross-country skiing in the winter on the forest tracks around Bonneval.

We weren't yet living in the house and still using the *auberge* when we saw the tall, robust figure of a man bending his head to enter through the doorway of the restaurant. His legs were so long they could have been attached to stilts. He had a narrow, angular face which sprouted a positive moustache and a voice which commanded attention.

'*Patron!*' he boomed and, seeing no one behind the bar, he then forcefully tapped his walking stick on the tiled floor. It was evening. Bill and I were the only customers, seated at a table studying some of Patrick's plans. Our attention was drawn to this character whose sudden appearance dominated the room. A woman, an image of femininity, dressed in a light summer blouse and flowing, floral skirt, stood demurely behind him. She was tall but, even so, only reached to his shoulder. In a low, husky voice, she bade him to be patient.

Thus beckoned, Jean-Pierre arrived from the kitchen, immediately bearing the attitude of a beta male. 'Jacques!' he greeted him in feigned surprise, as if the booming voice could have belonged to someone else.

'*Un whisky pour moi et votre meilleur demi-bouteille de vin blanc pour ma femme,*' Jacques ordered. In his company he only permitted the best wine to be drunk. Jean-Pierre disappeared into his *cave* to search for a half-bottle of white nectar which would win this expert's approval.

As if on centre stage, Jacques looked grandly around the room and spotted the two of us staring at him from our corner table. Pointing in our direction with his stick, he asked loudly, '*Vous êtes les Anglais?*' He had seen our car with its English plates parked outside.

Under his glare, we had to control our voices not to squeak.

'*Oui,*' we both said as naturally as we could.

'Aha!' He bellowed and moved menacingly towards us, but I noticed the warm smile on the woman's lips and knew, for the time being, we were safe.

A large hand was extended which shook ours with a firm grip. He introduced first himself, and then his wife as 'Claudine'. On hearing our names, he beamed down at me.

'Catherine,' he repeated, his demeanour softening. 'I have a daughter called Catherine. You remind me of her.' This was said in French.

'It's true,' Claudine added. 'You even look a little like her.' The daughter they were referring to was his from a previous marriage; Claudine had no children of her own.

'Tell him,' Bill asked me to translate, 'he's the spitting image of Jacques Tati.'

Jacques looked very pleased with this observation. Bill stood up, put both hands on his shoulders, gave him a kiss on each cheek, as de Gaulle would have done, and pronounced him, '*Mon Oncle!*'

Once it was established that we were the English couple who had bought the old *auberge*, I tidied our papers away and they sat down to join us. Jean-Pierre arrived with the whisky, an ice bucket and the half-bottle of wine.

Jacques studied the label. It was only opened after his approval, and Jean-Pierre poured a small amount into a glass which Jacques tasted. I also had a glass of white wine in front of me, but of the cheaper variety. Noticing that, he ordered Jean-Pierre to bring me a clean glass and, while so doing, for him to fetch another bottle: a full one.

We were set for a lengthy session. They spoke no English at all, and depended on my meagre French for translation. We managed, nevertheless, to converse for hours and to understand each other thoroughly.

It was the following evening, having been invited for dinner at their *moulin*, that we heard Jacques declare his feelings about Napoleon and Joan of Arc. He considered the former a murderer and detested his glorification, comparing his greed for conquest with that of Hitler. How he described the story of Jeanne d'Arc is too rude to interpret here. Suffice it to say, in my dictionary the word *con* or *conne* (depending on gender) has so many asterisks around its many meanings, depicting various degrees of vulgarity, that they look like a platoon of squashed fleas. I hear it used so often, though, that I consider it one of the most popular words in the French vocabulary; that and *merde*.

He explained to us in great detail how the martyrdom of the 'maiden of Orléans' was a myth; that she had been, most likely, a bastard daughter of a noble, or even, it was strongly rumoured, of the king. As a daughter of the nobility, she had access to an education that became evident in the manner in which she so eloquently defended herself at Bishop Cochon's arraignment.

The fact that she could ride a horse as well as any of the king's cavaliers and that he entrusted his army to her leadership also made it doubtful that she was just a simple shepherdess. Can one imagine a girl who, while guarding her charges, hears sacred voices commanding her to be the instrument of France's salvation in a war against the English? She then bravely approaches the king of a powerful country, to demand recruitment as commander of his forces. Even in the fifteenth century someone would have asked what kind of mushrooms she'd been eating. Charles VII may not have gone down in history as one of France's most glorious kings, but neither, Jacques believed, was he bonkers.

Her existence and many successes on the battlefield against the Anglo-Burgundian alliance were not in question. But the accepted story of her origins and her ending was suspect.

I was brought up a Catholic, and in my convent school there was a cult of Joan of Arc. I remember a painting above a side altar in our chapel in which she was portrayed astride a white horse, in her chain-mail armour. Her hand held a gleaming sword which she thrust upward towards heaven. A saintly halo crowned her pageboy hairstyle. She looked magnificent. So did the horse. Therefore, I was astonished when Jacques declared as balderdash her actual burning at the stake. The truth, he said, can be found in the municipal archives of the city of Orléans. There is historical evidence that she, in fact, married and became the Countess Montmorency, receiving remuneration until her death from the city in gratitude for saving them from the English. Jacques was not just voicing, as could have been expected, French Protestant disbelief for the reasons of her sanctification by the Roman Catholic Church, but was repeating the published studies of the historians, Las Vergnas (who, by the way, was a defrocked priest) and Amblem, whose works *Dramas and Secrets* or *Enigmas of History* can be found in most libraries under the publications of Robert Laffont. Jacques emphasised that these heretical illuminations have never been discredited.

When the decision was final that we would be emigrating to France, I knew my French was not up to the gravity of this undertaking, and so enrolled myself into an intensive course at the French Institute in London. As my end-of-term project, I chose to do a dissertation on the history of Joan of Arc, relying heavily, for colour, on Jacques's expositions. Surprisingly, I received an 'A'. I have a sneaking suspicion the professor was either a Huguenot or, dare I say without crossing myself, an atheist. I rang Jacques immediately afterwards to boast of my success. He was very proud of me.

Only ever from his lips did we hear a Frenchman state gratitude for Napoleon's final defeat at Waterloo and Britain's wisdom for his subsequent exile into oblivion on the isolated island of St Helena. These were courageous opinions to have of France's two most glorified heroes. As far as we were concerned, anyone who absolved the English of blame for the downfall of these icons would have to become a friend.

They were both interested in the locals' reactions to the fact that a dreaded English couple should have insinuated themselves amongst them.

'We've only had the best experiences,' Bill and I assured them.

'That surprises me,' said Jacques. 'France is rife with Anglophobia.'

He then related a story from his childhood. When he was eight, he and his younger brother were being walked by their grandfather through the streets of Le Havre. It would have been in the early 1920s. On the pavement, a little further from them, the two boys spotted a small group of people who seemed completely different. They were taller, broader, and dressed (to the boys' eyes) unusually. What was more, they uttered noises in a language neither of them could understand.

Fascinated and in awe of these strangers, the boys asked their grandfather who they were and where they came from. Grandpapa, who'd been studying some meat hanging in the butcher's shop next to where they were standing, was only made aware of these foreigners sharing the pavement by the boys' questions. Upon seeing them, he hastily gathered Jacques and his brother, shoving them protectively behind him.

'Quiet!' he commanded the boys. 'They are English, and the English eat little children.' He quickly turned around, pushed the boys in front of him and hurried them back home, glancing now and again across his shoulder to make sure they were not being followed.

'Surely he was joking with you,' I said to Jacques.

'No. I think he really believed it. And so did I, for a long time,' Jacques answered with twinkling eyes. His grandfather would not have been a veteran of the Napoleonic wars, but he would have been brought up in their wake, and listened to the malicious stories France's defeat by the English could have produced. I think by the latter half of the twentieth century such rumours had finally been dispelled. By way of proof, I have been asked and have accepted to be a godmother to two little French souls. Mind you, their parents were aware of my Hungarian origins.

Claudine admitted to us that, when she and Jacques told their friends in Le Havre that they had befriended an English couple, some eyebrows were seriously raised.

'If we speak of you to people,' she informed me, 'we must differentiate. You are not ordinary English; you are "our" English. Then they understand.'

When we opened our door to the many French clients we would receive, a barbed Anglophobic remark would be uttered now and again. If said in English, Bill would, in Basil Fawlty fashion, give a caustically humorous reply. If said in French, I didn't dare translate, but attempted to defend my adopted nationality with the politeness my silently fuming Tartar gene would permit. I have to admit, though, I was grateful that the French, on the whole, have a similar sense of humour to the English. They, also, can serve an insult in a candied pill of a joke. But more about that later.

Our moments with Jacques and Claudine became precious. He was finding it difficult to attempt the seven-hour journey from Le Havre every summer. Several hours every day of his first week in the Haute-Loire had to be spent at a doctor's on an oxygen inhaler. Too many Cuban cigars during his lifetime had given him a form of emphysema. The difference in altitude, from the sea level he had come from to the heights of Bonneval, put a stress on his elderly lungs. They put the *moulin* up for sale and our only opportunity to see them would be on our return journeys, taking the overnight ferry from Le Havre to Portsmouth, when we would stop and join them for dinner. For some of these occasions, Jacques delighted in going to the market to individually pick the shellfish they would serve as a *plateau des fruits de mer.* We would gorge on crab, oysters, clams, prawns and every sea mollusc available, with delicious mayonnaises Claudine conjured from her kitchen. The wine was always spectacular, cradled fondly in his arms as he proudly showed us the bottles.

I was still translating for Bill, but hardly needed to. He and Jacques had a rapport which superseded language. Jacques admitted to me that, although my knowledge of French was greater, Bill's accent in the few words he'd use and the appropriate guttural noises he'd make to accompany them spoke more eloquently than anything gleaned from a dictionary. So much for my concentrated efforts at the French Institute.

It was Claudine who alerted me to the hazards of driving in the Haute-Loire. 'There are too many old farmers,' she warned me. 'They are driving with licences that should be extinct. They have no idea of the new rules of the road.'

Unfortunately, my experiences on French roads had already made me cautious. I have driven in almost every European country and also in America. In France, though, I've had to cope with a distinctly different attitude the French have when in charge of their vehicles. I've never been a slow driver and have been known to exceed the speed limit by more than just a few kilometres an hour, but even if I were to accelerate with a turbo-charged rocket booster, speeding at Mach 3, there would always be someone glued to my behind as if their intention had been to mount my car. I've come across this aggressive pushing on German *autobahns* from the boys who are taking their Mercedes or BMW toys out for a spin. Unhampered by a speed limit for long stretches, they intimidate the drivers of lesser vehicles in their path by blinding them with megawatt flashes from their headlights. But at least there is a lane into which one can escape. In France this sort of driving can take place on narrow, winding mountain roads.

I am convinced that at some point my car had been stolen, sprayed with a paint which rendered it invisible, and then, as a cruel joke, returned to me. The *gendarmes*, traffic wardens, Bill and I are the only ones who can spot it. The amount of times its moving presence on a road has been ignored by other users has given me an inferiority complex. I have seen drivers look in my direction as I've been approaching an intersection where I have had the right of way, and they have pulled out directly in front of me or they have crossed my bows, as if my car hadn't existed. On a straight road, being pushed from behind by Alain Prost wannabes, I have often encountered an oncoming car speeding towards my bonnet in its impatient attempt at passing. I could only pray that the car following me had left enough distance to see the red glare of my brake lights. Once again, I'd obviously not been noticed. The approaching vehicles playing Russian roulette that I have met trespassing on my lane, and luckily avoided while negotiating a blind bend, I can't blame for not having seen me; but I can't excuse their stupidity. It is no wonder that almost twenty-four per cent of all accidents in France are caused by frontal collisions. When I now buy a car, I am no longer interested in its acceleration, but, my God, do I study the brakes.

Those large bouquets of flowers one can see at certain points on the roadside have not fallen off an Interflora delivery van. They are the families' shrines and sad reminders of lost loved ones who have joined France's shameful road fatality statistics which, at over eight thousand deaths a year, rank among Europe's highest. In order to promote a public awareness of these tragedies, our department, the Haute-Loire, has placed on its accident sites wooden life-sized human silhouettes. Their torsos consist of a large red heart which has a white arrow piercing it. Each figure signifies a death. I see too many on the routes that I take, sometimes even gathered in clusters of up to five, and I know that many of them represent someone's child between the ages of 17 and 25. I love my friends too much to bear the thought that they or their children would one day be depicted as these wooden effigies which haunt our roadsides.

Yet the driving course is very strict, and the exam fiendishly difficult. Having passed, the new driver is obliged for two years to stick an 'A', meaning apprentice, on the back of the car. They are restricted to lower speeds, but not yet, unfortunately (although it is being discussed), to more sedately powered motors. At the moment, if their parents are wealthy enough, their first car can be a Porsche. I have been aggressively passed many times, and forced to inhale the dark turbulent clouds from an exhaust while watching an 'A' disappear at breakneck speed in front of me.

As far as I know, France is the only European country that allows people who have lost their licences due to serious transgressions, or those who are incapable of passing the test, to sit behind the wheel of a car and use the open road. There are special Dinky-toy-like vehicles manufactured for that purpose. A little larger than the old 'bubble car', they have a maximum speed of 50 kph (downhill). Bill and I referred to them fondly as 'Zimmermobiles', but not when we were stuck behind one driving up a steep slope. On those occasions only curses came to mind.

It was my intention to buy one for Bill which would have given him more independence and the opportunity to indulge his craving to steer a trolley through supermarket aisles unchaperoned. I studied advertisements in the local papers. A used Mercedes would have cost less. Even if we could have afforded one, Bill decided he was too sensitive to other people's feelings. He would not have been able to take the stress, knowing there were irate drivers forming long queues behind him.

I accepted a ride once, for a short distance, in one of these contraptions. It was night, and I had just been informed that our donkey had escaped her fencing. She was gallivanting in the darkness on a road two kilometres away. Seeing me running in a panic, a woman kindly stopped to give me a lift. When we spotted the donkey in the headlights and I wanted to get out, the driver yanked the handbrake up, the wheels blocked and we skidded to a halt.

'Don't your brakes work?' I asked, astonished.

'But this is the brake,' she answered unperturbed, still gripping the lever.

I looked down at her feet and saw a pedal next to the accelerator.

'Why don't you use that?' I said, pointing down to it.

'Oh, no, I prefer doing it like this. It's less confusing using my hand.'

I don't think her driving instructor would have approved, if indeed she ever had one; but I thanked her for her kindness nevertheless, and wished her an uneventful journey home.

Through Jacques and Claudine we met more of the locals, some of whom became our staunch friends. There were those who'd led sophisticated lives and came back to their homeland to retire. Others were farmers, whose families had lived on the land for centuries.

The Auvergnats have a reputation for meanness. I would like, herewith, to put an end to these malicious rumours, although they themselves laughingly admit to it. '*Un sou est un sou et un chou est un chou*': literally, this Auvergnat saying means, 'A penny is a penny and a cabbage is a cabbage.' It loses its poetry in the translation, I'm afraid, but it tells you they're wily enough to appreciate the difference. I've never eaten a penny soup or seen them paying in cabbages. I think.

There is a legend attached to a certain bank. This establishment convinced the Auvergnat peasant farmers that the notes they were stuffing into their mattresses would actually be safer, and could even earn interest, if deposited into its safekeeping. Once the farmers had been converted to this wisdom, mattresses, pillows, socks were emptied and their contents taken to the bank, and thus was created one of the richest financial institutions in the world: the Crédit Agricole de la Haute-Loire. Occasionally, though, when old ruins were renovated, large stashes of paper money were still found hidden behind a loose stone in a wall. Frustratingly for the builders who discovered them, most of these treasures consisted of ancient francs, which were no longer legal tender.

I went to a meeting the Crédit Agricole hosted to enlighten us about the effects the introduction of the euro would produce. I'd been under the impression that a definite date had been stipulated for all monies to be exchanged. In certain circumstances, though, we were told, the bank would agree to change francs into euros for another ten years, giving as the reason the likelihood of inheritors discovering mattress money their relatives had scrupulously hoarded for them. Once exchanged, this money would be declared and, therefore, taxed.

The Auvergnats are not known to spend extravagantly on themselves, but seem to save this gesture for their guests. We have often been the grateful recipients of their generous hospitality; and it was on one of these earlier occasions that we also learned of a particular French etiquette practised in upper-middle-class homes.

Having been invited for lunch at Patrick and Marie-Christine's penthouse flat in Le Puy, we rang the doorbell, in consideration, ten minutes after the appointed hour, and were welcomed into their home where delicious aromas were already emanating from the kitchen. It was the first time we had met Patrick's wife. At first appearance, I was convinced she had been the muse to whoever fashioned the Barbie doll. Long, thick, blonde hair framed the perfect features in her oval face. She had a moulded figure, as if her creator had squeezed her waist, displacing the matter to form perfectly proportioned bosoms and nicely rounded hips. But beneath this doll-like appearance was a talented artist, a quick, inventive wit and one of the most spontaneously kind women I'd ever met. Beautiful, fifteen years my junior (the bitch!), she adopted Bill and me. It would be through her enthusiastic efforts that we were introduced to the very people who would give us advice and the necessary grants towards our future B&B venture. She and Patrick engineered our speedy integration into Le Puy society. We were still only dipping our feet into the waters, and it was through their warmth that the deep lake we would eventually plunge into felt mild and welcoming.

Having been given a tour of the apartment, and introduced to their three delicately beautiful young daughters, we were invited to sit at the dining table. The decor of the living area one could only describe as the ultimate in minimalism. A neutral-coloured imitation suede paper lined the walls, upon which was hung only one picture: a tasteful, architect's painted design of a villa. There was no sofa, nor were there easy chairs, nor coffee table. The living room was entirely devoted to eating. Time and again we would notice this was a French priority.

On this occasion, though, what struck us with a little apprehension was that we had been there for well over half an hour and not yet been offered drink. Minimalism, schminimalism, who cares, as long as there's booze? Having already been informed that the daughters would not be eating with us, I counted two extra settings at the table. We were obviously waiting for other guests. Conversation continued politely but, as Bill and I would later admit to each other, we had begun to feel a certain panic. Had we accepted an invitation to a teetotal household? *Quelle horreur*, Bill would have said. There were wine glasses placed at our settings which gave rise to a little hope, but the ominously large carafe of water at the centre of the table could have contained the only liquid to be poured into them. We could easily have passed the lunchtime without a drink, but we'd have liked to have been warned about it first.

After another quarter of an hour of sober chit-chat, the doorbell rang. It was answered and in a few minutes the awaited couple entered. She was presented to us as Kri-kri, and her husband as Li-li. More time passed with the sort of talk such new introductions engender. They explained their peculiar nicknames. Because almost every second woman within their circle of friends bore the name Christine, she had assumed 'Kri-kri' to avoid confusion. 'Li-li' stood for Helier, as in St Helier on the island of Jersey.

'Are their many Heliers amongst your friends?' Bill asked.

'None at all. But it rhymes with Kri-kri,' Li-li answered.

It was only then that Patrick opened a cabinet which contained a crowd of bottles, all standing, all bursting to show off their labels. Marie-Christine arrived from the kitchen with ice, lemon slices, nuts, sausages, pickles, crackers etc. The *aperitifs* could now be offered. Every distilled or fermented alcohol was on display and, if chosen, was poured copiously into a glass. We discovered the French preferred malt or whisky to cognac, and drank port before their meal, as opposed to the British, who sip it as a *digestif.*

Within moments, the atmosphere lightened and my French became quite fluent. Bill began making jokes in a language he could hardly speak, and, miraculously, everybody laughed. During the meal an enormous amount of wine was poured into our glasses. The afternoon ended with all of us having adopted nicknames. Bill became 'Bi-bi'; Marie-Christine, 'Mi-mi'; because of my maiden name, I became 'Chi-chi'; and so Patrick, unfortunately, had to be called 'Pee-pee'.

In an English home, a guest is offered a drink before they've even removed their coat. And if you are shown around someone's house, you will, most likely, make the tour holding a glass in your hand. In France a different attitude applies. They consider it impolite to begin a party until the last person is present. Whereas in England a latecomer is hurled into a scene already advanced in alcoholic boisterousness, and is forced to drink quickly in order to catch up, in France, the popping of a champagne cork, like a starting pistol, only happens when the participants are all gathered, and have an equal opportunity in the revelling that will follow.

Not long after having met Li-li and Kri-kri, we were invited to a rather grand midday 'do' at their impressive villa just outside of Le Puy. Once again, we arrived courteously a few minutes late. There were already quite a number of guests milling about, admiring the property and the almost Olympic-sized swimming pool. There was a large table groaning temptingly with unopened bottles in the centre of the garden. It was shaded from the heat by a colourful marquee. Discreet sounds of conversation hummed across the lawns like the gentle buzzing of bees. Our hosts introduced us hither and thither. We were all able to shake hands unimpeded, due to the absence of glasses. More people were arriving and for the next hour we continued to mingle, being guided by either Li-li, Kri-kri, Patrick or Marie-Christine to become acquainted with the professional classes of Le Puy. For a while I found myself listening in fascination to a female psychiatrist, who was discussing the various neuroses of her patients. I could not entirely understand every word she had said, and it was only later that Marie-Christine informed me that the woman's career was devoted to the mental stability of horses. I should have known from the way her feet had sometimes been pawing the ground.

When an hour and a half passed and still no drink had been poured, Bill was considering leaving. At two o'clock the last couple arrived. I'm glad to say we were not the only ones who let out a howl of glee when the first cork was about to be pulled. Waiters suddenly appeared and busied themselves around the bottles. Cheerful popping sounds were heard and a noisy swarm gathered around the marquee. The decibels had reached a higher pitch.

By seven in the evening, having eaten and drunk to bursting point, there were people bobbing like corks in the pool. Some of them had bothered to change into appropriate suits. Others were fully dressed, having fallen, been pushed or thrown in. In a corner on the surrounding terraces, Bill was entertaining a group of devotees with his theatrical stories. Every now and again, I could hear him mimicking the voice of Sir John Gielgud in perfect Franglais. Music was blaring from the exterior speakers. Someone asked me to dance. A surgeon? A lawyer? The chief of police? I no longer remember. It was a slowish number which called more for swaying than intricate foot-work. Suddenly everyone began to laugh and pointed hysterically towards my partner's feet. It was only then I realised I'd been dancing with a man whose dropped trousers were clinging to his ankles. No wonder he'd been shuffling so strangely.

I leapt away from him, put both palms on my cheeks and screamed, '*Je suis choquée!*' to the amusement of all present. It's true. I was shocked, but strangely enough, not in the least offended. Neither was Bill, nor the man's wife. Had it happened in seclusion, behind a bush, our reactions would have been different.

Tomorrow he would behave with utter propriety having donned his surgical mask, pleaded with a judge, or arrested a criminal, feeling better for the antics of the previous evening.

The experience taught us that, no matter how polite and controlled the behaviour at such French gatherings is to begin with, there is always hope this genteel veneer will be stripped to reveal their more earthy, uninhibited, anarchic natures. Coming from a profession whose individuals were mostly endowed with these virtues, we felt completely at home.

Our circle of acquaintances enlarged on every visit and we encountered the contrary to Anglophobia. Bill and I presumed this was due to the novelty factor. Our part of France was not overrun by the British. With our professional backgrounds, he as the director and myself as an actress (occasionally recognised on their TV screens), we were considered exotic. Strangers knocked on our door, curious to see how we had renovated the old *auberge* they had known so well. They were impressed with the yellow walls and the huge, round, blonde timbers which spanned the entire ceiling, supporting the bedroom floor above. They marvelled at the blue open staircase and the blue wooden arches which framed the window alcoves.

Nodding in reverence and a little in awe, we would hear them say, 'Ah, yes, English taste.'

'Actually, no,' we'd inform them. 'We stole the colour scheme from the French impressionist, Monet. He had a yellow and blue kitchen.'

A friend had made a birdhouse for us back in England. We hung it on the wall opposite our door. Bill painted a sign over it which read L'AUBERGE DES OISEAUX. The cylindrical cage at its centre was filled with crude, unsalted peanuts. People came and stared at it in wonder. It became a village curiosity.

'You feed birds?' we'd be asked.

'Yes, in the winter,' we'd reply.

'Be careful,' we were told. 'Someone may come with a hunting gun.'

Seeing me pale in shocked disbelief, they would add with broad smiles, 'No, no, it's just a joke.' But as some walked away, they turned back pretending to hold a rifle. They took aim at the feeding birds through the sights, pulled the trigger, and even managed an authentic jerk as the imaginary gun recoiled against their shoulder. Only a real shooter could have performed this gesture so perfectly; that or a student of the great mime artist, Marcel Marceau.

Bill suggested we should paint a target on the wall with the birdhouse as its bullseye. We decided against it, afraid the joke would be taken seriously. I'm glad to say, today there are many such birdhouses to be found in local garden centres, and they are not used for target practice. But we still have to ask our friends who are visiting from England to bring the correct bird nuts.

We were cannibalising our flat back in London, bringing bits and pieces with us on every trip. It's a miracle the car I was driving at that time didn't break an axle with the heavy weights we were transporting. On our arrivals it took hours, and sometimes a helping hand, to disgorge the car and carry the contents into the house. It was during one of these unloadings that we met 'Dents d'Or': the man with the golden teeth, and, for his age, the complexion of a baby's bottom.

He'd been having a drink with Jean-Pierre at the *auberge* above us when they noticed our overladen car bump by. Bill and I had already begun the emptying process when Jean-Pierre came down the path in the company of a man wearing bright blue overalls, and introduced him to us as a local farmer. From the pristine state of his clothes, I presumed he'd not toiled in his fields that day. Jacques and Claudine had often spoken of Dents d'Or, but this was the first time we had met him and been dazzled by his smile.

Normally, Jean-Pierre would have helped us unload. He enjoyed making comments and evaluations on the articles we were importing, usually telling us we'd have done better buying them in France. Therefore, we were always surprised when, on our return trips, certain things had gone missing, having been borrowed and made use of in our absence. These articles were usually returned to us in a damaged state, including a very solid Black and Decker Workmate.

On this occasion, though, he excused himself, stating he had customers to look after, leaving us with Dents d'Or enjoying the sight of our continued scuttlings between the car and the house. At one point Bill and I lumbered down to the eastern barn. We were each carrying a heavy box of books, which would later be unpacked and stacked on our intended bookshelves. Dents d'Or accompanied us on all of our movements, never offering to help, but making observations in his glass-shattering voice. Sometimes he laughed hysterically, which would bring on a fit of wheezing. Only much later, when I learned to understand some of the *patois* he spoke, did I realise his frequent cacklings arose from a self-appreciation of his never-ending stream of jokes. At that time, though, we thought it was an excuse to show off his expensive teeth.

Piling our crates in the eastern barn gave Dents d'Or an opportunity to examine the farming relics stowed there. Thinking it would be easier to cart the boxes back up to the house once the shelves had been constructed, we placed them on the two-wheeled low wagon which had attracted our attention when being given the original tour of the property. In order for it not to see-saw as we were placing the boxes on its planks, Bill wedged some wood underneath it. Dents d'Or turned from whatever he'd been scrutinising and crossed over towards us. He stood looking down on to the boxes, which were now positioned on the wagon, while emitting a flow of animated, high-pitched noises. Our boxes were not completely closed and some of the books they contained were in full view. For an insane moment, Bill and I thought he was enthusing over the literature we were bringing to France. But it was the wagon which had attracted his attention.

For his sixty-odd years, he was an extremely strong man. Bending down, he easily removed the heavy boxes from the wagon as if they'd contained tissue paper, and put them on the straw-covered floor. He knelt to touch the planks, the wheels, all the while muttering appreciatively, studying the object as if he were an expert. He pulled out the wood which Bill had wedged beneath it. Standing up again, he took hold of the shaft and began towing it forwards and pushing backwards.

We'd been watching in silence, and then Bill turned to me whispering, 'It's a wagon. It has wheels. They go round. The wagon moves. Why is he so fascinated?'

'I have no idea,' I replied, also in a whisper.

Satisfied that it was in working order, Dents d'Or shouted an incomprehensible question at us. (He always spoke at a pitch as if the listener was deaf. In time I discovered it was he who had the hearing problems.) Having asked him to repeat what he'd said, he assumed a loud, slow enunciation, the way one would talk to an idiot.

'Will you keep a pig?' I understood him to ask between hilarious laughter and wheezings, and repeated what I'd heard to Bill.

'Tell him probably not,' Bill said casually, as if the question were not out of the ordinary, and then went on to explain, 'Anyway, we built the bathroom where the pig used to live.'

I simply answered 'No' to Dents d'Or, at which he smiled so brilliantly, I felt I had to protect my eyes from the glare of his 18-carat gold teeth. He then proceeded, without asking, to pull the wagon out of the barn, up the gradient, past the house, up the hill towards the *auberge*, disappearing as he rounded the bend, while continuing all the way to talk to himself, to laugh and then to wheeze. We caught sight of him again between the trees on the road above towing the wagon, presumably to where he lived, still audibly amused.

Bill and I are not wimps, and yet we allowed him to walk off with the wagon without a single protest. It was as if they belonged together. We were in an area where farming was comparatively primitive. Anyone who owned a pig obviously had more right to the wagon than we; but we were still to be enlightened as to its use.

That would come later, when I'd drop in at his farm which was a pleasant walk away from our house, and where occasionally I'd buy, to serve at dinner for our paying guests, the goat's cheese his wife, Janine, produced.

When first meeting her it became evident on whom the dentistry budget was spent. Janine's ready smile in her plump, pretty face lacked the glamour of her husband's. The tooth fairy did not compensate her for her losses.

Far in the future when Dents d'Or died having omitted to make a will, and Janine, as his childless widow, suffered the consequences of this negligence under the Napoleonic Code, I'd learn the sad secrets of their marriage. During the long and complicated process of the probate, I would also witness the darker side to the natures of some of the peasantry who peopled the area in which we found ourselves.

But for the moment we were charmed by everything that surrounded us. It became more and more difficult to leave this completely different world. London beckoned, calling us to earn the money to afford our schizophrenic lifestyle. I was beginning to notice, though, that most of the calling came from Bill's agent. There were ominously long silences from mine.

Our partings only became bearable when we had something to look forward to: a happy visit with Jacques and Claudine in Le Havre, from whence we'd be poured on to the overnight ferry. As the heavy ship rolled and swayed across the channel, I slept, dreaming of going back to Bonneval.

After we moved definitively to Bonneval and had no reason to go back to London, we never saw Jacques and Claudine again, but we kept in touch with them via the phone or the post. With the passing of time, I learned that Jacques had become weaker; and worst of all, his mind had begun to wander. Claudine looked after him as a devoted mother would her child. During our last conversation she admitted that Jacques often didn't realise what was happening around him. He was sometimes unaware that his children, or even his adored grandson, had come to visit. Most of all, though, she missed his sardonic humour and his fiery, astute opinions.

But one evening she was rewarded when the two of them were watching the news. Jacques sat quietly, staring blankly at the screen. Claudine had no way of knowing how much he was taking in. Towards the end of the programme a lengthy interview took place with the then President, Jacques Chirac.

As if an internal switch had been turned on, Jacques seemed to come awake. Having listened for a while, and in a manner reminiscent of his past, he suddenly declared loudly, 'At least, Mitterrand, you could compare with Machiavelli. But this man, Chirac, can only be compared to Pinocchio.'

I wish Bill had been there to hear him.

Chapter Eight

DEAR HUGH,

Thank you for your kind invitation to spend a weekend at your charming mill house hotel. If work does not get in the way, we would love to come.

I must say, I've really appreciated our correspondence and enjoyed reading about the hotel project, and keeping you informed as to our French acquisition. (By the way, the photograph of the moulin in winter scenery is absolutely stunning.) I'm sorry we've never been able to take you up on your invitation to stay over on our forays into France, but, as I told you, we've tended to take the Portsmouth/Le Havre route. What a pity you've never stayed with us on your quick returns to London.

It's amusing how we discreetly introduced our partners to each other. You began by simply signing your cards as Hugh and then eventually adding Martine to your signature. I, then, added Bill to mine. So, now we know we both have other halves. I presume Martine is the great cook you mentioned some time ago.

Every year at Christmas we have wished each other well and success for the future. But, now, I have a very embarrassing question to ask: Who the hell are you?

I only know two Hughs. One is the 15-year-old son of very good friends of ours, and his parents have assured me that he is still living under their roof. The other is a Scottish laird, and I doubt very much that he sold his castle to open a hotel just across the Channel.

I've scoured the local libraries for the 'Who's Hugh of France' but it was always unavailable. Do you correspond with many people?

I hope you'll understand, before arriving at a definite decision, we would like to know exactly who's the Hugh whose invitation we hope to be accepting.
     Love, (as usual)
     Catherine

It was Bill who received the reply by phone. I was out, and on my return he explained who the mysterious Hugh actually was. Once Bill mentioned the Barbican, a light bulb in my mind illuminated distant memories. I recalled someone who had had a flat there. Evenings at the theatre came to mind. I remembered attending a crowded midday party in his tiny flat within the claustrophobic beehive complex the developers of the new Barbican were so proud of. I recollected the loud Hooray Henry and shrill Sloane Ranger voices which accosted my ears in that cramped space. He had prepared the expensive buffet himself: lobster salad, slices of cold roast beef. I'm sure there was even caviar. I know there was lots of champagne. But I couldn't conjure up what he had looked like, and was only left with a vague impression of a kindly, jovial teddy bear who had flown cargo planes. I'd also had the feeling he was too generous to the people who surrounded him.

Our acquaintanceship evaporated unremarkably to be lost into the ether of our different lives. I had completely forgotten him.

Knowing now who he was, we accepted the invitation and spent the weekend at his hotel. What we couldn't have foreseen, though, was how portentous this reacquaintance would be, and how integral it became to our future plans.

The hotel was on the edge of a rushing river which powered the exterior mill wheel. In the centre of the main reception area were the mill works, perfectly restored. Beneath them was a basin fed by the diverted millstream which flowed under the floorboards. You could look into the pool, leaning on the wooden barrier, glass in hand, and count the fat trout swimming lazily about. They only exercised when they'd break the surface of the water to gobble up a piece of toast someone threw in for their own amusement.

A second reception room had an enormous fireplace in which thick metre-length logs happily burned. Two large sofas and some easy chairs were conveniently placed for guests to absorb the warm glow of the fire.

There were eight good-sized bedrooms in the main building. In a converted pigsty, which served as an annexe, another four had been built with large windows overlooking the river.

Hugh was passionate about the hotel. It was entirely his creation. He'd bought the mill and its adjoining buildings in a total state of ruin, and then set about to expertly restore or convert them, doing much of the work himself. It had been a labour of love, and his enthusiasm in relating the project became contagious.

The weekend went pleasantly enough because Bill heeded my threats that if he insulted the other guests, he would be tortured in a manner even Vlad the Impaler would have recoiled in distaste from. It was a struggle for him, though. The poor baby had to bite his tongue so often it almost began to bleed. Given the choice, he would have recast most of the guest list. He had never been comfortable listening to those accents which had so irritated me at the party in the small Barbican flat, and things became even more disagreeable when those voices began expressing right-wing views gleaned from the nether side of cuckoo land. If it were not for Hugh's kindness and the interesting, witty presence of Peter Stothard, the then newly appointed young editor of *The Times*, and Sally Emerson, his novelist wife, Bill would have demanded that we cut the experience short; or to have, at least, the overweight, obnoxious executive with his screeching, bimbo, call-girl date shot.

We said our farewells to Hugh, thanking him for the entertaining week-end and promising to keep in touch. It felt a lot better being able to picture the person one was going to communicate with.

Bill was still working, albeit no longer directing the stylish television dramas on which his reputation had been based. Gone were the days when he dazzled the critics with such spectacular productions as *Orde Wingate* with Barry Foster in the title role; Molly Keane's *Good Behaviour* and *Time after Time*, the latter starring John Gielgud, Googie Withers, Helen Cherry, even Trevor Howard; and the Greek trilogy *The Oresteia* with Diana Rigg, Helen Mirren, Claire Bloom, Flora Robson, Billie Whitelaw etc. etc. There had been a time when the television companies budgeted for innovative, prestigious dramas, and Bill was often asked to direct them. He had been spoiled on occasion, managing the post-production editing for one pro-gramme while setting up the next. Well-established actors, actresses, dames and sirs had been eager to work with him.

But the companies had been forced by their accountants to change their priorities. Bill was now directing the popular soap opera *EastEnders*. And we weren't complaining. Our bank account was still in the black, although frequently dipping into a murky grey and threatening to slide into the red.

We had overspent on the renovations in France. The repayments on the £13,000 mortgage there, as well as our existing £24,000 in London, were becoming a challenge to meet, as were the ridiculous service charges we were expected to pay on the flat.

I noticed I had been 'resting' a little too long. My career seemed to have gone into a coma, to be only occasionally reanimated with poorly paid theatrical work or, every now and again, a cameo part on television. I didn't need to wear spectacles to read the writing on the wall.

Actors jokingly admit that there are five stages to their careers: 1. Who is Joe Bloggs? 2. We want Joe Bloggs! 3. We want someone like Joe Bloggs. 4. We want someone like Joe Bloggs, only younger. 5. Who is Joe Bloggs?

There was a time in my mid-thirties when an actress friend of mine, Linda Marlowe, went up for a commercial. She was ushered by the casting director into a boardroom, and asked to sit facing a long table, around which were seated the clients of the product, representatives of the agency, the producers, the designer and the director.

Having barely made herself comfortable in the chair, the first words uttered to her were, 'We're looking for someone like Catherine Schell.'

She happened to know I was out of work at the time and was tempted to say, 'Then why don't you ask for her?'

I knew then at what stage my career was. I was presumably considered too busy, too grand, or too expensive. How wrong these presumptions were. In 1994, though, I felt I was on the cusp of stage 4, soon to disappear into 5.

And then it happened. While walking up the North End Road, I passed a shop window which was full of television sets, all working, all tuned to the same channel. It was showing an umpteenth repeat of the mid-seventies film *The Return of the Pink Panther* in which I starred opposite Peter Sellers and Christopher Plummer. There was something weird about walking casually up a street and suddenly spotting one's face on multiple screens in various degrees of definition and clarity of colour. I stopped to watch Peter as Inspector Clouseau and myself in close-up as he, in yet another disguise, approaches me in a nightclub. He has just been accidentally socked in the face by a hyperactive mover on the dance floor.

As I was standing, looking into the window, fondly remembering that particular scene, a middle-aged couple slowed to a stop and stood next to me. They too were attracted to the images displayed on the many screens. Only the slightest sound was audible through the thick reinforced pane of glass.

Clouseau reaches my table, and wishes to introduce himself. He uses an assumed name which he can barely pronounce. I allow him to sit down and notice he is only wearing half a moustache. The other half, no doubt, was still sticking to the dancer's knuckles. We drink a toast to each other and he says in his Clouseau accent, imitating Humphrey Bogart in *Casablanca*, something which, at the time, sounded like, 'Ears leaking at you, kid.'

I knew the line and laughed privately in the street, which was exactly what I was doing, only louder and more obviously, on the screen. Blake Edwards knew it was hopeless to stop me corpsing and kindly didn't edit my laughing fits out of the film.

The couple next to me started giggling as well, even though they could hardly have heard the dialogue.

'That's a *Pink Panther* film, ain't it?' I heard the woman ask her husband.

'Yeah, that's Peter Sellers doing his Clouseau, all right,' said the man, still staring in the window. 'Can't remember who she was, though,' he added, and then as if thinking aloud, 'She's not Elke something, is she?'

I was tempted to prompt him, but before I could, she replied, 'No, it's Catherine...' At that point I wanted to kiss her for remembering, and then she finished with, '... Deneuve.'

I moved away from them with a cartoon-strip balloon bubbling silently out of my head. 'Actually no!' it read. 'That blonde, long-haired beauty you've been gawping at was Catherine Schell.' But even I noticed my unspoken thought had been formed in the past tense. It had been a long time since I'd appeared in a glamorous film like that. At least she'd remembered half of my name.

I don't know if it was that incident that sowed the seed in my mind that, in order to survive financially, our lives were going to have to change. Or the letter we had recently received from our flat's managing agents demanding a ridiculous £7,000 service charge for undertaking reparations due to the previous exterior decorating and roofing company's shoddy work. There was no claim to be made against the cowboy company as they had, in the meanwhile, gone bankrupt, but not before they'd received (so we were told) our £12,000 two years ago which represented our 25% liability for that year's outgoings on the Edwardian, double-fronted building our maisonette was situated in.

I was tired of paying lawyers to investigate the service charges imposed upon us by supposedly reputable managing agents and their clients, a subsidiary of an American bank, who owned the freehold and were our landlords. Bill loved the flat so much, though, he didn't mind paying the price. And then I answered a phone call while he was having a nap.

We were already aware that something akin to a *putsch* had taken place at the BBC's offices responsible for the making of *EastEnders*. Leonard Lewis, who had been the series' producer, and a long-time friend and frequent employer of Bill, had been ousted. Bill was due to direct another two episodes of the series but the contract had not yet been signed.

I found myself speaking to a female voice who introduced herself as the new producer. She was anxious for me to relay the message that Bill would only be contracted for one further episode. They were having problems with the script of the second, she explained nervously.

'You will tell him, he'll only be doing the one episode, not the two?' Then, as if instructing a child, she reiterated, 'Only the one. Do you understand?'

I understood perfectly well. A new broom sweeps clean. She didn't want to inherit the old guard when there was younger, less expensive, more impressionable talent to promote.

When Bill was 25, he too was discovered by the BBC, having come to their attention while employed as the artistic director of the newly opened Leeds Playhouse. He was trained by them and then set loose to command five cameras simultaneously during the nerve-destroying, alopecia-inducing days of live television. He learned his trade the hard way, directing episodes of *Z Cars* when decisions to cut from one camera to the next were irreversible. There was no safety net in the form of an editing suite to retire to and correct the mistakes after the episode had been recorded. The programmes were broadcast as they were being shot, warts and all. Actors frequently had to improvise, as did the director when things did not go as rehearsed. Doors stayed stubbornly shut when a character needed to enter a scene to deliver the important lines upon which the plot revolved. Dialogue was shouted through the jammed doors, and made to look as if that had been intended. On occasion when they did open a rogue camera could be seen framed squarely in the doorway. The director had to quickly cut to the next scene and another camera. Surprised at their premature cue, the actors jerked into action and began talking. All seemed to be saved until, realising it had been mis-positioned, the rogue camera could be seen gliding smoothly past a window against which the two emoting actors were framed. Even such a sight could be overcome by some quick-witted ad-libbing from the actors:

'Just ignore those cameras. The BBC is doing a documentary on the police force.'

'Yes. I've noticed, sir.'

Unfortunately, though, the office they'd been talking in had long been established to be on the fifth floor.

But the greatest test of everyone's composure and ability to extemporise had to be the unexpected appearance of a dead actor. It did happen. The poor man had taken his position and was seated behind a desk, waiting for the cue. All the cameras and the crew were busy on another set with the preceding scene. They then followed the actors through a corridor. As per script, a door was opened. Only on that day, it revealed a body slumped in a chair. At first, everyone thought he was dozing and unaware of the scene having begun. The cameras, one of which was always transmitting, positioned themselves into the three-sided set. An actor slammed the door shut in the hope of waking his colleague. The only response was a deeper crumbling into the chair. It became painfully obvious to all concerned that he had departed to the great green room in the sky. Undaunted, even by death, the show had to continue. The actors played their scene, compensating for the missing dialogue and any visible reactions from the corpse, and the director's discreet use of the cameras made it possible for the audiences watching their screens at home to remain oblivious to the real drama which had taken place in front of their eyes.

Today, the director would shout 'Cut!', the body would be removed, a production meeting would be called, and the writer asked to make some crucial alterations to the script. They don't train them like the old guard any more.

Without Bill's regular income from *EastEnders* and with the continued silences from my agent, it became apparent that some decisions would have to be made. We were not going to be able to afford the upkeep of two homes. The question was: which one do we sell?

The house in France was considered a *maison secondaire* and as such, if sold, a considerable tax would have to be paid on any profits. We had kept all the bills for the whacking £40,000 worth of renovations, but property prices in the Haute-Loire had not yet matched our investment.

Some of the French holiday homes we'd visited should have given us a clue. No matter how wealthy or sophisticated their owners were, they preferred to camp for those weeks rather than spend the considerable amounts to make their places more comfortable.

We were invited once to a farmhouse in a very pretty little hamlet. Our hosts were a retired doctor and his opera-singer wife. It was an evening in mid-August, and we sat hugging the warmth from the wood-burning fire. To have described the furniture in the downstairs kitchen/dining/living area as bargain buys from a junk shop would have made them sound overly expensive. The couple had not yet got around to doing the floor. My feet, only slipped into sandals, were freezing on the cold but not quite muddy ground. The white electrical cables looped across the stone-and-breeze-block walls were the only decorative hangings to alleviate the tediousness of the gloomy grey interior.

'So, how long have you had this place?' I asked.

They conferred with each other, making some calculations.

'It must be at least twenty-five years,' they both concluded. 'We do a little every time we come.'

'Little' was an exaggeration for the renovations that had taken place, but we were assured that, should we need to use the *waters* (French for loo), we would now have some privacy; on this trip they had hung a curtain across the cubicle, jerry-built into the stable. I have to say, though, she made an excellent *aperitif*: lemon slices marinated overnight in sugar and *kirsch* which were then transferred into a large bowl and doused with bottles of chilled sparkling wine. After having indulged in a few glasses, and making a couple of visits, Bill and I decided that the hideously patterned plastic curtain across the loo was an extravagance. The stables had not contained an inquisitive animal for a quarter of a century. The only peeping Toms were the spiders who lowered themselves on gossamer threads from the rafters, and made sure you did not overstay your welcome.

It seemed logical, in order to stay afloat, that we sell the London flat. When Jacques and Claudine put their house in Bonneval on the market for a mere £30,000 it took over two and a half years to find a purchaser. I had predicted at the time that only the English would appreciate the house at that price. I was proved correct. The French had thought it too expensive. It was an English couple who eventually bought it. We would have to sell ours at a higher price and didn't have the time to wait. I'd bought the flat with a ninety-nine-year lease of which seventeen had already been used up. The moment the lease dipped into the seventies, its value would diminish. The flat had previously been estimated at £185,000, but 1994 was experiencing a drop in property prices. Nevertheless, we were sure we could offload it in a shorter space of time and still make a reasonable profit. The question was, would we buy another (smaller, cheaper) flat and keep a base in London?

Then Hugh proposed an intriguing solution: sell the flat, put the money into an account earning interest, and work with him at his hotel. We would live for free. One of us would earn a salary and a share in the profits. It was decided, as the French speaker, it had better be me. The hotel was only a short distance from the Channel Tunnel so, should our agents suggest an important interview, or even a job, we were not too far away to consider returning. Hugh was quite willing to cope should one of us be absent. We had enough friends in London with spare bedrooms with whom we could come to a financial agreement. It would give us a breathing space to decide where our lives would settle. His season consisted mainly of the winter months, when the English would shoot across the Channel for long weekend breaks to stock up on cases of cheap booze and cartons of cigarettes. Some actually came to see northern France. During the summer months most of the clientele bypassed the hotel in their rush to spend time in the Dordogne, Provence, or on the crowded beaches of the Côte d'Azur.

It was a tempting prospect. We'd be paid and looked after for six months, maybe more, depending on the bookings. The rest of the time, we could holiday as per usual in Bonneval and, perhaps, toy with the idea of making the house there work for us. We could augment our winter earnings by opening a bed and breakfast during the summer high season.

We put the flat on the market with the most aggressive agents we could find, and began seriously discussing terms and conditions with Hugh. He had not kept it a secret that the hotel was in dire need of further investment. With the addition of the four extra bedrooms in the converted pigsty, it had outgrown its legal capacity. For the hotel to pass future safety inspections, various alterations had to be undertaken. He dreamt of converting the adjacent huge stone building into a quality restaurant which could welcome not only the hotel guests, but also the public at large. There was even enough space for wine storage at ideal temperatures, either to sell or to keep at a rental for the discerning clients who didn't have the room or perfect conditions back in England. As the wine became ready to drink, they would come, spend a night, collect their cases and enjoy their liquid assets at home. He wanted every square metre of the property to be gainfully employed. There was a large, fallow field on the other side of the hotel's back garden which also belonged to him.

'I can see a few horses grazing there,' he mentioned to my delight. 'We could advertise riding as another attraction. You wouldn't mind escorting the clients? There are some beautiful bridle paths.'

My eyes became orbs of desire.

It all sounded too good to be true; and yet, as Hugh quite rationally explained the possibilities, even Bill showed a degree of enthusiasm.

A lunchtime meeting was arranged with the manager from a northern branch of Barclay's bank with whom Hugh had already had dealings. The substantial loan that Hugh was seeking from him had been agreed and was only waiting to be signed. I was to be introduced as the prospective managing director of the French company which would be formed to run the business of the hotel.

I was conscious of the fact that, for the time being, Hugh was prohibited from assuming such a title. Due to an unfortunate incident of mistaken identity, he had spent some months in a Belgian jail during which time an insurance payment on the hotel became overdue. His wife, Martine, several months pregnant, was understandably distracted with the outcome of her husband's fate, and had omitted to answer the threatening letters from the insurance company.

Hugh was eventually freed through the intercession of friends in high places and the King of Belgium. All charges were dropped. However, in France it is a criminal offence to allow one's insurance to lapse; if a policy is not to be renewed, the insurer has to be told in writing at least eight weeks before the renewal date. Upon Hugh's return to France, he was forced to stand before another court which found him guilty of the heinous crime of non-payment of an insurance premium. His financial reputation was in ruins and he came very near to losing the hotel.

I had absolutely no idea of business and Bill's knowledge of money matters was even less. During our heydays, we'd become a company. Our affairs were in the strict, capable hands of Peggy Thompson's business management. We were not even allowed to touch our company cheque book. Peggy kept the books and guided us through the yearly, gruelling sessions with a chartered accountant who handed over our figures to the Inland Revenue. Bill and I pretended we understood the jargon. We donned serious expressions and did a lot of nodding. After these meetings we'd retire to a pub just to clear our heads of the alien vocabulary we knew we'd never come to grips with.

Hugh and the bank manager were already in the restaurant when we arrived. With Bill's direction, I had taken care to dress for the part. I had rummaged through my wardrobe to find an ensemble which hinted towards freelance business consultant with feminine overtones, and modelled my selection for Bill's approval.

'You're meeting a bank manager, Catherine. You're not going to a Tupperware party,' was his adjudication of my dress sense. I did a quick change, allowing him to choose my outfit.

A very decent Chablis and a St-Émilion were on the table ready to be poured. The manager had a very personable air about him. It was soon established that he and Bill were the same age and were the last generation to do national service. Over the meal, they shared their army experiences; but I doubted that he appreciated being teased for having completed his tour of service as a humble private, whereas Bill had been upgraded into the officer classes.

In between, we also discussed the hotel. I confessed to my ignorance of all things financial except for the logic of not spending more than one was earning. This ignorance naturally precluded me from any capability for committing fraud. I was assured of expert advice from the high-powered firm of accountants who were to be employed, and of course there would always be Hugh. We spoke in general of the duties that we would be expected to perform, and Hugh was adamant that the menial tasks, such as cleaning the rooms, would be left to a local village woman who was already in his employ. Until such time as the larger restaurant would be in place and a recommended chef be found, we would use a graduate from the Prue Leith school to do the cooking for the existing cuisine reserved only for the hotel guests. But of course, there would be occasions when we would all have to muck in. To which, of course, I agreed; I can make beds and I know how to cook, and Bill is very handy with a corkscrew. His aesthetic talents would be used to improve wherever necessary the interior of the hotel, and especially the garden for which Hugh had found very little time. We were to think of ourselves as the hosts of a large country house to which cherished friends would come to stay and all that that would entail. Funny, I thought, that's exactly what 'dragon lady' had always intended for me.

The bank manager was very impressed with me, and even stated so in a letter to Hugh. Bill and I made a few trips back to the hotel during which I was paraded as the prospective *gérante* in front of the local mayor whose

The ruin as I first discovered it from the terrace above. The note 'For Sale' is stuck to a shutter.

The south-facing façade which gives the true impression of the size. It was not a little ruin; it was a big one.

The writing on the front wall of the house that convinced Bill we had to buy it.

A view of Le Puy-en-Velay with the chapel of Saint Michel on a peak and, beyond, the terracotta virgin.

La Chaise-Dieu Abbey and its many steps.

My fellow conspirators on the terrace having lunch when I spotted the ruin. Seated, left to right: Sid Livingstone, Bryan Pringle and Jeremy Nicholas. Serving them is the *aubergiste*'s 'waif'.

Bill and I in December 1989 watching the roof being done. It was warm enough to have drinks on the terrace of the *auberge*.

The dwarves on the roof.

And later, in 1996, the collapsed roof of the barn where the Four Seasons were going to be placed.

Spring

Summer

Autumn

Winter

Early sunshine on the terrace awaiting the guests for breakfast, and the barn's entrance to the Four Seasons.

Looking down our field towards the little river and the bridge beyond.

The house in the snow with a curtain of icicle daggers hanging from the roof.

Daisy and friends.

A forest walk with a
guest, a cat, a dog and,
in the lead, a donkey.

A view from our
living-room
window when
autumn has
begun. It is why
I am here.

Me and my new best friend, another Catherine known as Kati. I will be forever grateful to her for helping me run the B&B after Bill's death.

Janine in her kitchen with Pierot, myself and Catie from Nantes behind her.

How I will remember him: (left) Bill before the stroke with puppy Olive on his lap and a bottle of fine red wine within arm's reach; and (below) the two of us on location.

Bill's bridge from where we strewed his ashes.

consent we would be seeking in enlarging the hotel's business. I was introduced to the accountants who would be forming the company. We had hour-long meetings, but the course I had taken at the French Institute didn't help me to understand the proceedings. If the vocabulary meant nothing in English, it would be doubly confounding in a foreign language. I did a lot of knowledgeable, expert nodding though. They, too, were impressed.

Even Bill encouraged this new role I was acting out, albeit with feigned bravado. He was already deciding which of Hugh's wall-hangings would have to go and which of ours would take their place to add a bit of gravitas to the establishment. He'd studied the garden and made a plan of shrubs, bulbs and climbers to be planted. He enjoyed entertaining the few paying guests whose visits coincided with ours.

The last time I stood in front of a camera in England was during the summer of 1994. Although 'stood' is, perhaps, not the correct description; 'struggled' would be more the defining word. For the financial reasons already mentioned, and with Bill's reluctant advice, I accepted a part in the TV comedy *The Wimbledon Poisoner*. The role consisted of wearing pyjamas and rushing hysterically around at night as part of a large group through Wimbledon's streets, and on the muddy lanes of its common. It could have been played just as well by a glorified extra. Even the director, Robert Young, who had been a friend for years, called me when hearing I'd been cast. The part was so insignificant, he'd left the mundane responsibility for its allocation to a casting director.

'You're actually willing to play that part?' he asked, genuinely surprised I'd agreed to the contract. 'I'd never have dreamt of even suggesting you for the role. It's far too small.'

'We need the money,' I replied to him in all honesty.

'Well, now I know it's you, I'll let the camera dally on your face a little longer,' he added sweetly.

It was during some of those dallyings that I had to struggle. True to his word, Robert included me in shots for which my part hadn't been mentioned in the script. My role was enhanced by becoming an appendage to a certain actor who didn't appreciate this invasion of his own private screen space. He resented his thyroidic-eyed, toad-like face having to share a two shot with a rather normal-looking female. With his impressively photogenic features, he had expected to have close-ups on his own. Every time we were pictured together, I suffered a thrusting elbow in my ribs, a heavy shoulder leaning against mine, and a knee shoving from his side to unbalance me. I held my ground exceedingly well, though. After all, I'd been trained by a horse.

But I hadn't enjoyed that experience, so when in October a young Dutch couple made a reasonable offer on the flat, I was eager to accept it. I was happy to have the means to begin another life. Bill hadn't worked since that episode of *EastEnders*; he, too, needed a challenge to concentrate upon. He was not used to 'resting' and spent too many of his leisure hours in the pub, and I don't think he was learning to play darts.

We exchanged contracts on the flat with the Dutch couple, stipulating the twenty-eighth of January as the completion date, and now needed to put our affairs in order. It was during our last meeting with Peggy and Ronald, our accountant, to wind up our existing company that the dreaded 'e' word was used.

'Now that you've decided to emigrate...' Ronald began.

Only then did we realise the enormity of our decision. Up to then it had seemed we'd only been planning an extended holiday, whereas in fact we were burning our bridges to become *émigrés*.

I felt a pinprick of fear pierce my stomach, although I'd been an *émigré* several times in my life. It had been forced upon me as a child, moving from one country to another with my family.

At the age of four, I was hoisted across the barbed-wired frontier between Hungary and Austria. My father was fifty when he took the initiative and the gamble to escape from the Communist regime with three small children and a much younger wife. After paying the guides, he retained the exact amount of dollars as his age in his pocket to secure a future for his family. On reaching Vienna, my father presented us at the American embassy seeking refugee status. We were denied that protection.

It was in 1949 when the dawn of the Cold War was casting its sinister light over Europe. Austria was a buffer state between East and West, occupied by the victors of the Second World War. Vienna was a quartered city with its zones patrolled in rotation by the four allies. As a family we were in constant danger of being picked up and interrogated by the Russian patrols. Without stamped documents, they could have simply made us disappear. The essence of those threatening times was captured exactly in Carol Reed's direction of the classic film, *The Third Man*.

But we survived intact. With the help of my father's pre-war diplomatic contacts, we eventually made the voyage to America along with thousands of other refugees, embarking at Bremerhaven on the troop transporter, the USS *General Ballou* in 1951.

When I was thirteen, my father was offered a position with Radio Free Europe at its headquarters in Munich. Our flight on that occasion was far more civilised. We travelled to Germany first class on a Pan Am Super-constellation, and dined on *filet mignon* served on porcelain plates and with the airline's embossed silver cutlery. It was the first time I was allowed to taste champagne. I savoured its effect and joined the 'mile high' club but in a more innocent context.

From Munich, at the age of twenty-three, I had come to live in London. I was a seasoned traveller, but England had been my home now for twenty-seven years. Leaving its shores and our family of friends was a daunting prospect.

But if my father could do it successfully at the age of fifty, so could I. Ours would not be a daring escape, but a comfortable cruise on the ferry; crossing the Channel, not barbed wire. We had a place to go to that we loved. We knew people there, and, in Hugh, had an accomplice to ensure our financial security.

I was aware, though, that the uprooting would be more difficult for Bill. '*Émigré*' had never featured in his curriculum vitae.

We sat shoulder to shoulder on Peggy's large sofa, listening to Ronald while he took us through the procedures which would terminate our company and eventual residency in England. Bill and I turned to look at each other and I felt his hand gently touch my thigh. I placed mine into his and we sat clutching hands for the rest of the meeting. His, normally warm, felt even colder than mine.

I knew we'd retire to a pub afterwards. I ordered a white wine and watched in horror as the bartender filled the glass from a dispenser. At least *that* won't be happening in France, I thought. Bill had asked for a pint of bitter and looked on in satisfaction as his glass was pulled from the pump. He took a taste from the golden liquid.

'I won't be getting any of this in France,' he said, a little morosely.

We found a table and sat quietly, digesting the consequences of the meeting we'd just had, allowing our ruminating silence to speak for itself. Bill became fascinated with the glass he was holding, turning it slowly from side to side.

After a while, I hazarded interrupting his meditation.

'So what do you think?' I asked inanely.

He lifted his head from his concentrations, put the glass to his mouth, drained its contents and replied with another question.

'Why didn't the brewers of Courage, ever call one of their beers "Dutch"?'

Chapter Nine

I F I WERE TO SAY THAT, SHORTLY BEFORE OUR ARRIVAL at the Moulin Blanc in the Pas de Calais, Hugh's ancient Labrador accidentally pissed in someone's soup, I'd be giving a subtle hint of the sort of debacles we would come to expect during our eight-week-long venture into hotel management. That was when I found out, beyond the other necessary alterations, that the floorboards on the first level also had to be replaced. The poor old dog was chasing a cat through the upstairs corridor, got overexcited and relieved itself exactly above the dining-room table. What seemed a never-ending flow from the contents of its bladder escaped through a crack in the warped wood and poured from the ceiling directly into the soup bowl belonging to a female Liberal Member of Parliament. The incident was a test to her sense of humour. She failed it dismally.

Our sense of humour would be tested as well, especially on the occasion when an irate plumber who had threatened to shoot Hugh, his wife and baby daughter because of a long-outstanding unpaid bill for services rendered, made a sudden and menacing appearance. I'd witnessed the phone call Hugh had had from the man. Hugh remained calm while I, from behind his shoulder, could hear rough squawking coming from the receiver. Just before hanging up, Hugh threatened the man that he would contact the police.

'What was that all about?' I asked, my mouth opening like the entrance to a tunnel.

'He wants his money and I refuse to pay him for the crappy job he did. It's cost me twice as much for the repairs.'

'Why the police?'

'Because he's threatened to shoot us,' he answered, almost nonchalantly.

'What!?' I went pale.

'Oh, don't worry. He's just a maniac. Shall we have another glass of wine?' He walked off into the kitchen to fetch another bottle.

I was left utterly dazed. This was a new experience. 'Don't worry. He's just a maniac…'

A few days later Bill and I were in the large lounge, sitting on the sofa placed at right angles to the blazing fire. It was early evening and the hotel was empty. We hadn't bothered to put any of the lamps on, preferring to enjoy a quiet relaxing moment in the semi-darkness. The only light came from the soft strobing glow of the flames reflecting on the pale walls. The lighting effect complemented perfectly Bill's choice of a particular Mahler symphony we were listening to on the stereo.

Through the large windows on either side of the door we became aware of a white van cruising slowly past the front of the hotel. Within a moment we saw it creep stealthily back in reverse gear, and the driver staring ferociously towards the windows. It came to a halt and we noticed a logo with something written in French to do with plumbing emblazoned on its side.

'Oh, fuck! It's the plumber,' I heard Bill gasp. Convinced the man was armed, we both slid off the cushions on to the floor and crawled quickly on our hands and knees to hide behind the sofa. Thereafter we communicated in hysterical whispers.

'Do you think he saw us?'

'I don't know, but he must see the fire, so he'll know there's someone here.'

I turned to Bill. 'Oh, my God! If he saw us, you're the same height and have the same dark hair as Hugh!'

'But you don't look anything like Martine.'

'I could, to a man blinded by rage.'

Edging one eye from behind my corner of the sofa, I saw a bearded man slowly get out of the van.

'He's getting out. He's getting out!' I squeaked.

Bill peeped out from behind the other corner.

'Oh, shit! He's reaching for something from the back of the van.'

'It's a gun. It's a gun. I know it's a gun,' I squeaked a little louder.

'It's too dark to tell, but it doesn't look long enough and it's a bit too fat to be a rifle,' Bill reflected.

'It's probably a bloody sawn-off shotgun!' I screamed in a whisper. I don't know what films I'd seen lately, but that was the weapon that came to mind.

Bill peeked around his corner again.

'Is the door locked?' he asked.

'Why?'

'Because he's coming towards it.'

'I don't remember locking it. Did you?'

'I wouldn't be asking if I had.'

'Oh, fuck! What do we do now? You were an officer in the army. You can't let us get shot like vermin behind the sofa!'

There were two seconds of silence during which we heard the footsteps approach.

'Retreat!' Bill ordered and pushed me towards an archway, behind us and to our left, which led to the kitchen. His side of the sofa had been closest to the fire, and before following me he'd grabbed whatever fire-iron was nearest to hand so that, if necessary, he would have a weapon for our defence.

Outsized vermin is what we would have looked like if the bearded man had been able to see us scuttling across the tiled floor into the protective darkness beyond the archway. We stopped just around the corner, crouching as low as possible to the floor. Bill hazarded another peek and saw a face peering through the glass panels into the interior. Whatever he was carrying was obscured by the bottom half of the door.

We headed to the kitchen, but there was nowhere to hide. The fridge was too dangerous and the oven was too small. But there was the service door we could exit through which led to the other reception room where the trout were swimming in their pool, blissfully oblivious to the danger an irate plumber with a sawn-off shotgun could cause.

A narrow fire-escape staircase led from that reception area to the rooms on the first floor. We climbed it and arrived in the corridor Hugh's dog (since demised) had used as a *pissoire*, and stopped at a window which overlooked the parking in front of the hotel. We were still on all fours and, placing our noses against the bottom edge of the window, could see the white van waiting outside. Aware that every movement could be heard below through the floorboards, we remained frozen, as if petrified, and perceived the sound of an ominous metallic click from downstairs.

Visions of a pump-action shotgun being primed invaded my already stressed imagination. For a horrible moment I thought my bladder would behave like Hugh's old Labrador's. That would have given our position away and made us an easy target for a blast from his gun through the leaking ceiling separating us from his murderous intentions. I made an extreme effort of self-control.

'*Il y a quelq'un?*' a gruff voice asked from below.

Bill and I clung to each other, hardly daring to breathe.

Not hearing a response, the same voice made some disgruntled mutterings, and we heard another click.

With our eyes just above the window sill staring down, we were relieved to see the top of his head begin to move towards the van. It's strange the images you remember; he had a round bald patch on his crown, which made it looked like he was balancing a beer mat on his head.

Whatever he was carrying was returned to the back of the van. He got into the cab, made a U-turn and drove away. We waited for it to disappear before getting to our feet and rushing downstairs. The fire was still burning happily. Light and shadows danced on the tiles, highlighting a white calling card on the floor. I picked it up. On one side was the plumber's name and logo. On the reverse a message had been scrawled. It was so illegible, I couldn't begin to translate it

While we were considering the risks of remaining in a place where our lives were threatened by a maniac plumber on the loose, we saw the headlights of Hugh's car approaching. He parked and walked to the entrance. The door had been locked. I must have done it automatically and immediately forgotten. We opened it for him from the inside. He'd hardly stepped across the threshold before we regaled him with our near-death experience. I showed him the card.

Hugh was more experienced in deciphering the tiny hieroglyphics which pass for French penmanship than I. He immediately read the message and translated it as: *Came to renew the section of downpipe causing damp on the wall to bedroom. No one was here.*

'It's another plumber,' he said, holding back a giggle. 'I'm so sorry, I forgot to tell you about those repairs, and I completely forgot he was coming today.'

'Great!' Bill didn't like feeling foolish.

'There were some frightening clicks! We thought he was priming a gun!' I added, dramatically.

Bill looked around for what could have been the source of that threatening noise. He walked to the door, flipped up the brass flap to the mail slot, and allowed it to spring closed again. The mystery was revealed.

On that occasion, we laughed so hard I had to rush cross-legged to the loo, most of the laughter being caused by my hero's hurried choice of weapon for our protection. It was a long metal-handled broom used to tidy the ashes in a fireplace. There were other times, though, when our sense of humour failed us.

And yet, the omens had augured so well. The sale of the flat went smoothly. The Dutch couple even offered to adopt our fifteen-year-old cat, 'Puskas', who was still thriving, albeit on occasional steroid injections. It would break my heart to leave her behind, but I couldn't risk her being torn from limb to limb by the pack of five dogs in Bonneval that the *aubergiste* had since accumulated which ran wild, nipping the bare calves of passing cyclists, or sinking their considerably large teeth into the tyres of moving vehicles. I dreaded to think what those teeth could have done if ganged up on my elderly, utterly unferocious pussycat.

Even the move was going to cost less than expected, as the Dutch were sharing the lorry. Having unloaded our furniture in France, it was heading back north to pick up their belongings already in containers waiting in a warehouse in Amsterdam to be delivered back to our old address from where their round trip had begun.

Two days before the flat was to be emptied, we received a phone call from our *Mairie*. Isabelle, the secretary, warned us that severe snowstorms were taking place and advised us to direct the drivers of the pantechnicon along the less tortuous route from Dore-l'Église to approach the higher altitude of Bonneval. The mayor, she said, would make sure the road would be cleared of snow, and he promised it a double gritting. It would be impossible to position the lorry on the slope in front of the house, so the mayor had arranged for it to be parked further up the hill, and he'd find some locals to help with the unloading. She continued to inform us that the western barn had been cleared and swept as promised, and was ready to accommodate all of our belongings. In exchange for that monumental task, we had made a deal with the mayor: he could keep all the wagons, tools and farming relics for use as exhibits in the retrospective rural museum he was planning to establish.

Bill and I were moved by their concern and offers to help. It made us wonder if these acts would have been reciprocated if, say, a French couple were moving to a little hamlet in the north of Yorkshire during a severe and snowy winter. Would they have had the considerations of a mayor and the local people to ease what could possibly have become a nightmare? I don't suppose they'd have had a Mercedes snowplough at their disposal. Anyway, it would probably have been the wrong kind of snow.

A few weeks before our January departure, we held what Bill called a 'house-cooling party'. At that time we'd given one of our spare bedrooms to a Filipino man called Joe, whom we inherited from our neighbour, Alastair. Joe was in between flats and needed a place to stay. Money didn't exchange hands but, when my back was turned, the flat was cleaned until it sparkled. Bill's shirts were ironed to such perfection that I was shamed and, if Joe wasn't working in the evenings, we feasted on the most exotic dishes which he'd prepare in my kitchen. Alastair also told us that having Joe around would give us complete security. No burglar would ever mess with Joe. His entire body, including his nose, was a lethal weapon. It was comforting to know we had our very own personal kung-fu fighter living with us who called Bill 'Boss' and me 'Lady'.

Joe did most of the catering and behaved like a butler during our 'cooling down' do, affording me the time to reminisce and shed some tears amongst our friends. You have to be Hungarian to understand that, when you're having fun, it's good sometimes to cry. Bryan Pringle and Jeremy Nicholas, my fellow protagonists in our French discovery, were there with their wives, Annie and Jill. So many faces we'd come to love were all gathered in our living room. They were laughing or weeping, speaking loudly in their theatrically trained voices. The whole room was vibrating with a sort of dramatic hysteria.

Every now and again someone would be heard booming above the din, 'End of an era!' and whoever Bill or I were speaking to gave us a sloppy kiss or a hug which would send me once again into emotional fits of sobbing. In a way, it *was* the end of an era. This chapter of our lives was coming to an end, but the book was far from finished.

We'd invited the Dutch couple, who had never been around actors, directors, writers or producers before. I must say, once they became accustomed to our friends' uninhibited behaviour, they fared terribly well. Hugh also made an appearance and was introduced to the crowd. Individuals posed questions about our undertaking to him. He replied to them with his usual charm and optimism.

Before taking her leave from the party, a close friend, the actress Gillian Raine, Leonard Rossiter's widow, took me aside. She held my shoulders with outstretched arms and looked into my eyes as directly as a surfeit of red wine would permit.

'Are you sure about this? You're leaving London to work for that man, and I've never even met him before!'

We counted Gilly as one of our most intimate friends. Bill had known her from the days well before she'd married Leonard. They had worked in rep together: Bill as stagehand/designer, she as the resident leading lady. Since Leonard's sudden death, our relationship with Gilly had become even closer. Bill liked to consider himself a surrogate uncle to her daughter, Camilla. We spent weekends at their lovely cottage in Bosham where he influenced the design of the garden, and where we managed to make large dents in Leonard's collection of fine wines that Gilly had inherited. Not long ago she had invited us to Venice, travelling there and back on the Orient Express. What splendid memories, what happy times we'd shared.

I tried to look back into her eyes as directly as a surfeit of white wine would permit and answered, 'It has to work out. We have no choice. The business has dumped on us. We can't earn a living here any more.'

'But you'll be so far away!'

I had to explain to many of our friends that day that we were not going to Mars. We were only going to that bit of land across the Channel which English armies had often visited in previous centuries, well before aeroplanes, ferry services and the Tunnel had existed.

My mother, the 'dragon lady', had also to be convinced that I was moving to the same continent she lived on; that, in distance, Bonneval was even nearer to Munich than London had been. I would no longer be dependent on the vagaries of labour relations to travel to her. Motorways, in my experience, never went on strike.

But there were moments during the party when I, too, had the daunting feeling that we were travelling to a faraway planet. When we kissed our friends farewell, I had no way of knowing when or where, or even if, we would see those beloved, familiar faces again.

In the days that followed the party we were kept too busy to contemplate the pain of severance. Once again, Joe was a miracle, helping us to pack and crate what I had accumulated since my arrival on British soil. Challoner Crescent was the only address I'd occupied since I was born that lasted more than five years. It had been bought because my previous much smaller flat in Fulham had run out of wall space to accommodate the pictures I loved buying, and also, to be perfectly honest, the wardrobes became far too cramped. Added to my life's acquisitions, there was also Bill's voluminous collection of CDs, books, theatrical posters and precious wine-glasses. Everything we were not junking or giving to charity shops had to be wrapped and stowed meticulously.

The movers arrived early in the morning of the appointed day, and we witnessed the three bedrooms, two walk-in wardrobes, office, two bathrooms, kitchen and a 27x19-foot living room emptied of all their effects as if someone had used a vanishing spray. Poor Puskas lay in a corner on a cushion glaring accusingly at me, distressed that everything she had become accustomed to rubbing or brushing her tail against was disappearing. I think she knew that I'd be disappearing too.

We were leaving London at 8:30 in the evening to drive to Portsmouth and once again, perhaps for the last time, to catch the overnight ferry. Joe was coming with us, helping with the driving and the unloading of the van at the other end in Bonneval. He was looking forward to a little holiday in France, a country he admired but had never seen.

I'd managed to reserve several fluted glasses from the packing. A bottle of champagne was cooling in Alastair's fridge. The Dutch couple arrived at about 7:30; they, too, brought a bottle of champagne.

The house contained six flats, our lower- and ground-floor maisonette on one side of the double-fronted Edwardian edifice, Alastair's on the other. Directly above him lived David McKee, the children's author and illustrator. On the top floor lived Margaret, a 78-year-old spinster and sitting tenant, who still never allowed any of us to help carry her shopping up the three flights of stairs. The flat just above us was occupied by a Polish gentleman who was also a sitting tenant but whom we hardly ever saw. Bill and I were convinced he was a spy and only maintained the address as a dead-letter drop. The other flat on the top floor was unoccupied. Margaret, David and Alastair were more than just neighbours: they'd become dear friends, and came to partake in this mini sending-off party. Puskas looked on, refusing to leave the security of her pillow, the only soft article remaining in the vast void of the living room.

For the lack of chairs, we stood elbow to elbow in that enormous space, as if we were at a crowded cocktail party, but the other guests were invisible. We all made promises that we would see each other again. Caroline and Hugo, who were now the owners of the flat, once again assured me of their devotion for adopting Puskas and that a spare room would always be available should we be returning to London for a visit. Alastair was already making plans to visit us on his BMW motorbike, and David who owned a property in Nice would drop in to see us on his way south. Margaret doubted that she would ever make the trip, but we'd remain in contact by phone and letters.

During these last-moment pledges, Joe maintained a discreet distance, keeping busy packing and rearranging suitcases, boxes etc. to make room for us in the interior of the car.

A few moments before leaving, I picked up the pillow with Puskas still lying upon it and carried it through to Alastair's flat where I set it down under a table. Alastair was going to look after her until Hugo and Caroline had settled in. She ignored me totally as I stroked her and bade for her to understand why I had to leave her behind. We'd become very attached to each other in the last fifteen years. The first and only time she'd had kittens, instead of retreating to a hiding place, she insisted on sharing the experience, choosing to give birth in front of me. I knelt on the bedroom carpet feeling panicky and useless as she howled and screamed, all the while staring straight into my eyes. I touched her belly and felt it contracting with the labour. Until that moment I had thought animals didn't suffer birth pains as humans did. I learned differently that night. Bill, who had experienced this natural feline phenomenon during his previous marriage, was fast asleep, snoring loudly in our bed. None of my shouting, 'Bill! What do I do now?!' roused him from his dreams to give me his accustomed directions. And then, finally, out slipped a tiny, bald, wet creature that looked more like a mouse than the predator it would become. She furiously licked it dry, carefully placed it into her mouth and carried it to the nest we had prepared for her in the depths of a walk-in wardrobe. I felt honoured when she came back and went through the same process twice again directly in front of me. At four in the morning, though, I was exhausted and had to crawl to my bed. The following day, through the curtain of clothes that I gently pushed aside, I saw Puskas in the dark corner suckling four little squirming kittens at her breast. She had had the last one in silence. I could never forget the special relationship we had, my cat and I. She lived for another two happy years being cosseted by Caroline and Hugo, for which I thank them sincerely.

As my fingers caressed her soft black-and-white coat, tears were stinging my eyes. For a fleeting moment she looked up to my face, and I thrilled in her brilliant citrine glare. And then, she stood up from the pillow and moved further under the table, out of reach of my hands. In cat body language she was telling me to piss off. What did I expect? A kiss?

Outside on the pavement, we hugged and were hugged by our two-legged friends. Not for the first time, I saw tears in Alastair's eyes and felt his shoulders heaving as I put my arms around him. He'd become like a kid brother to me from the moment he'd moved into the house, soon after I had. I'd lived through some of his disastrous relationships and consoled him when they had come to a bitter end. He seemed to have a penchant for violent women. One threw an iron at his head from across the room while he was in bed.

'Was it hot?' I asked him, horrified at the thought of the wedge-shaped metal sizzling into his handsome face.

'No, no. She'd have never used it for ironing,' he replied. 'Wouldn't have known how to turn it on.'

Another woman stabbed him in the leg with her stiletto heels. And then, there was the woman with the hoover… not to mention the one who left a part of her finger in his steel-framed heavy front door. I was going to miss Alastair, but not, perhaps, those moments of high drama.

Calls of 'Good luck!' and '*Bon voyage!*' echoed in the street as we piled into the car. Joe was in the driver's seat with Bill beside him. I was squeezed into the back, barely finding enough room to move my shoulders amongst the articles stuffed there to turn round and take one last look at what and who we were leaving behind.

Joe drove slowly away and I could see five figures standing on the steps that led up to the large front door, their arms waving wildly. And through the tall bay windows, partially obscured by the foliage of our giant *monstera* and umbrella plants that we were leaving behind, I saw the parsley-green colour on our living-room walls denuded of the many paintings that had been hung on them. The walls looked harsh, now only lit by a bare bulb hanging from an ornate central rosette that I remembered Bill painstakingly painting to reflect the shades of green, pale salmon and soft ivory, the colours we used in that space.

The only words spoken along the route to Portsmouth were to give Joe directions. What could have been a forbidding silence between Bill and myself was masked by the music he was playing. The excitement I had expected to feel and to share had turned to numbness. Not having to drive, I had the rare luxury of being able to stare out of the window. All I saw was a dark landscape of the beloved country I had adopted rushing by. I think I can honestly say I left England as a zombie that night and slept on the ferry as if anaesthetised.

But I awoke with vigour! We decided it was best that I start the long drive through France and allow Joe to take over once we'd reached the final autoroute to get him used to driving on the right side of the road.

I sped down the familiar route from Le Havre thinking of Jacques and Claudine, remembering that first time we'd caught the overnight ferry and disembarked before dawn. We'd arranged to meet Jacques beyond passport control, and spotted his tall figure wearing a cloth cap with the brim pulled so low over his face, only his moustache was visible. He leapt into his car and we followed him through the backstreets of Le Havre to their house which had a view of the Channel and from where he'd watched our ferry, lights twinkling from the portholes, slowly approaching the docks.

Claudine, having been told that the English feast for breakfast, had set a table which would have satisfied a rugby team. There was *charcuterie*, smoked salmon, boiled eggs, jams, brioche, croissants, warm *petit pains* and baguettes. For Bill, Jacques removed a vintage burgundy from his *cave* and, with a cloth, wiped the dust from the bottle before placing it on the table.

Not wanting to disappoint Claudine, I ate as much as I thought was wise. Normally, I only drink sugared black coffee when driving long distances. But Bill managed his share of the wine while he and Jacques studied the Michelin map for the best route to Bonneval which Jacques prescribed from years of experience. On all the trips we ever made, we hardly strayed from his original suggestion: Rouen, Evreux, Dreux, Chartres, entering the autoroute to Clermont-Ferrand just north of Orléans.

It was just south of Orléans that we decided Joe could take over the driving. We'd stopped for petrol at a service station as I needed my coffee fix. Entering the small cafeteria, it became evident we were in France. A controversial law had been passed the previous year forbidding smoking in all public places, and yet the air was thick with spent tobacco emissions. Three burly *gendarmes* with holstered pistols hanging from their well-padded hips stood against a wall. A tall round table holding their paper coffee-cups was in front of them. All around them cigarettes were being lit by the other clients in the cafeteria; I'd never seen such nonchalant disregard for an established law. But it was no wonder. The three *gendarmes* themselves were happily puffing in defiance of the glaring red-and-white NO SMOKING sign in full view directly behind them.

Nearing Clermont-Ferrand, Bill from the back and I in the passenger seat noticed Joe's head drooping heavily to his chest. I could see he was blinking a little too often and a little too long. But when we voiced our alarm, his pride would not allow him to admit to his tiredness. He'd obviously not slept through the ferry journey as well as I had. We insisted that he pull over and allow me to continue the drive.

The domed shapes of the volcanoes were covered in snow, which forewarned us of what we could expect in the loftier altitudes towards which we were driving. Bill wisely directed me to aim for Thiers, and climb up into the Massif taking the route to Ambert, which was wider and a more gentle ascent than our normal Issoire/La Chaise-Dieu itinerary. We had last been in Bonneval in late October, when, as a precaution for our return, I had exchanged my summer tyres for winter ones.

The mayor had kept his word. The road from Dore-l'Église to Bonneval had been cleared and the remaining tightly packed, icy snow which clung to the tarmac had been thoughtfully gritted. Huge mounds of snow had been shoved on to the verges, obscuring from view the smooth white fields beyond. We wanted Joe to appreciate the winter scenery. He sat in silence staring out at high white walls speckled with rust-coloured grit. The branches of the tall, dark firs which lined our route sagged under the weight of what looked like heavy dollops of whipped cream.

The house was as cold as if an iceberg had settled on it. We turned on the electricity at the fuse box and spotted a red light warning us that we were having an 'EJP day'. In our attempts at frugality, and because the house had served as a holiday home, seldom used in the winter, we had opted with France's electricity-generating company for the EJP contract which gave us the cheapest tariff all year round except for twenty-two days between the first of November and the thirty-first of March when we could be hit with an eighteen-hour tariff at ten times the normal rate. Our electricians had designated certain sockets for the heavy radiators which were connected to the EJP fuse. On such a day, they were automatically cut off, as was our water heater. There were to be no hot baths or showers that night. None of the radiators would heat until one in the morning, and then only until seven a.m. if we suffered two consecutive EJP days.

While Joe and I slid up and down from the car (which had to be parked further up the hill) in our efforts to unload it, Bill set to creating heat from the living-room fireplace. When our efforts were completed, I led Joe to his bedroom which was downstairs in the converted forge where we had established a suite. Our breaths turned to mist as I showed him around, explaining where everything was. Any comments he made were stuttered in between the chattering of his teeth. He was delighted to see there was a wood-burning stove in his salon which I began filling with kindling, but the matches at hand refused to strike. They were French.

It is a joke amongst our English friends who live around us how French matches are notoriously inadequate. At least three have to be struck before you get a light. Remember the shoe bomber? He was on a plane from Paris heading to the States and was only discovered due to the sulphurous smell of the numerous matches he was frustrated from lighting. The outcome could have been disastrous if his flight had originated from London with a pack of English Swan Vestas in his pocket.

Joe was visibly trembling with cold as he helped me brush the snow off the logs we were bringing in from outside the forge door. I was finally successful with one of the matches (the pile of spent ones added to the kindling), and soon a little ribbon of flame glimmered in the stove. I assured him that once it really got going, the stove was quite capable of heating the entire suite. I also promised him two hot-water bottles to accompany him in his bed.

An all-too-familiar blue veil greeted us as we went back up the stairs to join Bill. The living room was thick with smoke wafting down from the still-cold chimney. Bill and I were used to these initial discomforts when repossessing the house after a long absence, but poor Joe was going into shock. We had left the luxury of our centrally heated, magnificent London flat to be cured like herrings in freezing temperatures amongst volcanoes in the middle of France. I think he was hoping for an eruption, just to keep warm.

The furniture van arrived as planned the following morning. A team of locals had been gathered by the mayor to assist with the unloading. Helping them, Joe moved up and down the slope, slipping on the unaccustomed icy surface, trying desperately not to drop the objects he was carrying. His gloveless hands were turning blue and the socks in his inappropriate shoes were stiffening with ice. Within two hours, the cleanly swept western barn was filled with our belongings to await the purpose they'd eventually be destined for, be it a *brocante* or to furnish the B&B.

After that spurt of hectic activity, Joe spent the rest of the day shivering, often standing as near to the fireplace as caution would permit. I made frequent forays into the igloo of the barn, satisfying myself that the crates that would be emptied for our immediate needs were the most accessible.

Bill twiddled furiously with the knobs of the radio, but the BBC Radio 4 long-wave reception, his means of keeping contact with England, had disintegrated into an annoying static. This audial starvation caused him to behave like a growling tiger anticipating his canines being simultaneously drilled by an ambidextrous, psychopathic dentist. He consoled himself, though, by drinking tumblers of red wine and listening instead to classical works of music blaring from the ghetto blaster.

I quickly prepared a supper conjured from the ingredients we'd salvaged from our London fridge. We ate in reverential silence, Joe and I only daring to speak in whispers as the jangling notes from Saint-Saens' *Danse Macabre* mingled with the hissing and the spitting of the fire. Bill's mood had not improved. It was as forbidding as the freezing black night outside.

Joe helped with the washing-up and then disappeared to seek warmth in his bed. When I delivered the hot-water bottles, I found him buried under several layers of blankets, the duvet, and a doubled-over patchwork quilt. Only his head was visible beyond the mound of bedding. He had stretched a brown knitted hat over it which covered his forehead and was pulled almost down to his nose. We had a brief conversation during which I felt I was speaking to a coconut embedded into a white frilly pillowcase.

As I turned to leave the room, the coconut asked me a question.

'Lady, can I borrow a pair of your tights?' it whispered, bashfully.

'Of course!' I replied and rushed up the two flights to our bedroom to rummage through some drawers.

In height, Joe was smaller than I, but he made up for this lack of altitude with a muscular physique. There was no doubt that, by his appearance, he was definitely 'butch'. It must have been from extreme discomfort that he could have brought himself to ask for such a feminine article of underwear. I found a perfect pair of thick woollen tights that would keep him warm for the rest of his stay. He was grateful for that extra layer underneath his jeans, but he didn't stay the week. Having lived in the Philippines for most of his life, he was not prepared for the heat deprivation his body had to suffer during a severe Haute-Loire winter. It wasn't only the clothes he lacked; it was a certain will.

The following morning, I rang the station in Le Puy to ascertain the availability and times of trains for Joe's return to England. When he surfaced for his breakfast, I told him of the schedules and possible connections.

'Is train today, Lady?' he asked, his dark eyes shining with hope.

'Yes, there is one,' I answered, 'but it leaves Le Puy at eleven. It's nine o'clock now. I don't think we'll make it.'

'I pack my things very quickly,' he said and headed back down to his bedroom.

Bill and I looked at each other.

'Why not?' Bill shrugged. 'We'll put him on the train and I'll take you to lunch in the big city.' It was the first time since we'd arrived that there was a smile in his voice.

Bill opted to stay in a café near to the station while I bought Joe's ticket and explained the changes he would have to take in Lyon and then in Paris. I walked with him to the platform where the two-carriage train was waiting, and stuffed some French francs into his jacket pocket for food and drink along the journey and some surplus UK banknotes for when he'd arrive in England.

'Goodbye, lady. I hope you will be happy here,' he said, stressing the word 'hope'. His face, usually inscrutable, gave me a meaningful look. He shook my hand, and then boarded the train. I watched from the platform as the noisy diesel engine pulled the carriages out of the station. He was wearing the same woollen hat from the night before on his head as he leaned out of the window looking back at me, and a hand trained in kung-fu fighting gently waved until his carriage rounded a bend and disappeared.

He had promised to keep in touch, and even occasionally to send Bill his beloved *Guardian* newspaper so he could continue his cryptic-crossword puzzling; but, except for a phone call from Paris telling us that he had found the correct station and platforms for his onward journey, we never heard from Joe again. I sometimes wonder if he's still wearing my tights.

Lunch was orgasmic. And the siesta afterwards, great. Or should I have put it the other way around?

Chapter Ten

RAAAAAH-DA-DAH
DA-RAH-DA-DAH
RAH-DA-DAH
DA-DAH-DA-DAH-DA
BOOM
DA-RAH
BOOM
DA-RAH
BOOM
DA-RAH
BOOM
DA-RAH
DA-DA-DAH-DA-DAH
DA-RAH-DA-DA-DAH...

Depending on the sort of lives you've led, some of you may recognise the above as the raunchy rhythm from the music most 'artistes' prefer to strip to. I don't remember how the tape came into my possession, never having had to prepare for an audition to play such a role. I had discovered it years ago amongst a pile of ancient tapes, and sometimes played it secretly. It helped to keep the hip joints oiled.

The tape must have been slipped into another cassette cover by mistake. Bill was planning to hear Berlioz's *Symphonie Fantastique*; he was treated to a striptease instead. The ghetto blaster was set to do exactly that, in anticipation of the symphony. When it blasted out this more erotic noise, I couldn't help but begin to disrobe. Joe had gone; we were alone. The curtains were drawn against the cold. The house had warmed up a bit and, in celebration, I began to tease off my winter wear. The heavy pullover was pulled up over my head, and tossed defiantly in the air. Wool-lined suede boots with tractor-tyre rubber soles were slipped out of, and discarded into far corners of the room. Thick corduroy trousers were peeled below my hips, then my knees, then my ankles, then daintily stepped out of, and thrown to join the other scattered debris. All of this was done in faithful accompaniment to the boom-booms. I sat on a stool to roll down my knee-length woollen socks, bending my knees, crossing my legs to the rhythm, pointing my toes. When stripped off, I dangled them sexily across Bill's chest, sliding them teasingly down his lap. I was trying to be as professional as possible, and had the advantage of being backlit by the blazing fire which added a certain frisson to the gyrating silhouette Bill was attentively studying.

And then, the phone rang. I answered it in the only remaining clothes still covering my body: cream-coloured thermal underwear.

It was Hugh. Through the sounds of 'The Stripper' and in between the boom-booms, I could hear him telling me that the very pleasant bank manager we had met, who had excellent taste in wine, had just been arrested for suspicion of fraud. Hugh had heard it that morning on the BBC and recognised the man's name and the location of the branch as the one he'd been negotiating with. He doubted if the loan which had been agreed and signed would now be honoured.

But not to worry, he continued on the phone. His lawyer in France and the accountants were dealing with it. Bill had turned the music off and was listening to my end of the conversation. We should still come. He had already set up some dates for the English press and travel agents to come over for a junket. With the extra publicity, the hotel would gain on bookings and, with this added turnover, another loan with another bank could be negotiated. His tone, as usual, was optimistic. I could imagine him smiling like a chipmunk, cheeks puffing out from the corners of his mouth. It was then, and in the same happy voice, that he told me of the disastrous behaviour of his Labrador.

I don't know whether it was the revelation about the bank manager, the dog story, or that I'd been sitting on a window seat in only my thermal underwear, but upon hanging up the phone something strange happened to me. For a good ten minutes afterwards, Bill told me, I made no sense at all.

Perhaps I'd been hyperventilating from excitement and the cold. I tried to relate to Bill what Hugh had just told me, but it came out as gibberish when I babbled that the bank manager had peed into someone's soup which a liberal MP did not find funny, and his poor old dog was in jail. I couldn't remember names, and even denied them when Bill prompted me. I refused to admit the names Bill gave to the lawyer and the accountants because they didn't fit the faces I could see in my mind's eye. It wasn't until Bill had gathered my scattered clothes, helped me back into them, and then placed a glass of neat scotch into my hands that I began to calm down and assume normal speech.

Two days later, I answered another phone call; this time from Li-li. We had spoken to our French friends of our plans, and he was ringing, urging me to be very careful in accepting the position of *gérante* (manageress) of the hotel. Having been in business all of his life, he had experience of the dangers such a position could produce. He'd been worrying for my lack of knowledge in such matters, and therefore had spoken to a lawyer friend of his, detailing my situation. The *avocat* strenuously warned against my accepting such a post. A *gérant(e)* in France can be held responsible for any debts incurred by an establishment under their control, and thereby can run the risk of being forced to repay those debts by forfeiting any property they own. Bill and I were joint owners of the house. Although I would be contracted as *gérante*, in the absence of a marital agreement declaring a separation of wealth, Bill would share in any financial mishaps that could befall me. I could lose the roof over his head.

Our decision to go to Calais regardless was driven more from a need for comfort rather than common sense. Although the house was warming up, our supply of wood was getting dangerously low. The snow beyond our door was stubbornly refusing to melt, making another delivery impossible. EJP days were hitting us unabated during the week, which meant we couldn't turn our electric radiators on. Long daggers of icicles hanging from the roof threatened to pierce our craniums every time we ventured outside. We felt it a little too soon after arriving from civilised London to have our survival skills challenged. We had the choice of moving in with the *aubergiste* and his family, and suffering his gloating at our ineptitude in unspeakable English, or taking our chances in the Pas de Calais. It was hardly a contest. We opted for Hugh and his centrally heated hotel. But I was not signing a contract.

We headed up north in mid-February, having made a reservation for a night at a *chambre d'hôte* in the region of Sancerre. Our intentions were to spy. If we were going to open our own B&B eventually, we wanted to know how the competition worked.

Over an *aperitif* offered by our host before the evening meal we'd reserved, I admitted to the reason for our presence. On hearing we were spying, he initially went pale; but when we told him why, his relief was such that he poured us another drink, to the surprise and instant disapproval of his silent wife. Perhaps he thought we were agents from the local VAT disguised behind our English accents, and perhaps he had something to hide.

We were the only guests that evening eating with our hosts. The food was very good and the conversation lively, if one-sided. We noticed all of our relevant questions as to the running of a B&B were answered by him. Her participation at the table seemed to be that of a servant who was permitted to partake of the meal she'd prepared, to discreetly remove the used plates, carry them into the kitchen, re-emerge with the following course, place it silently on the table, take her seat and delicately begin to eat. The only sound she made during the meal was an uttered smirk when her husband chided the English for their avoidance of such French delicacies as snails and frog's legs.

Bill donned a charming expression as he replied in English, 'It's difficult to find something delicious that looks like the cooked contents winkled out of somebody's nose.'

I didn't translate that. I just grinned stupidly.

'And if the French think,' he continued to my embarrassment, 'that seeing the lower halves of embryos swimming in a butter and garlic sauce on a plate is appetising, let them eat it. I prefer toad in the hole, actually.'

I was still grinning and not translating. Notwithstanding the embryo bit, *'crapaud dans le trou'* would not have evoked the deliciousness of tasty English sausages baked in a Yorkshire-pudding batter. Then again, we had just eaten *crottins de chèvre chaud* as a starter. Literally translated, it means warm goat's turd. The things the French eat. (I was recently asked to translate our local restaurant's menu into English, and had some difficulty with one of their entrées: *pied de veau en crepine*. Somehow, 'calf's foot in an oil-sump filter' wouldn't do the dish justice.)

We left the next morning not too much the wiser; but he had given us advice as to which were the most important guides to appear in, and we were impressed with the decor of the rooms. A beautiful, bleached terracotta-tiled floor was underfoot. The furniture was genuine, rustic antique, which she had inherited from her family. With such pieces as a dowry, he had made a very good match. I hope he appreciated that when they were alone.

It was mid-afternoon when we drove up to the hotel. The parking area was deserted, as was the building. Rain fell heavily from a gloomy sky. The tall windows on the ground floor yawned darkly at us. We'd been warned of the possibility that Hugh would not be there to greet us. I went to the appointed window-box to retrieve the keys, and we let ourselves in. At least the lounge was warm, if not very cheerful, which Bill immediately remedied by lighting a fire. There was a distinct air of neglect to the place; the tiled floors needed cleaning, the occasional tables dusting. I wondered what had happened to the maid. We knew where the booze was, and settled on the sofas, drinks in hand, waiting for Hugh's appearance.

He arrived with great excitement, telling us the good news that he'd approached another bank, and in a few days' time we'd receive a visit from this new bank manager to study the accounts, and that the mortgage was bound to be agreed. In the meantime, our first punters were arriving the next day. They'd be eating in, and five bedrooms would have to be prepared. Unfortunately, we had lost the cleaning woman. She was afraid of being denounced and wouldn't work without a proper contract, which at the moment he couldn't afford.

I excused myself early to the guests the following night. After showing me where the linen cupboard and the cleaning materials were, Hugh had gone off to do the shopping for that night's meal. I did the five bedrooms, cleaned the two lounges and, that evening, while helping Hugh in the kitchen, I witnessed him slicing through a frozen salmon with the used blade of a wood saw. I lost my appetite. Lying in my bed upstairs, hearing the river rushing past my single-glazed window, I almost lost the will to live. The day had not been the most auspicious beginning to a career in hostelry.

Not being able to sleep, I heard Bill's unsteady footsteps approaching his room. Because of the length of our intended stay, and the amount of clothing we had brought with us, we had opted for two rooms next to each other, rather than one crowded one. A light was left on in the corridor which made me aware that the door to my room was three inches off the carpet, allowing a glare from the exterior to reflect brightly on the chalk-white wall facing my pillow. Until I finally placed a coat across the space to block out the light, I had to be prepared to receive some strange nocturnal visits: a river rat, dormice, ordinary mice, the resident cat's kittens, shrews, and other rodents I was not expert enough to recognise.

They always announced their entry by making their distinctive noises. I often wondered if these creatures had tried all the other rooms before finding mine the most convenient. Or did my room have a particularly attractive smell for them which my olfactory sense had not perceived? It's just as well that I'm not squeamish about little furry mammals; but later, in Bonneval, my courage would be tested when invasions of more dangerous species had to be dealt with.

For the moment, though, Bill and I were coping with the human variety entering Hugh's hotel. I wouldn't say they were coming in herds – they weren't exactly crowding the entrance as at a Harrods sale – but, for the time being, their sparse numbers suited us. I was still trying to come to grips with the enormous and heavy linen sheets I had to make the beds with. The nuns in the convent school I'd gone to had taught me how to make hospital corners. Only, I remembered those mattresses were lighter, more pliable, as were the sheets. Hugh had not skimped on the sleeping comforts for his guests. Making the beds became a back-breaking experience. During our time at the hotel, out of sympathy for me, Bill coined a reverse euphemism for more sheets as 'more shits' every time new guests arrived. As Hugh catered to a 99% English clientele, Bill had to refrain from calling them 'shits' within hearing. When we opened our B&B, and would work predominantly with the French, he would shout it with impunity: 'Another load of shits coming down the hill, darling!'

It was in the Pas de Calais that I first saw Bill wielding a broom. On occasion, I was even surprised to catch him manoeuvring a mop. His decision one day to tackle the windows made me almost faint with worry. I had visions of him falling from an upper-floor sill, until I remembered: all windows open inwards in France.

Bill was an early riser by nature. He had inherited the 'day hunter' gene. I was exactly the opposite. It took time for the smog in my brain to disperse, for the liquid lead in my legs to transubstantiate back into blood. I didn't walk in the morning; I shuffled. I could trip over a needle stuck in a carpet. During my golden days, many a driver employed to get me to the studios at dawn could have attested to my early-morning condition. One in particular, Steve, who drove me during the making of the series *Space 1999*, had my permission to hoist me over his shoulder, should I not make it from my front door to his car.

Hugh and Bill decided, for the safety and comfort of the guests, I would be disqualified from serving breakfast. I was grateful for their sensitivity. But there was one thing that would wake me: Guilt. That was something else the good sisters in the convent taught me. From the age of eight onwards, we were expected to attend Mass and receive the Eucharist before breakfast, as a sort of *hors d'oeuvre* before the porridge. It was not obligatory, but those of us who preferred to remain under our blankets were shamed for the rest of the day.

Our rooms at the hotel were near enough to the conservatory below, where, when we had a certain amount of guests, the breakfasts and dinners were served. When they were fewer in numbers, meals were served at the refectory table at the far end of the lounge, the table that the Labrador had watered. With the lack of sound insulation between the floors, I could hear the morning's preparations. I could hear Bill folding the napkins into triangles and stuffing them into the juice glasses. The sound of butter knives and teaspoons being placed on to a tablecloth thundered into my conscience. More times than not, the mattress lost the battle to guilt. I descended the stairs in a stupor and found Hugh and Bill coping quite adequately without me. But there was always something to do: trying to remove a dead mouse that the cat had placed behind an immovable cupboard before its cadaver began to reek, kicking the dishwasher door to cajole the machine into action, or helping Hugh unload a lorry delivering seven cubic metres of logs.

When that particular job was completed, Hugh had walked off to his office calling over his shoulder, 'Catherine, you sign for the delivery. I'll pay when he sends me the bill.'

Forewarned by Li-Li, I signed in a scrawl: *Heidi Brunchburger.*

It was not very long before the unfortunate fact became obvious that, based on his collateral, Hugh was not going to get the money he required from the numerous banks he approached. But he was very resourceful, and another plan was embarked upon. Through his numerous wealthy contacts, the idea of a rescue package in the form of a syndicate was broached. An acquaintance arrived, an executive from a financial institution based in the city of London, who proposed the following resolution. He could find five to six members who would generously donate £5,000 to £6,000 each and underwrite certain guarantees to the bank, thereby permitting Hugh to borrow the £150,000 mortgage he required to buy back the hotel from the administrators. Did I not mention? Oh, yes. The hotel was already in receivership. With this initial investment of £30,000 from the syndicate members, Hugh could pay off the outstanding debts owed to builders, suppliers etc. (including, hopefully, the maniac plumber for the sake of everyone's safety). The syndicate in return would receive 25% of the hotel's turnover, leaving Hugh needing only to pay the mortgage, the staff, all outgoings, taxes, etc. from the remaining 75%. As I've mentioned earlier, Bill and I were not experts in business matters but it seemed to us that, if this was a rescue plan, it was a little like offering Hugh a life raft which rats had gnawed enormous holes into. As things turned out, the syndicate never materialised.

Bill was becoming more and more unhappy. It was not the season to be creative in the garden. For days on end, the skies were grey and depressing. The mop and broom had lost their initial novelty. He was missing his friends. He was missing his life. At ten o'clock in the morning, he could be seen clutching a tall glass containing a clear liquid with ice cubes and a lemon wedge. It wasn't Perrier. Sometimes in the evenings, after a long nap, he'd come into his own. Hugh and I would hear his voice entertaining the guests in the lounge, and their responding laughter, while we manically prepared the dinners in the kitchen. We were often grateful for his ability to amuse because the dinners were not always served on time.

Bill's mind could assess a situation immediately. Without having looked at the accounts, he instinctively knew the hotel as it was being run could never make a profit. There were too many invited guests. The buzz Hugh enjoyed from seeing his hotel peopled to capacity was the same as an actor experiencing a full house for his performance. For Bill, though, it was a little too like 'papering the house', which alludes to the free tickets offered by a theatre to friends and family of the cast, putting bums on seats to create an audience during the run of an unsuccessful play. The only weekends we were ever full were those when a few paying guests shared the hotel with the non-paying travel agents, press and their extended families. Bill referred to these freebie reservations as 'bums on free sheets'. I noticed him more often with the same tall glass refilled with more clear liquid, and it still wasn't Perrier.

Possessing a nature more inclined to lead rather than follow, to create rather than accept what has already been established, he became morose, complaining. I was witnessing the beginnings of an implosion. Bill needed to organise. He'd been used to platoons, later to stagehands and film crews being inspired by his directions. At the hotel he was not in charge.

One Thursday afternoon in the second week of March, we were accosted by a representative from EDF. He had come to cut off the electricity supply. The hotel was empty of guests, but we were expecting a full house at the weekend, although only six guests would be paying. I was unaware that red reminder notices had turned to scarlet, and they had been ignored due to lack of funds in the hotel's account. Paying the bills was not one of my responsibilities, especially as I was determined to withhold my signature from any official document, and a cheque in France is sacrosanct. I pleaded with the man for a few further minutes of indulgence and quickly phoned Hugh at his chalet house nearby. Bill was convinced the outcome to this crisis was going to be negative and had already gone up the stairs to pack his bags while he had the daylight to do so. On his way up, he suggested I did likewise.

Relieved to hear Hugh answer the phone, I explained the situation with controlled hysteria. Within two minutes, he arrived waving a company cheque book; only this one had nothing to do with our *moulin* hotel. It was an SARL (a kind of limited company) bearing the name of an altogether different *moulin*. The secret of this surrogate account was never revealed to me. Perhaps I didn't really want to know. The EDF man accepted the cheque made out for over FF7,000 (£700) and drove away. We would have an electricity supply for the twelve occupied rooms over the weekend; or, at least, that's what we thought.

On the Saturday night when a northern wind howled, threatening arctic conditions, and the conservatory dining room was full with guests halfway through their meal, the hotel suffered a blackout. This is not unusual in France. Depending on the weather conditions, many outlying villages can be plunged into a sudden darkness. It was also not unusual for the hotel. Hugh had had to, on many occasions, find the reasons for an overload on the circuits. The guests were not overly bothered, as every table was already lit romantically by a candle; but we three in the kitchen were at a grave disadvantage. The electric oven and the grill were quickly cooling. Only the blue flames from the gas stove heating some pots offered a minuscule glow. It was not enough to keep us from bumping into each other as we all headed off in different directions to unplug whatever machines or radiators could possibly be overloading the supply.

Much of the main house was heated by an oil-fired boiler, but even that needed electricity to run. The four rooms in the converted pigsty were entirely dependent on electric power for their hot water and radiators. If we couldn't get the supply back on, there were going to be some very cold bums on freezing sheets that night. With most of the rooms occupied by travel agents, this was not going to be the best publicity. After establishing that the problem was being caused by an overload, Hugh came back from the four annexe rooms. Their radiators had been turned on to maximum. He had lowered them to a convivial 3 and tried the fuse box again. He pressed in the tripper switch. For a brief flash the lights went on, and then immediately off again. Bill was given a candle to light his way into the dining room and jolly the guests while Hugh searched for more apparatuses to switch off.

I was left in the kitchen considering Plan B. Some of the main courses had not yet been served. The salmon, doused with butter and herbs and wrapped loosely in foil, would have to be removed from the oven, and the fish placed into a frying pan. *Crème brûlées* were definitely off, as we'd need the grill to caramelise their tops. (Those handy flame guns had not yet become universally available.) I didn't relish the thought of having to mix a batter by candlelight to make two *crêpes* apiece for twenty people.

Hugh came back to the kitchen, the light from his torch bouncing about like an iridescent tennis ball. During his absence, the lights continued to play their teasing trick, causing a moment of jubilation from the guests in the conservatory, followed immediately by a long sigh of disappointment. It was as if Bill was waving a baton and conducting an audience during a pantomime performance.

'I can't understand it,' Hugh began saying. 'I've turned off, or at least down, anything that could have tripped the supply. We have over forty kilowatts of power in the place, for God's sake.'

'Is there a short circuit somewhere?' I asked, holding a candle while rummaging through the dark and overladen fridge for more butter.

'Not according to the circuit fuses. They all seem all right. It's a mystery.'

He left me to join Bill and apologise to everyone for the inconvenience. I could hear the cheerful sounds of the 'bulldog spirit' emanating from the diners, which may have had something to do with the champagne Hugh had offered.

The remaining guests were served their pan-fried salmons on cold plates, brought to them via a path lit by strategically placed candles. Everyone had ice cream for dessert. It was the logical solution as the deep freezer was getting warm.

The guests were invited to partake in after-dinner drinks around the warm, crackling fire, while Hugh disappeared again to try to solve the riddle of this long-lasting darkness. Once they had made themselves comfortable, Bill announced that the blackout was actually a fake; that it had been stage-managed, and that all present were meant to participate in a murder-mystery event. On hearing this, some people giggled. Others murmured appreciatively. I wondered what on earth Bill was up to, and edged myself discreetly into an obscure corner where I could watch the proceedings without having to take part.

'When the lights come back on, a skeleton will be found,' he elaborated on the theme. The firelit faces of his audience, marbled by flickering shadows, glowed attentively towards him. He continued to describe the scenario. 'The skeleton's flesh has been gruesomely devoured by crazed piranhas which have been secretly slipped into the fish pool amongst the docile, overfed trout.' There was another burst of giggling which Bill put a stop to by raising his hand. He waited, until only his voice, and the sounds from the fire, invaded the hushed silence. Such a well-behaved cast/audience was every director's dream.

He looked at each of the faces and asked accusingly, 'Who dumped the body into the pool? With only bones to look at, who, in fact, was the victim?' If we were going to play this for real, I thought, how the hell were we going to create a skeleton at the bottom of the pool? Hardly anyone had had chicken that night. Was Hugh in on this? If so, why didn't anyone tell me?

'And who, recently, amongst you, visited a tropical fish store?' Bill asked, pointedly. People were actually beginning to look suspiciously at each other.

'But all will be revealed,' he declared. 'My good friend Peter Falk, better known to you as Lieutenant Columbo, and with whom I've worked many times, will be arriving shortly to solve this case. We invited him as a surprise for you.' Now I knew that Bill was indulging in one of his Piscean flights of fantasy. All men born under that sign have an irresistible urge to delude. He had never met Peter. How was he going to get out of this? Especially as everyone was now shouting with excitement, 'Columbo's really coming?' 'I can't believe it! We're going to meet Columbo!' At which point the front door happened to open, more violently than intended due to the wind which was now up to gale-force strength. A dark bulk crowded the threshold, wiping its shoes on the mat. All faces with their eyes as round as dishes turned to the entrance, and an expectant gasp hung in the air.

'Cue, Columbo!' Bill shouted in his directorial manner.

'Awfully sorry folks,' said the figure, struggling to close the door behind him. 'I've been around the village to see if other houses are suffering electricity problems, but it seems we're...'

'That's not Columbo!' someone exclaimed with disappointment.

'No, it's me,' Hugh said stepping further into the room, nearer to the light from the candles and the fire. 'Why Columbo?'

'He's supposed to come and solve the murder,' said another from the group.

'What murder?' Hugh asked, bewildered.

'The skeleton in the fish pool.'

'There's a skeleton in the fish pool?!'

'Eaten by vicious piranhas,' a woman intoned as if stating the obvious. 'We don't know how they got there, and we don't even know whose skeleton it is.'

'Good God.' Hugh paused, his brow wrinkling with worry and confusion. 'But what about the trout?'

Bill could not have asked for a better line to extricate himself from his fabrication. There was a startled silence while everyone considered Hugh's priorities, and then a sudden violent explosion of laughter, to the extent that some of the flames from the candles were blown out.

When everything calmed and the candles were relit, a lively discussion ensued about what an ideal place the hotel was to produce such a murder-mystery entertainment. After glasses were further replenished, the guests were eventually escorted to their rooms and given more candles to light their way to bed. Up until then, they had enjoyed their adventure in the dark. Only time would tell if their good humour would last after waking up in a freezing cold room.

As it happened, the electricity came back on during the small hours. Hugh had hardly slept, fiddling with the switches, unplugging and re-plugging the machinery until he finally found the culprit on that occasion. We had been working both of the dishwashers at the same time. The one I was wont to kick into action caused an overload if the well-behaved one placed directly on top of it was also in use. I never realised machines could have such egocentric natures.

The next morning, Bill was even more adamant that we were leaving. He threatened to go back to England alone if I refused to return us to Bonneval.

I thought he had been in his element the previous night, that he'd enjoyed it, but to him it was only like making the best of a sorry situation – an amusing interlude hiccupped into a series of disasters. He was sick of the guests. He was sick of the weather. He was sick of our sleeping accommodations.

I realised our time at the hotel would soon have to come to an end if our marriage was to be saved. Hugh was aware of Bill's discontent. There was no contract to bind us. We had been paid for the first four weeks; God only knows from what funds. His arguments on the office telephone with the various bank managers he'd approached were overheard by us. They always ended with disappointing news for Hugh. Bill had lost all confidence in the initial plan of our working at the hotel during the winter months and doing our B&B in the summer.

But I still felt a certain commitment to the place, and could see that, with extra investment, it could become a success. On many afternoons, while Bill napped, Hugh and I would talk, he straddling the saddle of the bum warmer with his back to the fire, and I lounging on one of the sofas. Hugh painted his dreams for the hotel on a canvas with enthusiastic brushstrokes. He didn't need oils or acrylics. I could imagine the finished product in a gilded frame through his passionate descriptions. And I was often very tempted… to write out the cheque he required.

Hugh never asked, or even hinted, and I knew Bill would never have agreed. It did not become an option.

To pack our bags and leave immediately seemed a little too ungrateful to me. We had, after all, received a lot from Hugh's hospitality. Besides which, I was gaining a precious apprentice. Some of the freebie weekends had borne fruit. The reservations were picking up. They were not enough to make a difference to the overall debt, but I felt it was unfair to leave Hugh to cope alone. Bill and I struck a compromise. He would grin politely and continue to charm the guests, and I would drive him to Bonneval in early April, where we would concentrate on organising our future.

Hugh understood perfectly the reasons for our departure. Our friendship remained intact. He visited us with his wife and daughter during the following summer; and on one of our return trips from a visit to London, we stopped off at his chalet. The hotel had been closed and officially padlocked. But he knew of a secret entrance, and one night with a torch, he snuck in to remove from the walls the paintings we had loaned him, saving them from the bailiffs, and returned them to us.

And Bill returned to the person I knew and loved once we were back in Bonneval. The snow had melted. The yellow buds of the daffodils he'd planted were beginning to peek through. More wood had been delivered. We'd replenished the bird feeder, and delighted in the squabbles of the dandily suited tits; black ties over yellow shirts, and their wings jacketed in blue – the same blue as the sky above us.

We went to our local DIY and had some wood cut for Bill to paint a sign: CHAMBRES D'HÔTES VALENTIN, PREMIÈRE À LA GAUCHE. The letters were painted in a soft green on an off white background. The 'o' in HÔTES was red, shaped as a heart, with the circumflex accent squatting like a roof above it. We attached it underneath the much larger sign advertising the *auberge* at the entrance to Bonneval. The only room to let was the suite. We were planning a rehearsal for the eventual more important production. Well, we had to start somehow.

Chapter Eleven

'YOUR HOUSE IS LIKE AN OLD MACKINTOSH with a mink lining.' This was the judgement of our abode stated to us by our first clients.

The sign was in place at about three in the afternoon. At five o'clock Bill had retired to our bedroom upstairs for his usual nap. I was downstairs in the sitting room of the suite, occupied by my favourite pastime: playing house, rearranging objects, redirecting lighting to attract attention to our paintings, as well as casting interesting shadows on the stone walls. I thought I heard a gentle tapping on our front door. It was before we had a dog whose barking would have alerted us. Thinking I'd imagined the noise, I continued my pleasurable 'tweakings'.

A second tapping, this time a little more insistent, took me up the stairs to our living room. The fire, for once, was behaving: the air was clear of smoke. I opened the door. An extremely tall man, with high cheekbones jutting from a broad Slavic face, bent the top of his body down towards me and asked in French, 'Do you have a room?'

He was accompanied by his wife whose smile was so delightful I could hardly believe our luck. The sign had only been in place for two hours, and already two strangers exuding warmth, even affection, were standing on our threshold asking to be our very first guinea pigs.

Losing my cool entirely, I shouted with excitement, 'Yes, of course! Come in! Come in!' In my enthusiasm to drag them inside, I'd forgotten to point out the low lintel of the door. There was a painful *thonk* as the tall man's forehead collided with the underside of the skylight in which the building's date appeared. I watched the spot on his brow growing red, and thought,

'Oh my God! Our first punters, and I've already managed to give one of them concussion!'

His wife began rubbing the bony area, making soothing noises. 'It's all right,' she said, turning to me. 'It happens all the time. He's just too tall.'

Once she'd lowered her healing hands from him, they began to look around them. Appreciation for the room oozed like honey from their lips. They loved the rich yellow colour of the walls, and the streaked-blue arched frames around the windows. They even noticed the patina we'd painted to simulate a lived-in look. They admired the great round beams of the *bois massif* which stretched along the ceiling, their natural blonde colour now turned with age to a deep gold. Their awed utterings were music to my ears.

There was a creaking from the bedroom floorboards above us. Bill had become aware that I was not alone, and called down to ask who was there.

'Guests!' I shouted up to him.

'What, already?' he replied in disbelief.

Giving Bill time to dress and make his appearance, I ushered the couple downstairs to the suite. There, too, they gazed about them in appreciation. Not expecting clients so soon, I'd omitted to turn the radiators on. The rooms were perceptibly chilly, for which I apologised.

'No matter,' he said. 'We're not afraid of the cold.'

I suggested they make a fire in the stove and turned the radiators on for them. 'Do come upstairs for a drink while all of this is heating up,' I offered, leaving them to deposit their suitcases.

It was then that I realised, they'd never even asked how much the experience was going to cost. As the letting of the suite was still very much in an experimental stage, Bill and I hadn't yet decided on a price. Because it had been arranged and decorated to accommodate friends and family, we'd never bothered to close it off from us with a door at the bottom of the stairs. Our conversations from above in our living room could be heard by them below in their salon. Bill had placed a tape into the ghetto blaster and was now putting another log on the fire when I whispered to him, 'How much should we charge them?'

'What?' He couldn't hear me over the music. I turned the volume down.

'Why did you do that?' he asked, a little annoyed.

'We have people downstairs and they can hear everything from us up here,' I hissed.

'They should be so lucky to be listening to Offenbach,' he replied.

I normally enjoyed *Gaîté Parisienne*, but I wasn't sure whether the bawdy orchestration of the cancan was the most appropriate music to accompany the mood of our establishment. After all, we were not running a brothel.

I posed the question again.

'If we're going to talk money, we'd better do it with the music playing.' He turned the volume up a little and said, 'I think we should charge at least the equivalent to £50 a night.'

'Never!' I insisted. 'We're not in England.'

'But they're in a suite and breakfast is included.'

'Still! We can't.'

Before we could agree on the sum, two heads floated up the open staircase, one much loftier than the other. I wondered if our beams which were suspended at two and a half metres above the floor would cause another injury, and bade them immediately to take a seat on the sofa in front of the fireplace.

'*J'adore cette musique!*' she said, closing her eyes in pleasure, waving her hands about to the rhythm, pretending she was clutching the multiple layers of a crinoline petticoat. Had she been standing, I'm sure she'd have been kicking her legs into the air.

Bill gave her an appreciative smile.

I poured drinks for them, and only after the obligatory toast of '*Santé!*' did we do the formal introductions. We learned his name was Stephan and she was Dominique. His last name was of Polish extraction, ending with a 'ski' which explained his pronounced Slavic features. He even spoke some English, endearing him immediately to Bill. She had an adorable giggle and liked a drink, which endeared her to me. They lived in Paris and had escaped for a few days from the demands of their late-teenaged son and daughter.

I continued to fill their glasses as we talked like long-lost friends. We mentioned the improbability of attracting our first customers only two hours after our sign had been placed. They replied with the improbability of driving through a forest on a narrow country lane, seemingly leading to nowhere, but enjoying the adventure, and then ending up in the surprising comfort of our house.

'I must admit, though,' Stephan said, 'we stopped first at the *auberge* and asked where the *chambre d'hôte* was, and the *aubergiste* directed us to you. As we came down the hill to your house, we had serious doubts about staying.'

It was before Bill had restored the façade. But for the new roof, not really visible from the ground, the building's external appearance was still like the ruined hovel we'd discovered while filming in 1989.

'To tell you the truth,' Stephan continued with a hint of embarrassment, 'from the outside, when I knocked on the door, I expected an old, bent, little peasant woman to open it. When it was not answered for a while, I thought that she must be deaf. I knocked harder the second time, but then felt guilty because, perhaps, she was also lame, and it was taking her a long time dragging her leg to reach it.' While talking, he had stood up and bent double to re-enact what he'd imagined. His performance was grotesque. But hilarious.

'And then the door was opened by a beautiful woman, and behind her was a beautiful, big room. It was so unexpected. That's why I bumped my head coming in.'

We loved them. They stayed for three nights, exploring the region, coming back in the evenings when we'd talk and drink some more together before they'd go to the *auberge* for dinner. Jean-Pierre came down on one of those evenings while we were in mid-flow, having a happy conversation, to call them up to their table. He noticed their glasses were filled with an *aperitif*. I saw a brief flicker of a scowl, like the shadow of a bat's wing fluttering across his face. This was the first hint of a future battle we would have. It had nothing to do with our guests arriving a few minutes late for dinner, but everything to do with our particular hospitality. Bill and I continued to offer drinks to our guests. It was a convivial way to become acquainted with people who were, after all, strangers sleeping under our roof. Our welcoming routine eventually led to a confrontation between Anna Magnani and myself when I went up to the *auberge* one evening to reserve some tables for our guests. She furiously pounded the top of the bar with her fists, shouting that we were stealing food from their mouths. This was the Italian actress in her most dramatic guise. We had no right to pour drinks for our guests because it stopped them from having *aperitifs* in the restaurant. They were losing money through our insensitive behaviour. I pointed out that they wouldn't be eating at the restaurant if our business didn't exist. The little we offered them didn't preclude our guests from having another drink at their place. But perhaps their prices did.

Since the *aubergiste*'s children were now teenagers, each had a room of their own. Another member had been born to the family. The local gossip, gleefully spread, was of the child's uncanny resemblance to Jacqui's, when his were of a similar age. For the lack of rooms, the *auberge* no longer accepted an overnight clientele. Everyone we sent to them for meals was a bonus in their pockets. But the first arguments we had with our neighbours were only skirmishes compared to what would follow when we became obliged by our guests to cook dinners.

When Stephan and Dominique were leaving it was like losing old friends. Because we had so enjoyed their company it was difficult to give them a bill.

'Business is business,' Stephan said to me, drawing a wad of notes out of his pocket. We charged them under half of Bill's original suggestion and still felt guilty. They came back to visit us many times. We had phone calls from them asking for our news, giving us theirs. Then there was a long period when we heard nothing until, eventually, we received a black-framed memorial notice from Stephan and the children. Dominique had died. I rang him on receiving the notice and we had a tearful conversation. But we never saw him again.

During the time we ran the B&B we'd have other, similar experiences. Some of our guests would become friends, and they too would keep us informed of their events, their marriages, births and, sadly, deaths. It was the difference between our form of welcome and that of a hotel. Can you imagine ringing the manager of a Hilton and shouting down the phone, 'I've just become a grandmother!'?

With the help of the tourist office and some of the already established local *chambres d'hôtes,* we worked a surprisingly successful season. It was a good rehearsal. Even the *auberge* continued to send us clients. But the money wasn't enough for us to survive. And it was time for us to become legal.

The *Mairie* had advised us that, as we were living permanently in France, we would require a *carte de séjour* (resident's permit). This came as a surprise to us, as Bill was a British passport holder, and under the impression that all citizens of the European Community had the right to reside in any of its member countries without undue complications. I was a naturalised American, but his wife. We were already registered at the *Mairie*, and to us that seemed sufficient. On our request, we asked Isabelle, the secretary of the *Mairie*, to confirm the necessity for the *carte de séjour*. She phoned the *Préfecture* in Le Puy and received the reply that it was definitely obligatory, and proceeded to advise us on the *dossier* we would have to complete. Oh God! Not another *dossier*! We'd already had the suitcase full of papers in London that we took to the bank for the mortgage.

We then had the nightmare experience of exchanging our GB licence plates for the left-hand-drive Renault I'd bought in England and reimported into France. That took a good two weeks, being sent from one office to another until, finally, it was established which town's bureaucrats held the authority to issue the plates to a resident of Bonneval.

The car, which had only done 8,000 km, then had to undergo an MOT inspection to determine if its specifications adhered to France's demands. I pointed out that it was of original French manufacture. Nevertheless, it was minutely examined, no doubt to determine if its short stay in England had given it some sort of contagious disease.

This new *dossier,* we learned from Isabelle, would consist of information similar to that which we'd supplied to the bank. She generously offered to do any photocopying required. No, we did not have to supply fingernail clippings. But all documents would have to be translated into French and stamped by the offices of an official translator. She couldn't say for certain, but the fee would probably come to FF800; a mere bagatelle to be allowed to live in our adopted country. Anyway, our bridges had been burned. Certified copies of the originals were duly sent off to Clermont-Ferrand. Most of the documents were duplicates of each other, varying only in our names, dates of birth and our social security numbers. In time a heavier, larger brown envelope was returned to us. Every piece of paper, regardless that the printed word upon it was identical, had been scrupulously translated. As, in effect, we were establishing two *dossiers*, the fee was doubled.

Isabelle made an appointment for us at the *Préfecture.* Armed with our *dossiers* and brand-new passport photographs, we announced ourselves and handed over our documents. We were ushered into a vestibule where there were a few chairs pushed against a wall and told to wait. And so we waited. And waited. Only two of the three offices whose doors opened on to the vestibule seemed to be occupied by an official. They were directly next to each other. At regular intervals, either of the doors would open. Their occupants, one a male, the other a female, would pop out, take a look at us and go back into their office. On occasion, she would open her door to march into his office, stay a second, and then march back into hers. He would do the same. Weirder still was when they'd both open their doors at the same time, cross one another in the vestibule, and enter into the other's office. Somehow, they'd synchronised their timing, so that they'd cross each other again on their return trip. There was no music, nor were there bells to accompany these movements, but their strange behaviour was reminiscent of watching the mechanical actions of a *Glockenspiel*.

After over an hour of this amusement, Bill had had enough. We weren't even sure why we had been told to wait. Were we to be interviewed by the *préfet*? Did we have to take an oath? Bill told me which bar I could find him in, should that have been the case, and left me. I continued to watch their extraordinary performance in the knowledge that at least my eyes were being exercised. At exactly noon, both doors opened and the two officials left for lunch. I was told to return at 14:00.

And so we did. This time the wait was a little shorter. The woman appeared from her office. As if congratulating Bill for having passed an exam, she told him that his card would be issued. Then she turned to me.

'But you, Madame, have a problem,' she said.

'*Moi?*' I asked, astonished. '*Pourquoi?*' And then I realised; of course! The absence of my birth certificate. I obviously had no right to exist. But when Isabelle had telephoned earlier about the *dossier* we would have to submit, she explained the lack of this document. It was not unusual due to my past refugee status.

'You are an American,' the woman said, almost accusing me of a crime. 'You cannot have a residency permit.'

'But I am married to an Englishman,' I pleaded. 'All of my papers come from England. I have lived most of my life in England!'

'Your passport is American. You cannot live here,' she insisted; and to prove it, she once again entered the man's office and reappeared carrying a heavy old tome. She leafed through its pages until her index finger found the paragraph that concerned my situation and pointed to it.

'Here!' she said emphatically. 'It is written here!'

I looked at the blur of tiny print. It meant nothing to me.

'Are you sure this book is still in date?' I asked, wondering if these statutes had been issued during the time of de Gaulle, who was notoriously anti-American.

The look she gave me was enough of an answer.

'What can I do? I have to live here with my husband. This is my home.' I was begging now.

Bill had been keeping up with our discourse, even though it had taken place in French. He'd heard the word American several times and realised there may have been a problem.

'I'm not allowed to live here,' I told him.

'That's insane!' he shouted. 'You're my wife.'

The woman then suggested that I leave the country and go to a French embassy abroad to apply for a permanent visa. Until I received such a visa, I was only permitted to remain in France for a period of three months at a time. From the day we left London to the time of this meeting, I had already become an illegal alien.

She smiled glowingly at Bill as she handed back his *dossier*. 'Your *carte de séjour* will be issued very soon. We will ring you to collect it.'

Looking somewhat apologetic, she handed me mine. We turned to go and had taken a few steps when from behind us we heard, 'You could always become British, Madame. Then there would be no problem.'

Why hadn't I thought of that before? I know exactly why. I'd been tolerated as an American living in England for twenty-seven years. I had married an English actor in 1968 and, immediately after, travelled with him to Spain where he was filming on location. I'd taken advice from the Home Office to carry my marriage certificate with me. On our return we queued together at Heathrow's passport control. My then husband showed his British passport. I showed my American one, and handed the immigration officer our marriage certificate. We were asked to wait in a side office and offered tea. By the time we had finished our cups, another officer had arrived and handed back my husband's passport and the marriage certificate. He congratulated us belatedly on our wedding and stamped a page of my passport with the magical, short sentence: GIVEN LEAVE TO ENTER THE UNITED KINGDOM FOR AN INDEFINITE PERIOD. That was the extent of bureaucratic control I underwent to be able to live and work in Britain. Mind you, it was 1968. I don't think it would be that easy today.

In France, who you are is only as important as who you know. We'd had the good fortune of having met the *sous-préfet* of Brioude. Every *département* in France, of which the Haute-Loire is one of ninety-five, has a *préfet*. He is a high-ranking civil servant appointed by the Ministry of the Interior and charged to assure that the laws which have been issued by central government are duly applied. He has authority over the *gendarmerie,* the internal security service and all centres of administration within his domain. He is a big cheese. And we know how much the French appreciate their cheeses. The departments are subdivided into smaller areas of administration. These have *sous-préfets*. This was decided during Napoleonic rule to make it possible for every citizen to be only one day's journey by horse or coach from their bureaucratic centre. They are pretty big cheeses. Ours was especially delicious.

On one of our holidays in Bonneval, during a balmy autumn, Bill was playing some Chopin. Our door was wide open, allowing the music to waft up to the terrace of the *auberge*. I spotted two men through the window, making their way down the path to our house. The one leading had dark hair combed back from a handsome face. He wore an expensively tailored jacket which was draped loosely across his shoulders. His eyes were covered by dark glasses. His confident walk matched the brazen chic of his attire.

'Don't get excited, Bill,' I said, glued to the window. 'But I think Alain Delon is dropping in to say hello.'

The man arrived on the threshold; his companion (who, we would learn, was his chauffeur) stood a little behind him.

'This has been an extraordinary experience!' he declared in impeccable English. 'I've been sitting on the terrace above you, admiring the magnificent view, and then suddenly I could hear my favourite piece of Chopin as if it was being carried on an enchanted breeze.'

Bill and I were too stunned to speak.

'I hope you don't mind this intrusion. I had to ask that funny fellow, the *aubergiste,* where the music was coming from.'

We moved towards him like robots with extended arms.

'My name is Hubert Blaison, and I am the *sous-préfet* in Brioude.' He bowed his head almost imperceptibly and removed his glasses.

We shook hands. I would have curtsied, but the removal of his glasses wiped ten years off his appearance. I stared into a face that every mother would have murdered to have as a son-in-law. I'd noticed he wasn't wearing a wedding ring, and regretted that Bill's daughter, Joanna, was not with us to be presented to him. So young and already so smooth.

We invited them in, and soon Bill and Hubert talked about music. He admitted to being the great-nephew of the French composer Bizet. Bill immediately inserted a tape of one of the *Carmen Suites* into the machine and, accompanied by his great-uncle's passionate score, we became better acquainted. Through our conversation we learned of the paths he had taken to be appointed to his present position. He had even been a judge. We had to assume that he was older than he looked. Or he'd begun his career while still wearing short pants. His chauffeur sat with us, silently smiling. He spoke no English. We liked the way Hubert included him by translating what we were saying. He was a democrat.

'I hope we will meet again,' he said just before leaving. 'I am so glad to have met an English couple with whom I can practise the language. You must come and have dinner with me at the *Sous-Préfecture*.' He gave Bill a charming smile. 'I will play some special music for you from my collection.' Once again the hint of a bow as he kissed my hand, and the two of them left into what was by now the night.

On seeing the headlights of the car with the official licence plates drive away, Jean-Pierre came running down the hill to us.

'Do you realise 'oo that was?' he asked, gasping for breath. 'You 'ave been 'onoured by such a visit. 'Ee his a very himportant person!' We didn't care. It had been his company that we'd enjoyed.

We did meet Hubert again, many times. He came to us to dine, or we to him. He offered his help in any capacity, should we ever have problems, as long as we had not broken the law.

I phoned him regarding my predicament as an 'illegal' in the country.

'That is ridiculous!' he pronounced. 'There must be some mistake. I will speak personally to the *préfet*.'

The following day, he rang back, apologising profusely. As much as he would have liked to, there was nothing he could do. It was the law.

I contacted the British embassy in Paris and explained my situation, asking if my lack of a birth certificate would bar my right to citizenship. The kind woman I spoke to on the phone didn't think it would matter, and promised to send me immediately the forms to fill in. I returned them with the few required documents, photographs and an emotional letter stating the reasons for my desire to become one of Her Majesty's subjects.

A little over two weeks later I received a letter bidding me to present myself at the British Consulate-General in Lyon. I made an appointment and arrived well within time. With a lump in my throat and a slight stinging in my eyes, I took the oath to be faithful and bear true allegiance to Her Majesty Queen Elizabeth the Second, Her Heirs and Successors according to the law. I then watched in fascination as the vice-consul clicked back and forth on the combination lock of an armour-plated safe and retrieved from its depths a seal with which he stamped the document that I had sworn to and signed. It would be sent to the Home Office in London. My Official Certificate of Naturalisation arrived shortly afterwards; I had become a Brit.

I took the document, emblazoned with the Crown's heraldic emblem which includes the French words *Honi Soit Qui Mal y Pense*, to the *Préfecture*. In red ink, printed boldly, it read CERTIFICATE OF NATURALISATION. The words 'British citizen' appeared many times. The woman took one look at it, and told me it would have to be translated.

'But it would read virtually the same in French,' I told her.

'Yes, I know. But it still needs to be translated. That's the law.'

Eventually, I deposited the certified French translation of the certificate with the same woman. It read: CERTIFICAT DE NATURALISATION ET DE CITOYENNE BRITANNIQUE. Huge difference. But I finally became legal in France.

After our ordeal, we met another English couple living in the Haute-Loire. They had been blissfully existing unaware of their need for a *carte de séjour*. From our experience, we told them it was obligatory. They, too, presented themselves at the *Préfecture*. In their case, all of their documents were accepted in their original English form; no need for translations. Later still, I accompanied another English couple to the *notaire*. They were buying a plot of land to build a house as their permanent residence in the neighbouring department of the Loire. The mayor of their town also attended the meeting. I mentioned the necessity for their *carte de séjour*. Both the mayor and the *notaire* emphatically replied that it was utterly unnecessary. They were British and belonged to the European Union. They'd never heard of such nonsense. It seems the law is interpreted on a whim, depending on the official, and possibly on how well they had slept the previous night.

Our *Mairie* had kept a blind eye to our rehearsal activities. The earnings barely covered our vices. I'm sure the mayor secretly enjoyed the old Auberge Valentin coming slowly back to life. But we were told our occupation would have to become official. That was already under way.

Patrick, our friendly architect, had drawn up the plans to create five bedrooms (all with bathrooms en suite), a lounge/breakfast area, a small kitchen and utility room to be situated on the two floors in the eastern barn. As the structure was built into the hillside, each level was accessible from the ground: the upper level from a northern entrance, the lower from the west. Of course, an interior staircase would have to be built to join the two floors. Much of the plans' configurations incorporated Bill's preliminary drawings. The intention was to keep our living quarters separate from the clients, allowing us some privacy, and, for our guests, a feeling of independence. The suite would, once again, become available for family and friends.

The work was put out to tender, but we were fairly sure we'd be using most of our original team. After all, we wouldn't dream of doing another roof without Roger Rabbit.

Prices for the entire reconstruction of the barn began to be presented. When they were all submitted, the costs came to over FF700,000 (£70,000). VAT would be added at 20.6%.

It had not been a good year for sterling. We had placed the proceeds from the sale of the flat safely into a deposit account; and then we listened with horror to the doodlebug drone of the plummeting pound, transmitted to us via the BBC news. First the currency speculators (led, no doubt, by fellow Hungarian Mr Soros) took chunks out of its flesh, and then came the collapse of Barings Bank.

We had counted on transferring £100,000 to our French bank for the expenses of our first year, which included the renovations for the B&B, hoping for a rate near to ten francs to the pound. With the little we already had in our account in France, Bill and I were looking forward to becoming, for a short time, French-franc millionaires. Sterling seemed to be in freefall, plummeting down a precipice. We held off making the transfer, desperately hoping for a recovery. When financial experts were predicting it would finally level off at six to one, I panicked. With Bill's consent, I rang the bank to make an immediate transfer. The exchange rate on that day had already dropped to the pound only buying FF7.20. We lost more than a quarter of our savings on that transaction and counted ourselves lucky. Of course, only a few weeks after our decision, the pound struggled up the cliff face and found a foothold somewhere near FF8.50. It would go further up again. Timing was not a talent of mine. Perhaps that's why I was no longer an actress.

We realised we couldn't afford to do the works as originally designed. We had to make some savings on the plans. The first expense to go was the creation of five windows, one for each of the en-suite bathrooms. The building already had a few openings which we could use or enlarge for some of the rooms, but another five would have to be battered through the stone walls. We tried to make more savings by replacing the shaped stone surrounds for these windows as drawn by Patrick, and using heavy oak instead. This suggestion caused a fit of temperament during a lunch that we were hosting at our house for Patrick and his wife, Marie-Christine. He threatened to tear up the plans. Li-Li and Kri-Kri had also been invited and, because of their soothing intervention, he ended up only throwing the papers across the room. After a second helping of tiramisu, he calmed down completely, and we spent the remainder of the afternoon in an amicable atmosphere. The stone surrounds remained as part of the design. We didn't want to lose him as a friend.

Patrick introduced us to an *économiste* whose job it was to study the project and come up with alternatives which could save us money. But most importantly, he and Marie-Christine introduced us to a man at the Ministry of Agriculture from whom we could obtain a grant. Our region was designated as a *désertification* zone. The establishing of a business which lured tourists, who would spend their money in the drought-ridden local economies, attracted subsidies; very generous ones. We would have to adhere to the national association of *Gîtes de France*, originally founded in the 1950s to help rural tourism by encouraging owners of derelict houses to convert them into viable properties for seasonal lets. The association expanded to include *chambres d'hôtes*. With a proper rating from them, we could also be offered a further grant via their offices. We calculated that, if we met all of the demands, our subsidy would come to FF200,000. It was not quite what we had lost on our disastrous currency exchange, but very nearly. This gave us the impetus to compile yet another *dossier*.

My French was still not up to business- and financial-speak. The dictionary was thumbed through until the pages almost shredded. Marie-Christine offered to do the photocopying in Patrick's office. I had instructive meetings at the Ministry of Agriculture in Le Puy with two charming gentlemen who did everything possible to ensure our undertaking deserved a grant. I had to prove that I had some sort of business acumen. Had I made a budget for the necessary outgoings compared to our prospective earnings? After all, the grant was like an investment from the state. It was not going to be wasted on a dilettante. I was given forms to fill in with percentages. I didn't understand them. They kindly filled them in for me.

'Do you know how much you'll be spending on breakfast?' I was asked.

I looked blank. I had no idea.

'Are you going to do English breakfasts?' This was asked with a hopeful expression on both of their faces. I could hear the faint murmur of tummies grumbling. The French may not think highly of English cuisine, but the combination of fried eggs, sausages, bacon, mushrooms, tomato, black pudding and hot buttered toast is greatly appreciated. They love it!

'No,' I answered. The two looked disappointed. 'Besides the time it would take,' I explained, 'I can't find English bacon or sausages in France.' Which was true. They have nothing like our bacon, and their sausages reek so strongly of garlic, I didn't think my stomach could take it that early in the morning.

'Pity. But you're right. Too much time. Too expensive.'

We stuck to the calculations of a continental breakfast. They ticked the items I intended serving, added the prices (I didn't even know the cost of a *croissant,* never having memorised it) and totalled the amount. As the breakfasts were included in the price of the room, I should not spend more than FF10 per person, I was told. I would learn that was an impossibility.

They were extremely helpful and, without some of their advice on the entire project, I'm sure we'd never have obtained the grants or made an eventual success of it. We had a similar experience with the director from *Gîtes de France.* She, too, looked at our request enthusiastically. On a visit to Bonneval to examine the site, we invited her into the house and gave her a tour which included the suite. She was very impressed with our use of colour. Our taste is anything but bashful, and we are certainly not mini-malists. She loved the objects, carvings and statues scattered around that Bill and I had acquired on our many foreign journeys. In France they are called *bibelots.* And I don't care what the house doctor says, a home without *bibelots* doesn't have a soul. I think we convinced her that, as far as our decorating qualities were concerned, the rooms would never be boring.

We were sent a pamphlet detailing the strict specifications with which all members of *Gîtes de France* aspiring to a higher classification were expected to comply. On the whole, there was nothing we objected to. Most of the criteria it contained had already been part of our conception. Although, later, we did have an argument as to where to situate the loos. They wanted an independent, separate facility. We argued that to divide the bathroom from the lavatory would make two claustrophobic spaces in which no one could relax.

There were new regulations happening in Brussels, we were told, which could risk our classification being lowered. On the whole there were only two people to a room, we argued. One presumes they would know each other quite well. Perhaps the bureaucrats in Brussels had certain complexes. We were sure our guests would not. The way the wall directly opposite us and several of our bushes had been unashamedly watered by men who were total strangers had convinced us of that. Besides, the extra outlay for dividing walls, electrical fittings, five more doors, five more ventilators and the labour costs all of that entailed would have eaten up most of the grant that they were offering. We stuck to the one comfortably sized bathroom, which included the loo, for every bedroom.

All the *dossiers* were completed, copied and handed in. We were advised that on no account should we begin with the works before receiving notification of our successful application or the subsidies could be in jeopardy of being annulled. Patrick had set a starting date for early March 1996. Knowing that we needed to be up and running for the summer season, he inserted a penalty clause in the builders' contracts. Bill and I had to be able to start decorating at the beginning of June. This gave only three months for all of the heaviest reconstructions. But the artisans seemed quite happy to accept the challenge.

The tourist office had given our number for certain enquiries and we were already taking tentative bookings for mid-July. Besides the annual summer festivals which took place locally, 1996 was the year of the great *Equirondo* when thousands of horsemen and women would ride their animals from all over France, some even from abroad, to gather in Le Puy. The city would be transformed into one vast corral. All along the route, they would seek a bed for themselves and a field for their horses. We were ideally situated. I was extremely excited.

Waiting for the works to begin was an anxious period, not helped by Jean-Pierre's constant pessimistic prophecies, which always began with his favourite expression, *'Méfie-toi!'* (Beware!) We would not get the grants. Even if we did, the notification would come too late to begin the work for us to be opened for the coming season. The subsidies would take years to be credited to our account, by which time we would be completely broke. He predicted severe weather, and with snow on the ground work could not start.

As it happened, a nasty eastern front blew in blizzards all the way from Moscow. Once again, we were buried under two feet of snow. It was during the latter half of February.

Bill and I stared out of the window feeling victimised by the deep, white blanket outside. Jean-Pierre smiled sagely. 'I told you so,' he cackled.

The authorisations for the subsidies did come through. We were told how and when the payments would be allocated. It suited our budget perfectly. After certain stages during the works, a percentage of the costs would be reimbursed. The final payment would be withheld until the building was completed and verified.

In theory, the renovations could begin. Patrick had conversations with the mason who would be the first on the site. Would the snow be a nuisance?

No problem, he was told. The mason's first priority was to clear the ground in the lower barn of the centuries of cow dung and any protruding rock. He would then prepare the surface to later pour the cement foundation. It was all interior work.

We'd managed to overcome all of Jean-Pierre's gloomy predictions. I phoned the people who had tentatively booked for July to give them the good news. The rooms should be finished on time. I was writing their reservations in our diary in ink. A bottle of champagne was opened. We shared it smugly with Jean-Pierre.

Chapter Twelve

PERHAPS THE POPPING OF THAT CHAMPAGNE CORK was a little premature.

On the Monday when the works were due to begin, Bill and I woke up to a cloudless, cornflower sky. The snow that remained on the roofs gleamed in the early-morning sun.

We heard a large lorry arrive and park further up the hill, out of our sight. There was a loud clatter as if a ramp had been dropped to the ground, and then the sound of tractor engines. We saw the mason and his mate come hurtling down the path in front of our house. They were astride two extraordinary vehicles. The mason was riding a machine on caterpillar treads which looked like a miniature mechanical dinosaur with a beak-like conical protuberance thrusting from a long metal neck. His mate was on the back of what seemed like a Palaeolithic hippopotamus, its enormously deep jaw hanging agape ready to swallow anything in its way. They headed down towards the back of the house and then along towards the entrance to the bottom of the eastern barn. All morning we listened to the noise of scraping, digging and metal pounding on to rock. The sounds vibrated into our living room through the metre-thick walls, but we were thrilled to hear them.

At noon the dinosaurs fell silent. The mason and his mate walked past our door giving us a wave, and shouted they'd be eating at the *auberge*. Bill and I relaxed in the peaceful quiet and sipped a glass of wine in celebration of how well things had gone so far.

Suddenly, there was a sharp, penetrating, thunder-like crack followed by a long growling rumble.

'What on earth was that?' Bill asked slowly.

'I don't know,' I answered. 'But it wasn't one of those jets flying over.' We were used to hearing the French fighter pilots skimming the humps of our volcanos with their jets, and the explosive boom which rattled our windows when they attained supersonic speeds. But that was not the sound we heard.

And then it dawned on us. We rushed outside in time to see an enormous dust-cloud billowing high into the air, just above what used to be the roof of the eastern barn. The snow-covered structure had entirely collapsed. Broken tiles, planks, huge timbers lay splintered in a heap, having caved into the building. Even some of the stones the roof had been resting on had tumbled to the ground. We were looking at utter devastation. I tore myself away to run up to the *auberge* and tell the mason.

He was putting a piece of sausage into his mouth when I gave him the news.

'*Mon Dieu! Mes machines!*' he spluttered in alarm.

I'd never seen Frenchmen leave their lunch so quickly. The two sped down the hill followed by Bill and myself. We approached the dark entrance to the lower barn, terrified the rubble would have buried their machines. By a miracle, the floorboards of the upper level had not given way. The dinosaurs were not affected, and immediately removed to safety.

It was not the disaster that might have happened. The rotten floor above could have collapsed. The mason and his mate could have been working below. Those consequences hardly bore thinking about. A frantic phone call was made to Patrick. He was not too bothered. The old roof was going to be replaced in any case. It would only take a little more time now to clear the rubble. The crane would have to be ordered earlier than intended and, instead of lifting off the timbers neatly from the stone walls, it would remove their broken carcasses from the interior of the building. He came out to check if the walls had been weakened, and had a meeting with the mason. It was decided that once the caved-in roof was removed, and the floorboards demolished, the mason would consolidate the walls by building the concrete floor on the upper level. That work progressed with astonishing speed.

Unfortunately, though, bad news was to follow. With a concrete ceiling above him, the mason returned to the lower level with his dinosaurs. Another meeting was held with Patrick and a structural engineer. The barn was built into the hillside which was composed mainly of granite, jutting out and supporting some of the walls. These boulders had been used as its foundation by the original builders centuries ago. The mason dared not disturb them further. When the deep layer of cow dung was removed and the surface underneath revealed, it became evident that most of the ground was solid granite as well. To find the height required for the rooms planned there would have called for using dynamite. We were all agreed that that would not be a good idea.

Patrick returned to his drawing board. It was decided to scrap the lower floor. The upper level would contain the four bedrooms originally planned. The staircase, now defunct, was erased, making the entrance lobby larger. Downstairs would remain what it always had been: a vast, dark, cavernous stable minus the cows. We called it the 'depot', and it soon filled up with garden paraphernalia, discarded furniture, everything we wanted to ignore but couldn't bring ourselves to throw away; and then, later, the donkey's winter hay.

The only problem we had with just creating four bedrooms was that the grants we expected were attached to the creation of five.

We contacted the woman from *Gîtes de France* and the helpful men at the Chamber of Agriculture. It was she who came up with a simple solution which would meet all the conditions the subsidies depended on: incorporate the suite as the fifth bedroom. Use our living room with the large fireplace as a reception area. The pine dining-table, built for us by Jacqui and placed at the far end of the room, could be used for the breakfasts.

It would mean losing our privacy, but we were, by now, too committed to do otherwise. The people whose reservations I had hubristically inked into the diary were phoning regularly to hear how we were progressing. One, a woman who had already paid a deposit and booked all the five bedrooms for a highbrow socialite wedding in La Chaise-Dieu for the first weekend in August, was becoming particularly nervous. That may have had something to do with one of her visits which coincided with the day after the collapse of the roof. We had to lie to her, explaining that the crumbled mess she was looking at was actually intentional. Another woman was coming from the Swiss border with two companions; they were doing the journey across country on horseback. I wasn't too worried about that lot. They loved their horses so much, they'd have slept with them in the depot, or in the fields if the weather permitted.

To save time for some of the decorating, Roger Rabbit delivered the four bedroom doors and the wood panelling to enclose the bathtubs for Bill to paint. We had discussed doing the rooms to a theme. Earlier, when we thought all five bedrooms would be contained in the barn, I had suggested that Bill paint playing cards on to the doors. The rooms would be called 'The Queen of Hearts', 'The King of Spades' etc. But we were warned against this idea, as some of our guests may have had certain superstitions. We listened to this advice. Pity: we'd had a wonderful time dreaming up the interior of a room called 'The Joker'.

When we were left with only the four rooms to decorate, Bill found the perfect theme: the four seasons. Naturally. He painted the doors in his particular neo-art-deco style with a scene of Bonneval clinging to the hillside, the fields flowing down to the river, and in the foreground a Botticelli-like tree depicting the different seasons. On the bath panels he painted a *trompe-l'oeil* of tiles, again with a seasonal theme. The design wickedly starred frogs and what they would be doing: so that, in winter, they're skating; in summer they are punting; in spring they are flirting; and in autumn, they're fishing. Back in England, we had amassed a collection of frogs which we brought with us to France. I dotted them around in all the rooms. Most people would get the joke, but some did ask, 'What is this thing you have for frogs?' We'd just smile and they'd understand.

'Pity we can't play a similar joke on the English,' they'd reply. 'But roast beef on a bedside table doesn't look so cute.'

I eventually placed a couple of frogs on a bathroom shelf in 'Spring'. Considering that room the most romantic, they were always faced nose to nose, kissing. When the occupants of the room had gone and I went to clean it, I was often left in no doubt as to the antics that had taken place the previous night. What those frogs got up to! The positions I found them in! Shocking!! I'd also be told if the night had not been satisfying. Some couples arrived for breakfast with a distinctly chilly air about them. When they had paid their bill and left, I'd sometimes find the frogs back to back and very wide apart. I used to look forward to receiving these messages, but then one morning one of the frogs disappeared. As they were a pair, I've never found a replacement, and so my poor little froggy sits on his shelf all alone. Ironically, it went missing immediately after a woman had checked out who had warned me of the dangers of welcoming people who could, after all, be kleptomaniacs.

But I am leaping ahead, as, fortunately, the renovations did. The workmen arrived very early in the mornings to begin, and didn't lay down their tools to leave until much later than usual. It's amazing how the threat of a penalty clause will concentrate the mind. But we liked to think their speedy completion was in consideration of our need to begin earning in the coming season.

Losing the lower floor of the barn was actually a blessing in disguise. Looking back now, I can't imagine how the entire project, as it was originally planned, could ever have been completed for a mid-July opening.

We were able to bring our tins of paint and brushes to begin decorating the walls in early June. Some of the builders were still there, but somehow we managed to work around each other. On the thirteenth of July, the day before we expected the riders to arrive, the room 'Autumn' which slept three was furnished and ready for its guests. Two days later, having worked late into the night, 'Summer' was ready to receive, and immediately occupied. And so it went with 'Winter' and with 'Spring'. Throughout our hectic decorating we were still also working with the suite. By the beginning of August when the wedding party had been booked, we were already old hands at coping with a full house.

The mason had prepared an area in front of the house for a terrace. We prayed for sunny mornings. If the Four Seasons and the suite (now christened by Bill the 'Vivaldi Suite') were occupied to their full capacity, we could be serving thirteen guests at breakfast. The pine table could only accommodate eight comfortably. We had hoped to stagger the breakfasts between eight and ten in the morning, quickly removing the used settings to make room for those still to come. Invariably, they would all arrive at the same time. For a nation that is known for its meagre breakfasts, we were amazed at the eagerness shown to be the first to sit down. In good weather, at least, we were able to put some people on the terrace. In bad, though, I had to unfold my mother's old bridge-table, place chairs around it, and seat the last few guests. Our living room soon resembled a crowded café. Rosalie would have liked that, but we discovered it could lead to a major embarrassment.

Our bathroom was directly above the pine dining-table. And we had no sound insulation. It had never mattered when there were only friends or family staying. Someone was always kind enough to whistle… rather loudly. But the sound of tinkling just above a stranger's head while they were quietly sipping a cup of coffee could be disturbing. The predicament led to a coded message that Bill and I devised. When one of us had to disappear urgently, we'd mutter to the other, 'Wee watch.' The one who'd escaped rushed to one of the bedrooms of the guests who were still eating breakfast. The one remaining had to do everything in their power to keep them there, even if it meant feigning a serious *malaise*. We couldn't imagine the guests could be so heartless that they'd step over a prone, immobile body on their way back to their room. They would have lingered a while showing concern. Somehow we managed without resorting to this extreme deceit. But it and other realities would convince us that further investments had to be made. We'd have to enlarge and encroach into the western barn. But that feasibility depended on our first real season's earnings.

Our living area, which included an open-plan, galley-sized kitchen, had been designed for holidays which we enjoyed sometimes with friends. If the bedroom of the suite had been occupied, and the futon in its salon had been opened as a bed for another couple, we could still never have been more than six people in the house. The installation of a dishwasher had never occurred to us, nor a washing machine for the linen. We simply took the laundry back with us to London and dealt with it there. Washing up thirteen breakfast settings now by hand took a bit of time, but it was not impossible. Washing the used sheets and towels of thirteen guests in a bathtub was.

We bought a machine which was plumbed in and placed on a plinth in the western barn. It was worked so hard, it sought to escape by walking off its plinth to head towards the exit. The rubber tube it was connected to yanked it back and tipped it over, dislocating the drum. Until a technician could come to repair it, our bathroom was turned into a Chinese laundry. We didn't have a tumble dryer either. When I couldn't hang the laundry outside in the sun, I had to depend on the goodwill of some friends in La Chaise-Dieu who made room for my numerous sheets and towels on their lines, strung from the beams in their pristinely clean attic. Climbing four flights of stairs carrying a heavy load and pegging the laundry became my morning's exercise before I leapt back into the car to drive off to the baker and buy the baguettes and croissants for breakfast.

I've mentioned my horrors of the morning. The French tend to be early risers. We had to be prepared for them by eight o'clock which sometimes meant for me a 6:30 ungluing from the mattress. I was forced to bite that bullet; but often those dawn excursions rewarded me with privileged sights. The playful prancing of wild boar piglets as they crossed the road with their mother. A glimpse of a black woodpecker on a fallen tree, only visible because of its scarlet crown. The red deer leaping out of the forest, then rushing ahead, flicking their tails, showing off their white behinds. An arrogant fox, richly furred, trotting casually across my path. The buzzard that swooped on to the bonnet of my car and then spread its magnificent wings to fly forward just a few inches from my windscreen, near enough that I could marvel at the convoluted pattern on its feathers.

In the autumn I could be treated to the crystalline beauty of a hoar frost, when the trees are veiled in an intricate, white lace and every blade of grass stands upright like a brittle shard of glass glinting within the frozen landscape. The entire scene is painted in soft sepia tones, sparkling under a cobalt blue sky.

Those journeys could be a joy, and I'd return much happier than the grump who had left Bill behind setting the breakfast table for the guests.

We had to register with the local Chamber of Commerce to legally practise our new profession. For once, the procedure was quite simple, but I was not prepared for a particular insult. The woman I had the meeting with looked in her early twenties. I was surprised that someone so young would be in such a responsible position. Somehow, during our conversation, I learned she was the mother of teenaged children. Astonished, I complimented her on her extremely youthful appearance.

'Yes, well,' she said coolly, 'I have noticed that French women tend to look much younger than English women of the same age.'

'Oh, really?' I replied, feeling my hackles rising under the rather nice silk blouse I was wearing. 'Do you know many English women?'

'I spent a little time in Brighton,' she replied, as if that was the criterion all English women should be judged by. What a bitch! And I was going to have to give her my date of birth. She did not reciprocate my compliment, writing down the date with an expression that read, 'I told you so.'

Bureaucracy in France can work very quickly when the state has something to gain. It seemed as if I'd hardly returned from the meeting before we received letters from various organisations demanding money. There was UTIM (health and social security), URSSAF (welfare and benefits), ORGANIC (pension), and there would be many more to come once our accounts had been submitted. Being self-employed is a very expensive business. We discovered we even had to pay a 'professional' tax as well as an 'apprenticeship' tax. The devious percentages of our income these taxes were related to made it imperative that we employ a firm of expert accountants.

When eventually I was forced to hire a woman to help me do the rooms, the structure of payments I had to send on her behalf to yet further organisations was so confounding, I begged the accountants to deal with that nightmare web of tax collection. They did it happily for a further fee.

Because of our important outlay for the construction of the B&B, it was suggested that we register with VAT to receive a reimbursement. We duly did. The reimbursement arrived promptly, inflating the business account to make it look as if our endeavours had been very worthwhile. But it meant keeping precise accounts: another talent I was not endowed with, but one I had to learn. It was one more bullet I had to bite, and yet another reason to extend into the western barn. My 'office' was the pine table around which people had their breakfast. Untidy piles of ledgers, bills, used cheque-books, receipt pads etc. were scattered across its surface and had to be cleared away regularly. In my haste to do so, some of the bills or other papers would disappear. If I was lucky, I'd find them in a sock drawer or in a picnic basket. Bill became used to my constant, grim-faced searchings.

'Have you tried the oven, darling?' he'd suggest helpfully. 'I found your reading glasses in there yesterday... or were they in the fridge?'

I had to buy a calculator – the first one ever in my life. I'd managed for fi... fif... fift... (no, I still can't say it) for a very long time to live without one. Back in England, we'd hired a business manager and an accountant to employ such instruments on our behalf. I had to be taught how to use it and the formula to extract the different rates of VAT which exist in France. My slimline, elegant calculator became indispensable but, alas, was regularly confused with Bill's TV remote control, and sometimes with the portable phone.

The incident which finally precipitated our decision to incorporate the western barn into the business happened in January 1997.

We received our third visit from Stephan and Dominique. It had snowed liberally and the temperature had dropped to minus twelve degrees Celsius. We were, of course, on EJP which made it impossible to heat with the electric radiators. The stove was lit in the suite hours before their arrival. The *auberge* above us was closed for their annual holiday, so we'd invited our guests to have their evening meal with us.

While Stephan and Bill were pleasantly chatting in front of our fire, I was preparing the supper in the little kitchen with Dominique hovering at my shoulder. Normally, someone so close to me watching my method of cooking would have disturbed me. But all her hints and suggestions were well founded. She had entered my kitchen on Stephan's recommendation, and I was happy to learn from her. We *flambéed* a great deal of cognac that night, encouraged by our frequent 'chef's nips'.

The following morning Stephan suggested that he would drive up to La Chaise-Dieu for the bread. Bill went with him to show him the way to the bakery. They were gone for a considerable time, having made detours to the various bar/cafés that were open in the town. It was just as well. There'd be no coffee I could offer them on their return. When I attempted to fill the kettle, all that issued from the tap was a rheumy cough. We had no water.

I went down to the old stables on the ground floor of the western barn to check the water meter. It had frozen overnight. The meter had been placed, unprotected, very near to an arched hole in the door that the chickens would have come and gone through. A freezing draft blowing through that hole could have done the damage. Dominique and I gathered snow, packing it into all of my pots and casseroles. We put them on the stove to warm, but it was amazing how little liquid the snow produced. I'd watched natural-world documentaries showing the milder temperatures of spring causing mountain snows to melt. These droplets trickled into streams, which flowed into rivers, swelling them to dangerous flooding dimensions. Rubbish! We were having to collect snow to melt from an entire hillside just to fill a kettle. When that was finally achieved, I poured the warm, precious water, making sure it was not too hot, on to the glass window of the meter in the hope of melting the ice which was blocking it. I then placed a hot-water bottle wrapped in a towel on top. We waited half an hour, but there was still no water. No one had been able to even brush their teeth yet. Dominique pointed out that, thank God, this calamity had happened when only they were there, and not other guests with whom we were not so friendly.

Whatever differences we may have had with the *aubergistes* above us, if we required it, they never denied us their help. I ran up the hill and explained our emergency. Jean-Pierre immediately offered to come to the rescue. I was sent back down again, much relieved, while he searched in his garage for the exact implement with which to free the flow in the meter. He arrived with a blowtorch. Even I, who had only recently learned to change a light bulb and to use a screwdriver, had doubts that this was the correct method to employ. I was right. Within seconds, the glass exploded. The meter was rendered useless for ever more.

Jean-Pierre studied his handiwork. 'There's nothing more I can do,' he said to me, and left rather hurriedly.

I did what I should have done to begin with – I rang Jacqui. He arrived, took one look at the meter and pronounced it *foutu* (buggered), adding the German expression which is popular in these parts, *kaput!* Before he could admonish me for ruining something which belonged to the commune, I hastily told him that the shattered glass and the burnt bubble of the plastic dial protruding from the meter was not of my doing.

Jacqui just sighed and gave me an expression which meant that I should have known better. 'If you need anything else fixing, please come to me,' he begged.

He returned in the afternoon with a working meter which he'd cannibalised from a deserted house. We covered it with a mound of straw for insulation, but that was never going to be the ideal solution.

Our plumbers were called out. Bill had already toyed with some drawings for the conversion of the western barn. If different channels for the pipes were going to have to be dug anyway, in order to move the meter to an inside wall, we might as well get an estimate to plumb the entire building.

Savings had been made in the eastern barn by the elimination of the bottom floor. Our 1996 season, short as it was, had succeeded beyond our expectations. The mayor had found us another grant. The regional park, Livradois-Forez, in which Bonneval was situated, were willing to give us another subsidy for FF25,000. The following season would even be better. Besides appearing in the guide *Gîtes de France*, we had been chosen for the *Guide du Routard* who visit clandestinely, a little like Michelin does for restaurants. Besides the French edition, this guide was also translated into Dutch, which meant we could be welcoming visitors from Holland and the Flemish part of Belgium.

Most of the guests had promised to return, but they begged us to do dinners. Many of them complained about the *auberge*: not so much about the food, as Anna Magnani was an excellent cook, but about the theatre which sometimes accompanied their meals. When Jean-Pierre was feeling extrovert, which was whenever he had a captive audience, he could behave in a manner that the French clientele did not find appropriate for a *patron* of a restaurant. They did not like him pulling up a chair and joining them uninvited. As amusing as he could be sometimes, they were not always prepared for his particular sense of humour, especially if they were discussing the imminent departure of their great-aunt from this world and the implication of her will. They didn't always appreciate a Shakespearean performance when the menu was read out to them, nor, indeed, when *l'addition* was produced and sometimes argued over. Our future English guests, though, found him extremely entertaining. They'd not even be too bothered when he'd hand them the wrong bill. His manner of apologising kept them laughing all the way to their rooms. There is a noticeable difference between the French and the English in their attitude to food. For the French, a meal out is a serious business. They only demand that their taste buds be entertained. The English, on the whole, will excuse a mediocre meal if the experience in the restaurant has kept them enthralled.

In early 1997, the renovations to the western barn began. To recapture our privacy, a large dining room, an office and a second kitchen with the necessary machines plumbed in were planned. The old stables below were converted into another bedroom with a huge bathroom. A private terrace with a beautiful view of the valley was arranged in front of its entrance. I reverted to my Hungarian roots and painted tulips on the beams, the doors and a dressing table. We didn't have to think very hard to find a name for it. We could now work with six rooms.

Besides our guests requesting that we cook, a friend from La Chaise-Dieu who ran a B&B herself advised me that doing evening meals was the best formula for success. Our bookings would increase if we offered *tables d'hôtes*. As we were going to have to live off our earnings, we had to do everything to entice a clientele. I went off with her to obtain a licence for this venture. Oddly enough, it was a local bar that furnished it.

The *aubergistes* were not pleased when they heard of this new development in our little commercial enterprise. Within days, I received a phone call from the Customs and Excise offices in Le Puy. The conversation went a little like this:

'It has come to our notice, Madame, that you are serving meals to your guests,' the official began.

'Yes, that's correct,' I replied.

'You are aware you need a licence for that.'

'Of course; I've received one.'

'Good! Good! May I ask where from?'

'A little bar called "Le Cezanne" in Craponne.'

'Excellent! Excellent! You do realise with that licence you will have to register with VAT.'

'I am already registered.'

'Marvellous! Marvellous!'

'Would you like the name of our accountants who deal with our affairs?'

'Well, perhaps. If you don't mind.'

I gave him their name.

'Wonderful! Wonderful! We know them well.'

'Is there anything else you wish to know?' I asked him.

'No, it's good. You've done everything as it should be. If you have any problems, don't hesitate to ring our office.' We said goodbye.

All denunciations must lead to an investigation, but I had the distinct feeling that he was happy not to have to follow up our case. As he was even unaware of our having taken out the licence, how did he know our telephone number? Denunciations had spread like a virus in this part of France during the war. I had a suspicious feeling our *aubergiste* was infected with the same complaint.

By the beginning of the season in 1997, the western barn was entirely renovated. For our brand-new, spacious dining room, Roger Rabbit had given us an enormous folding wooden oval which we could place on top of an existing table to enlarge it by six more settings. Bill painted the oval beautifully with little mosaic tiles, depicting a pond with water lilies, the centrepiece of which consisted of four golden carp.

With the extra bedroom, and if there was a bum on every bed, we could accommodate and cook for eighteen people. We must have been mad.

Chapter Thirteen

IF YOU ARE A 'PEOPLE WATCHER' BY NATURE, open a B&B. Do it, preferably, in a foreign country that is frequented by many nationalities, and where you yourself are counted as an immigrant. This way, you can study in almost laboratory conditions the behaviour of the natives towards their fellow natives, the natives towards foreigners, and foreigners towards other foreigners. Besides housing them under your roof, invite your subjects to sit together around a table during a meal, and scrutinise their particular idiosyncrasies, their table manners, favourite topics of conversation, body language *vis-à-vis* each other, etc. If you took your research seriously, you could end up with a degree in anthropology. We did it just for fun.

Up until the time that we opened our door to strangers, we had entertained many people. But they had been friends; we were aware of their little foibles, and they of ours. The people who were crossing our threshold now were unknown to us. In London, our guests didn't notice dust (as far as I know). They never complained about our cooking (not to our faces). But here, because it was a business, we would be judged by stricter standards. If a girlfriend had noticed a half-eaten mouse with some of its entrails scattered underneath a chair, she'd have commented on Puskas' hunting abilities and her lack of appetite. She would not, as happened here with the remnants of our French cat's dead mouse, have become hysterical and threaten to have a vomiting fit. We tended to know our friends' tastes in food and pandered to them. No one back in London ever screamed that their mouth was on fire, demanding gallons of water, because of tasting a little bit of English mustard along with their meat. The *monsieur* had been warned, but didn't want to believe that the English were capable of producing hot mustard. There would be a great deal for us to learn.

Not all of our clients were as easy as Stephan and Dominique. I have to admit though, the vast majority were the most kind, sensitive, considerate, charming, polite and all the other superlatives one can think of. I never realised how wonderful the human race can be. But as we are living in an age of political correctness, I must not ignore the tiny minority, those few who would make us bite yet more bullets until our mouths tasted of cordite.

The 1996 season had gone brilliantly. I can't remember a single unpleasant incident. Our guests had been so encouraging, they'd given us the energy to work those incredibly long hours without a moment of fatigue. Even when the double bed in 'Summer' collapsed while its occupants were lying in it, we were not approached by irate expressions the following morning, but by two people who were howling with laughter and asked for a screwdriver to repair it. Not wanting to disturb us, they'd moved the mattress on to the floor and slept like that for the rest of the night.

'It reminded us of when we were students,' the wife told me, still giggling. He did an excellent job repairing it, as it has never collapsed again.

The 'Vivaldi Suite' had a nasty habit of flooding after a heavy downfall. The rain rushed down through the rocks in the hillside and seeped through the walls on to the carpet of the salon. It didn't always just leave an unattractive dark stain; the wet carpet could suck your shoes off. We had mentioned the problem to the mason when that part of the building was being restored. His solution was to build a false wall. Unfortunately, he had built it with holes at the bottom so the water could flow through. I bought a special vacuum-cleaner to draw the water up from the soaking carpet. Until this problem was remedied by cutting a trench and evacuating the water via a pipe, our guests insisted on using the vacuum cleaner themselves, freeing me to do my other duties. I'd see them on their hands and knees rubbing the carpet with the nozzle until gallons of the water was sucked into the cistern of the machine. Most of them refused the discount we offered for this inconvenience.

The 1997 season, though, would be a little more challenging to our stamina. Besides our advertising at all of the local tourist offices, we were now in two national guides, receiving reservations as fast as we could write them into the diary. And everybody wanted to eat. I was forever grateful for my experience at Hugh's hotel in Calais, as I don't think I'd ever have had the nerve to cook for strangers – especially French ones.

A woman, Mme P, phoned from Marseille. She wanted to book a two-week holiday at the beginning of July for her husband and herself. Did we accept dogs? In the previous summer, we had acquired a kitten which we called Valentine. He had now grown up to be a cat with attitude, and didn't seem to be frightened of dogs. He bullied them. But I wasn't sure of his chances against a Rottweiler.

'As long as your dog doesn't eat cats,' I told her, 'he will be very welcome.' She had a poodle and proceeded to describe its good manners and its eating habits in minute detail. The French love their dogs, perhaps even more than the English do. There is hardly a restaurant I know where you cannot bring your beloved companion.

I was asked if she would be able to use my kitchen for a few minutes every day, as her poodle required freshly cooked food which consisted of meat, vegetables, and either noodles or rice. I told her that could be arranged as long as what she was preparing for her dog would not be confused with what I was serving to my guests.

M and Mme P arrived. It is true what they say about owners and their dogs. They do look alike. She had the same short, curly, faded-apricot-coloured hair as her poodle. Monsieur P had resisted being coiffed in that style. The healthy head of hair he'd retained as an eighty-year-old was brilliantly silver, a little like aluminium foil reflecting the sunshine. Bill and I were waiting at our opened door to greet them. We were taken aback a little by the initial two-fingered rude gesture he was waving at us as they approached the house. It was only later when he proudly showed us his hand that we realised it was missing the pinkie and ring finger. He'd lost those digits while working as a master carpenter, and it was he who had fitted the kitchen for the Shah of Iran in his villa in the south of France.

Theirs was the first two-week reservation we had taken. I'd given them a discount and the room 'Winter' with the little terrace, which I thought was more practical for the dog. In gratitude, Mme P immediately asked me where the broom cupboard was, as she intended to look after the cleaning of the room herself. Perfect guests. They had taken possession and felt at home. It was that which would cause the problems.

They had booked dinner with us for the first night. Because they had no English at all, I placed them next to me, leaving Bill up the other end to entertain those guests who had a smattering of the language. All the nights that would follow, they insisted on the same placing at the table, regardless of any seating plan I may have considered. Likewise at breakfast. We'd been given two delicate tea-settings, from a well-known Bavarian porcelain manufacturer, by a sweet German couple who had stayed with us. Wanting to make our Marseillaises feel special, these were placed on the table for their breakfast. If ever they found someone else in front of those settings, they were told, in the harshest of terms, to move. If the people had begun eating, I'd be asked to wash the saucers, cups and plates and reset them for their exclusive use. I remember having to apologise to a lot of people during their stay.

I needn't have worried about Valentine. Their poodle was never allowed to touch the ground. He was either perched in the crook of an elbow or splayed across a lap. The few minutes she had asked for in the kitchen expanded to a good hour. A different stew, either with noodles or rice, was cooked for it every evening.

Before their stay was up, they asked if they could prolong their holiday for another two weeks. We were only too happy to accommodate them, but we began to notice a barricade of rocks and bits of logs being built along the edges of their terrace. There is a public path which stretches along the length of our property and passes next to 'Winter's terrace. It appears in the local maps and, very occasionally, a hiker or a rider insists on their right to use it. On the ground, it is unmarked because it is hardly ever trodden, but it takes a steep descent between outcrops of boulders, heading towards the river below. I can only imagine it was established when the locals, maybe, herded mountain goats. Bill or I, if we were there, tended to discourage its use, especially for people on horseback, and pointed out a more gentle descent. But sometimes, someone escaped our notice. It was then that we heard Monsieur P shouting furiously at those he considered as trespassing too near to the privacy of his terrace. I often had to explain to him that those people were perfectly in their rights to do so, and apologise to the shocked strangers for the abusive language they had been assaulted with. The barricade grew higher. Monsieur P may have been eighty, but age hadn't softened his Mediterranean temper. He may also have been protecting his seventy-year-old wife from prying eyes while she was sunbathing in the nude.

His temper was eventually directed towards us, when, at the end of their seventh week, we had to tell them to leave. The music festival was taking place in the abbey at La Chaise-Dieu during the last two weeks in August. We'd been fully booked for it for months. He took it very personally, that they would finally have to vacate their room. And I would have to dismantle his barricade.

It was during their stay that we began to notice a strange ritual the French perform with their medication. For Monsieur P's advanced years, it was not surprising that he would be on prescription drugs. His wife, at seventy, would also be taking some pills. It was the amounts that astonished us, and their blatant pride in positioning these brightly coloured capsules and pills in ostentatious rows at the front of their breakfast settings. These rows swelled in numbers when other guest would arrive. If the majority of our clients were sixty or over, the table was covered with armies of various medication. It was as if they were positioning their troops in readiness for the battle of Waterloo. Until all the pills had been swallowed, we hardly found space to put the bread baskets down.

Bill and I have worked with many film units, sometimes numbering sixty people or more, and would have had breakfast with them. We'd never come across this habit before. Perhaps someone at the table would drop an Alka-Seltzer into a glass of water; but that was only conspicuous through the noise of its turbulent fizz.

When we had clients who came from the UK, we were not made aware of their pill-popping habits. Do the British swallow them discreetly in a closet?

Once there are pills placed obviously on a table, someone will recognise one or two as the same that they are taking. It's a way of breaking the ice. The amount of animated conversation we could hear about varying degrees of illnesses made us believe that the French enjoyed being sick. They like comparing their goitres. One could think there was a competition around the table for who had the highest blood pressure, or how many units of insulin had to be injected every day. There was a great deal of discussion about which joints in the body suffered the most amount of pain if afflicted with arthritis. The hip was dismissed because it was replaceable. I think it was agreed that the knee was operable, but the surgery did not always lead to success. Whereas the shoulder, as demonstrated by a woman while flailing her arms about doing gymnastics in front of everybody, could become as good as new.

We were surprised about these intense conversations relating to their maladies. On the whole, we'd found the French extremely healthy, particularly in old age. After all, Monsieur P had scoured his vicinity for large rocks and heavy logs to build his barricade, and carried them back to his terrace, seemingly without effort. Maybe those abundant potions did work miracles, but their cost was ruining the state health system.

Bill and I observed with fascination the interaction between the different nationalities, or even between the different ethnic groups of a single country such as Switzerland and Belgium. We can boast that we have housed a Swiss revolutionary, which is almost a contradiction in terms. He spoke passionately as he tried to convince us of the inevitable uprising that would happen if the German part of his country continued to move all of the major industries away from the French. Bill's face was a picture of concern as he asked, 'What? All of the cuckoo-clock factories are being moved to Bern?'

The revolutionary paused for a second from his zealous rhetoric to give Bill a peculiar look of incomprehension, and then continued in the same fiery manner to threaten civil war and the breaking away of the French cantons to join their true motherland, France.

I am ignorant of all matters political concerning Switzerland. Having had to drive through that country on my regular visits to my mother in Munich, I can only vouch for the cleanliness of their cows. We happened to have a Swiss couple from Zurich at the same time as our man from Geneva. We made sure they were seated as far from each other as possible at breakfast.

There were sometimes similar problems with the Belgians. The Flemish who make an effort to learn languages complain about the Walloons who insist on only speaking French. We had two couples one morning from both divides. The Flemish ones, who could speak fluent French, refused to speak it to the Walloons unless the Walloons answered them in Flemish. When, eventually, I heard a reluctant conversation strike up between them, their communication was entirely in English.

Around the table for supper, though, all harboured animosities were put aside. Bill and I had to ensure a pleasant course of conversation. When Germans were present we noticed the war was never mentioned... Beethoven, Wagner, sauerkraut, yes. But never the Maginot Line or Alsace-Lorraine. And I forbade Bill even a hint of a goose-step as he marched the guests into the dining room. The war was a tricky subject with the French as well. Bill was accused one evening as if he had personally abandoned the French population when the British retreated from Dunkirk, and that he had single-handedly sunk the French fleet anchored off the coast of north Africa. The person had to be reminded that Bill was only a child when those events took place.

It was interesting to notice how different the French palate is to that of other nationalities. We were not going to compete with nearby restaurants who offered exclusively French fare from the region or beyond. Sometimes I included a local recipe. Being near to Le Puy which is famous for its green lentils, I did of course make certain dishes using that ingredient. On the whole, though, we offered Hungarian, Chinese, Italian, Austrian, Indian, and even some English favourites. We discovered the French adored shepherd's pie. But they had difficulties with curry and paprika. My goulash had to be made extremely mild, as did any curry dishes I attempted. Vindaloo was definitely off the menu. The French loved the flavours, but didn't like their tongues to sizzle. The other nationalities didn't seem to mind strongly spiced food; the hotter, the better.

I did make a grave error once: serving chilli con carne to a mixed group of French hikers. But they were a sour lot, anyway. In my reply to their reservation, I had mistakenly written *matelot* (sailor) for *matelas* (mattress). Not wanting to start over again, I left the letter as it was, hoping they'd have a sense of humour. In describing the rooms and their sleeping capacities, I'd mentioned that three single women could all share the room 'Autumn' which contained a single bed and another bed that had an enormous, six-foot-wide sailor (from Harrods) that the two women could sleep on. They were not amused. Because chilli con carne is a mixture of ground beef and kidney beans, the men made rude jokes throughout the meal, alluding to being gas-propelled on the following day's hike.

When the tourist season is over and the locals are exhausted, we B&B practitioners like to get together to compare our horror stories. We all agree that groups, although financially interesting for us, can be the most difficult. Their behaviour depends on the mood of the most dominant person within that group. If they are jolly, so are the rest. If they are belligerent, the group follows suit.

The worst can be hikers, who tend to be the most demanding. I think that's because they all arrive with very sore feet. They are followed very closely by groups of more than three doctors, because they can be as arrogant to us as they are to their nurses. Then come the cyclists, only because they want pampering for their bicycles as if they were thoroughbreds. Oddly enough, the nicest are the swarms of bikers who come buzzing to us on their Harley-Davidsons. Once that menacing helmet and black leather gear are removed, a most charming, polite and appreciative person is revealed. We were amazed at how often we were asked if it was all right for them to park their bikes in front of the house. Why not?

'Ooh,' we were told, 'many *chambres d'hôtes* won't even accept us. They think a motorcycle in front of their establishment will give it a bad reputation.' Their loss was our gain. We met some very pleasant architects, lawyers, airline pilots, pharmacists etc. who arrived on that mode of transport. I think the film *Easy Rider* has a lot to answer for.

The most sinister experience we had, though, was when two strangers arrived out of a misty night. It happened to be the eve of Halloween. For all we knew, they may have flown in on broomsticks.

We were entertaining four paying guests. Two were women who had discovered us during the summer and whose company we'd enjoyed very much. They were teachers from Lyon and had decided to take advantage of the half-term holiday to come back to us. Two male friends accompanied them. One was a jazz saxophone player; the other an undertaker. The latter was ostentatiously gay and prone to hysterical exuberance.

We were sitting around the pine table in the living room having dinner, when there came a mysterious tap… tap… tapping on the door. It was well past nine o'clock. We were off the beaten track. The tourist season had closed long ago. The only reservations we were getting were by phone from people who knew us. We didn't think it was Jean-Pierre, as he tended to just barge in without knocking.

I went to the door and, upon opening it, was met by an eerie sight. Two very tall, very thin men in long, dark cloaks were silhouetted against the mist. I almost expected to hear them say 'Trick or treat.' They lunged across the threshold, almost knocking me over, and came to an abrupt stop in the middle of the room. Everyone around the table had stopped speaking and was staring at the two strange men. The older one's pale face was luminescent, as if the skull beneath his tightly drawn, translucent skin was shining through. He would have been perfect casting for the grim reaper. The younger one could have been a highway bandit. The lower part of his face was hidden by a straggly beard; he had long, brown, uncombed hair and his eyes were dark and penetrating.

The bandit asked in accented French if we had a room for the night. He mentioned that they had stopped at the *auberge* and that they had sent them to us. He apologised for the lateness of the hour and spoke in a manner more civilised than his appearance.

189

I walked them down to the Four Seasons and offered them 'Winter' because it had two single beds. I could not have foreseen that the offering of that room would precipitate the bizarre events that followed, events which would make us feel as if we were all players in a darkly brooding Ingmar Bergman film. On the way to the room, I'd learned that they were father and son, and that they were Danish. When I'd opened the door and put on the lights, they seemed quite pleased with their accommodation. By then, the son had been speaking in English to me. His father didn't seem to speak at all. From the redness of their eyes, I gathered they were either terribly tired or had had a great deal to drink.

They were going back up to the *auberge* to have something to eat. Out of politeness, I invited them to join us later for coffee and watched the two cloaked figures being swallowed by the fog as they made their way up to Jean-Pierre's.

Rejoining Bill and our little group, I was relieved that this strange interval had not disturbed what had been, up to that point, a happy atmosphere. But they did find it weird that people knocked on our door at that time of night, and asked if we were ever afraid. It had never occurred to Bill and me that one day we could be threatened.

Our meal continued with much laughter. I'd warned our guests that I'd asked the two to join us for coffee. The undertaker was in high spirits, joking loudly that he'd been certain of having recognised the ghostly face of the father as belonging to one of the corpses he'd recently buried.

We were having our coffee and a bottle of cognac was being passed around when they returned. Bill invited the English-speaking son to pull up a chair and sit next to him at the head of the table. I made room for the father to sit next to me at the opposite end. To begin with all went well. We found out the son was an artist and that he had a house thirty kilometres away. They'd been driving back from the south when he'd taken a wrong turning in the fog. Seeing the signs to the *auberge*, he'd decided to stop for the night. He spoke either French or English, depending on who was asking the questions. They had both helped themselves liberally to the cognac.

While the son conversed, I became aware of his father beside me beginning to mumble; at first, only to himself. His white head was slowly lowering from a long thin neck towards the table. I wasn't sure if he was going to faint. But then, his mutterings became more agitated. I had placed the saxophone player to my right and the undertaker to my left for the dinner. Being so near, it was difficult for the three of us to ignore his behaviour. The son didn't seem to notice, or perhaps didn't wish to.

Suddenly the father reached for my hands and clasped them into his. They were cold, white, and skeletal. I felt as if my hands had been plunged into a tomb, and tried to release them. That only had the effect of him holding them even tighter, all the while muttering incoherently. He seemed to be pleading with me with his eyes bulging from the liverish shadows of his sockets, imploring me to do something. But it was impossible to understand him. He finally let go with one of his hands to dig for something in his trouser pocket. He brought the object out enclosed in his fist and placed it slowly and meaningfully into the palm of my hand. The undertaker and the saxophonist looked on warily during this gesture. The women, Bill and the son were still oblivious to what was happening at our end of the long table. The object he'd given me was the key to 'Winter's door. For a ludicrous moment I thought it was an invitation to visit him later in the room.

With the decorations of the Four Seasons completed, Marie-Christine had given us a gift. She had thoughtfully bought key rings for each room. As Le Puy was also famous for its lacework, she had chosen a tasteful design of a white lace heart glued on to coloured paper which was held in place within a transparent, plastic rectangle. This was attached to the ring which held the key. Aware of our theme, she had chosen the colours which she thought would best evoke the seasons: a sap green for the trees in spring, blue for the sea and sky in summer, a yellowish bronze for the turning leaves in autumn. But unfortunately there was not a dark green which she would have liked for the pine trees in winter, so she chose a black background for the little white lace heart. We found it quite suitable as, in winter, with the snow on the ground, the landscape could appear as if photographed in monochrome.

The father's long, bony finger began pointing at the black-and-white rectangle. He had begun to whimper like a frightened dog. It was now impossible for the rest of the table to disregard his behaviour. Bill gave me a look asking if I was all right with what was happening. The two women, seated either side of him, were glancing nervously towards our end of the table. The undertaker and the saxophone player were coiled backwards against their chairs in readiness to pounce.

The son said something in Danish from the far end of the table to his father. It sounded low and growling. Suddenly the father leapt up from his chair and began furiously to point that bony finger towards the son. With a voice that came from the grave, he shouted accusingly, stabbing the distance between them with his finger. He then lunged towards the son with out-stretched arms. The son jumped up from his chair, and we witnessed the two of them swaying on unsteady legs with their hands around each other's throats.

Now, I suppose, as perfect hosts, Bill or I should have said something like, 'Come, come, gentlemen. Do sit down and behave yourselves!' But we couldn't. We were mesmerised. We were watching a theatrical performance being played to the hilt in front of our eyes. I'm sure Bill would have loved to have directed them. The others around the table, waiting for our lead, could say nothing either.

The son eventually removed his father's hands from his throat and held the sobbing man upright. He turned to us to apologise, saying he would take his father to the room.

'Good idea!' said Bill.

He retrieved the key and the old man was dragged away, howling with fear, screaming something over his shoulder at us. We were too stunned to move. There was an exhalation of relief as the two went through the door.

Within minutes, the son returned alone. 'I have to explain,' he said on entering. 'Please, may I sit down again. I've had a rather difficult time.'

We were all ears and fascinated. He started telling us that the two had never got along. His father disagreed with his becoming a painter and moving to France. He hadn't seen him for years. Suddenly, the father arrived on his doorstep without warning. There was something about the mother having died and he not returning for the funeral. He had vowed never to go back to Denmark, and now this man that he'd hated all of his life was begging him to return to the family home. Tears streamed down his cheeks as he described the beauty of the landscapes here in France which inspired his paintings. He couldn't live without them.

We listened to him in silent sympathy, but I couldn't help wondering what was being left unsaid: the history behind his torment.

'My father has always behaved…' – he paused, searching for the word – '… strangely.' That was what I wanted to know more about, but he was unwilling to expound further and stared, brooding, into his glass of cognac.

Somebody asked why the father had seemed so frightened.

'Because he's convinced I have brought him to this place to be killed,' he replied.

'Here?' Bill asked, 'to our little *chambre d'hôte*?'

'Yes. He believes that the detour was on purpose. And that you will all be his murderers.' The son looked at me. 'He was begging you to save him.' That's why those imploring looks, I thought.

'But why?' we all asked in amazement.

'The key,' he answered. 'It's black with a white heart. To him it looks funereal – an omen.'

The undertaker nodded in agreement to that.

'He believes I have brought him here to die.'

'That's a first,' Bill said. 'Usually people come here to have fun.'

We had all calmed down. The mood was back to normal, and we were saying soothing things to the son, when the door was violently opened. There he was again, standing in its frame with the darkness behind him, a vertical corpse, screaming hysterically, pointing at each of us in turn.

The saxophonist was the first to crack. 'I'm sorry, but you're being too polite,' he said to Bill and me. 'This can't go on any more.' Perhaps not as tall as the Danish, but certainly broader in the shoulders, it was he who commanded them to leave. Getting up from his chair, he confronted the son and ordered him to take his father off to the room and to stay with him there, or to leave entirely. They had ruined our evening and he'd had enough of the drama.

His manner was not aggressively threatening, but neither would you have wanted to argue with him. He was the perfect bouncer.

And so it was that the son approached his father, staggering slightly, turned him round, and the two vanished into the night.

We waited for a while with bated breaths lest the nightmare would restart. When we were sure they had really gone, we all raced down to 'Winter'. I was afraid to open the door, terrified of the havoc we would find inside, and only very slowly pushed it open. The light was still on. The room was perfectly tidy. The black-and-white key ring was broken and lay shattered on the floor. An old brown leather suitcase was left on one of the beds.

'Open it! Open it!' everybody shouted excitedly behind me.

I allowed Bill that honour. He approached the case like a bomb-disposal expert. First, he sprang one clasp. Nothing exploded. Then he sprang the other clasp. We were all gathered behind his shoulders, staring down at the battered case. And then, very gently, he lifted the lid.

All it contained was one pair of trousers and two rolls of pink toilet paper.
We decided to buy an entirely different key ring for 'Winter'.

This incident happened at the very end of October, when we are sometimes treated to a most beautiful hoar frost which can cover like icing sugar the rust- or gold-coloured leaves still clinging on to the trees. Driving back down from La Chaise-Dieu on my bread run the following morning through the piercing shafts of a sunrise, I saw the Danish son kneeling in front of one of these dramatically frozen images, and stopped my car.

He was weeping. When he saw me, he stood upright and apologised for his father's behaviour of the night before. Still through flowing tears, he begged me to understand why it was he could not leave this landscape. Pointing to the frozen tree with orange leaves glinting like thin, oval glass beads hanging from the twigs, he told me this unexpected beauty was his inspiration as an artist. He followed me down the hill, disappeared into the room 'Winter', collected the father's suitcase and left without even accepting a coffee for his journey back... to where?

Chapter Fourteen

I WAS SPEAKING TO A WOMAN ON THE TELEPHONE. She was French, but her English was superb. There was only the slightest trace of an accent. She had been asked to ring on behalf of a couple who had left that morning. They were too embarrassed to phone themselves, she said.

'Have you been to the room yet?' I was asked. She was referring to 'Winter', the room the couple had recently vacated.

'I haven't had the time yet,' I told her. 'Why?'

'Ah… then you won't have noticed that the cords which keep the curtains in place are missing,' she informed me.

'Missing?' I asked. We knew the couple very well. They were called our 'lovers', and a theft would have been out of the question.

'Well… not exactly missing; they are just not in their usual place,' she explained. There was a hesitation, and then she continued, 'You will find them tied to the bed legs.'

There was another pause, as I considered the implications of her last statement. I'd never have imagined that our lovers were into S&M.

'But it's not what you think!' she hurriedly added. 'It was just that the beds kept moving apart while they were… you know. And Jeanette kept slipping down between the mattresses. Twin beds, even when pushed together, are not ideal, especially if the legs are on castors. The cords were the only things in the room they could find to keep the legs together. You do understand, don't you?'

Of course, I did. They were in too much of a hurry to get back to their individual homes and had forgotten to untie and replace the evidence. Our lovers had first appeared during the 1996 season. They had followed Bill's signs, attracted by the hearts and the name 'Valentine'. It was obvious from the start that theirs was an illicit relationship. Once they knew our whereabouts, they visited us as often as they could find excuses to be separated from their spouses. We usually received a phone call at the last minute, asking if we had a room. They'd disappear immediately after arriving and not re-emerge until they'd go to dine at a restaurant. On this occasion, the only room available was 'Winter', which did not contain the usual double bed they'd have preferred.

They were not the only illicit couple we welcomed. It was not our policy to ask for marriage certificates when we showed people to their rooms. And more than once, I had to fend off an irate spouse and even a mother who telephoned, enquiring if their partner or daughter was sleeping in one of our rooms. I can only imagine that someone had left our brochure in a place where a suspicious wife, husband or mother could have discovered it. We always feigned ignorance and discreetly warned the person involved that they had been asked after.

The trickiest situation of all, though, was when a man arrived with a woman who was obviously his wife, and the mistress called asking me to give him a surreptitious message. It had to do with a future rendezvous that she was unable to keep. As his wife never left his side, I couldn't find the opportunity to relay that message until he came on his own to pay. He looked disappointed on hearing the news, but was so grateful for our discretion that he left us a handsome tip. I was beginning to wonder if *Gaîté Parisienne* wasn't the ideal theme music for our establishment after all.

The *Guide du Routard* had given us a wonderful write-up, eulogising about Bill's paintings of the four seasons on the doors. They mentioned our previous professions – Bill having been a director, I an actress – and named some of the films I'd appeared in. This attracted a certain clientele. A mini *Space 1999* convention booked all of the rooms for a weekend to seek interviews and autographs. I'd co-starred in that 1976 science-fiction series beside Martin Landau and Barbara Bain as the resident extraterrestrial with metamorphic powers. Over twenty years later, it still had a cult following. Bill had a wonderful time watching the French fans parading around the property dressed in the series' costumes which they had all faithfully copied and sewn together themselves. The experience was surreal, but the fans were always polite and considerate, which I cannot say for a particular woman who arrived with her star-struck husband on another occasion.

It seems her husband had been attracted by the blurb in the guide, and had booked a night out of curiosity. They were a middle-aged couple. She was a twinset-and-pearls type with a heavily powdered face, hardly smiling, even during our greeting. He was much friendlier, and upon our introduction had gripped my hand so firmly I thought my knuckles would break. She had offered me a limp fish to shake.

They had booked too late to be able to eat with us in the evening and had taken themselves off to a restaurant. The next morning while serving them breakfast, I noticed him watching my every movement, and smiling broadly at me whenever our eyes met. Her eyes, though, followed me about like a sniper's would through the sights of a rifle.

There is a code amongst us female *chambre d'hôteans*: we never flirt with the husbands of our clients. It is strictly forbidden and very unwise, as it is usually the women who make the decision to come back to us. But I was finding it more and more difficult to avert his attention and eventually asked Bill to finish serving their table.

They came to pay the bill and, as we were saying goodbye, the husband turned to his wife and, to my embarrassment, said excitedly, 'Do you realise who she is? Who we've had the honour to stay with?'

Her bland expression was set in concrete as she faced me and said nothing. Her husband, urging her to make some recognition, continued to prompt her. 'She's a film star. I've seen her work, even here in France. She's made many famous films!'

For the first time, I could see a hint of a smile. It was not generous enough to crack her powdered make-up, though.

'Really?' she asked me, feigning interest. 'Were they in black and white?'

Before I could explain to her that Technicolor had been invented before I had started my career, her husband quickly said to her, 'Don't be so stupid. Of course they were in colour.' To avoid further embarrassment, he walked her rapidly away to their car.

She wasn't stupid. She had a doctorate from the university of insults.

They had spent the night in 'Spring' and, when I went to do the room, it was the first time I'd noticed the frogs separated and placed back to back. I didn't think much about it at the time, presuming she had needed a lot of space for her jars of unctuous, anti-wrinkle, day- and night-masks.

Such behaviour was extremely rare. I reiterate that 99% of our guests were adorable. But she did occasion a silent cartoon-strip balloon to bubble out of my head. '*La vache!*' (Cow!) it read. My smile, though, undoubtedly cracking my face with crow's feet, never left me.

Bill and I became very adept at recognising those few who could be difficult. Sometimes I'd be alerted by a tone of voice on the telephone.

'What sort of sheets do you have?' I was once asked snootily.

I was very tempted to say, 'White.' Instead I responded politely, 'One hundred per cent cotton, Madame.'

'Are you sure?'

'Quite sure, Madame.'

'It's just that I stayed a night at one of those other *chambres d'hôtes*, and had to sleep on nylon sheets. It was most uncomfortable.'

'You'll sleep very comfortably here, Madame.'

'I had better. Now, what's your best price?'

'All my prices are the best, Madame.' I had finally learned to say no to bargain pleaders.

She accepted the price of the room, condescended to reserve for one night, and arrived with her husband on the appointed day in the newest, most expensive, top-of-series BMW.

We could immediately recognise Parisians, because they were the ones who complained about the trees. 'We thought we'd never get through that forest! All those trees! Aren't you afraid to live here?'

'Don't you have trees where you live, Madame?'

'Yes, but they have been planted in an orderly fashion in Paris. They do not grow wild, like here.'

'Don't worry, Madame. They won't attack you.' Which was a lie. Bill and I had had a tree attack driving up to La Chaise-Dieu. Two loggers were in the forest cutting down trees. There was a CAUTION: WORKS IN PROGRESS sign at the side of the road. A few metres later, we spotted a 70 kph speed restriction sign. We could see a mess of fallen branches scattered all over the road ahead, and I decided to drive far slower than the permissible speed in order to negotiate the debris. Suddenly Bill gave out a yell in alarm and an enormous tree smashed down on to the bonnet of our car with a terrible crunch. We were unharmed, and even the engine was not affected, but the front of the car was badly dented.

I thought it best to remain silent about that incident when talking to the woman from Paris. She was staying for a week and would have risked having a nervous breakdown every time she had to get into her car. There is not a single road either to or from Bonneval which is not at some point overlooked by trees.

Others would complain about the curves in the road coming down from La Chaise-Dieu. 'Yes, it's a little mountain road, Madame. I wish I could stretch it straight for you, but that's not really possible.' There are exactly nine noticeable bends over the distance of five kilometres. I've counted them. They are not of the hairpin variety, but they do demand a slight turning of the steering wheel.

When such pronouncements on meeting us were negative, we knew an extra effort had to be made to please these guests. One couple complained they couldn't sleep. I was horrified. Everyone sleeps like a log here. It's obligatory!

'Was it the bed?' I asked.

'No.'

'Did the owls keep you awake?' We have different breeds of nesting owls that hoot to each other across the valley. It's a wonderfully soothing sound.

'No. There is not enough noise. We are used to noise. This silence is abnormal. It makes us nervous.'

Bill suggested we make a tape of traffic sounds and play it all night outside their window. 'That'll calm them,' he said.

In the end our efforts to please must have been successful, as many of these guests returned; some even sent their family and friends. They grew to appreciate the winding roads, the fairy-tale forests, and even the silence.

From the middle of June to mid-September, we could have bookings every single night. All the guests wanted to eat. This could require, depending on their nationalities, eighteen-hour workdays. We discovered the English and the Italians loved to linger over their meal. They considered the atmosphere round the table like a dinner party. We would often have to tell them politely after midnight that it was time to go to bed. When the table was cleared and the washing machine stacked, it could be one o'clock before we went to sleep. After the heavy season, the reservations decreased, but we would still work with a few rooms during the week and large groups at the weekends. We couldn't complain; after all, it had always been our intention to succeed. Only time would tell how this furious, unrelenting activity would affect our health and humour.

I was already noticing a strange habit I'd assumed, which could have been stress-related. I'd begun counting. Everything. While buying vegetables: one potato... two potatoes... three potatoes; one onion... two onions... three onions. Thank God peas came in pods. I counted every dish, knife, fork, glass I was stacking into the dishwasher. Did I think someone had walked away with their plate or a spoon? When hanging up the washing: one pillowslip... one towel... two pillowslips... one fitted sheet. I'd even begun to count the clothes pegs. How banal can one be? But it was when I began to speak to my laundry that I really became worried. 'Naughty towel! How dare you fall on the grass!' When shaking it out, 'All right, I'll forgive you. But only because you're dark blue.' I'd pick a white pillowcase out of the basket to examine before putting it into the machine. Someone had used it to polish their shoes. 'You're disgusting! You're going to have to be boiled!'

If our guests had ever witnessed my conversations with the laundry, they were too discreet or embarrassed to let me know.

I'd never realised how pampered our lives in London had been. Besides accountants, we'd always had a Mrs Mop to clean for us. Even when we could no longer afford her, I only had to do the work for the two of us, which was a little lighter than the workload here. But, never mind. Besides my aberrations of counting and talking to the bedding, we were coping remarkably well. When faced with the millions of monster, red-bellied black ants that decided to colonise our expensive insulation under the roof, or the wasps that had constructed a nest in the attic of the Four Seasons, and the hornets who had drilled through the stone preparing to multiply a few inches from our bedroom window, we coped. We telephoned the professionals to deal with it.

Unfortunately there wasn't, so far as I knew, a number to phone if we were presented with a snake. The first one brought to us was a gift from our cat, Valentine. It was grey, about fourteen inches long, and had a bright yellow collar which came to a 'V' on its forehead. The creature lay in the shape of an 'S' completely still, as if dead, on the carpet. The yellow 'V' screamed at us, advertising *Vicious... Viper... Venomous.*

Bill went to get the broom. I found a short-handled shovel and a pair of his thick gardening gloves. He poked it about with the broom. It remained motionless and we both presumed it was dead. He swept it on to the shovel and I carried it outside. I wanted to take it up to the *auberge* to show it to Jean-Pierre, but as it was Sunday lunchtime, and the terrace was crowded with clients, I thought I'd behave as a good neighbour and not cause a panic. We had been warned of the venomous varieties in the area, but neither Bill nor I could recognise them. The seemingly lifeless serpent was placed on a low stone wall at the end of our terrace with the sun shining warmly on its scales. I couldn't help peeking through the safety of a window at its sinuous shape, and was very startled when it began to move. Coming back to life, it slithered slowly off the wall, on to the tiles of the terrace, and disappeared into our overgrown clumps of mint. All the while, it had been playing 'doggo'.

From its description, we were later told it was a completely harmless variety of grass snake. A friend in La Chaise-Dieu explained how to recognise the venomous kinds. The *vipère* (adder) is greyish brown with a darker, twisting pattern along the scales on its back. The *aspic* (asp) is of a reddish colour like mahogany. They are both quite thin, not very long, and have a narrow, tapered tail. Harmless species have round eyes, whereas the poisonous ones have eyes shaped like a rugby ball seen vertically. It was just as well I'd had this lesson, as the next one that entered was an *aspic*.

While taking some guests to their room one evening, I'd spotted a narrow zigzag shape on the tiles inside the entrance of the Four Seasons and was immediately alerted by the dark reddish brown of its colour. As I crossed the threshold the snake suddenly recoiled, lifting half of its body off the floor. Its mouth gaped open as if ready to strike, and the two dagger-like, evil fangs were horribly visible. I did not go near enough to examine the shape of its eyes. After that hideous grimace, it immediately lay back down and remained motionless. Telling the guests to stay outside, I ran off to get the gloves, shovel and broom. Bill was entertaining some other guests on the terrace, and saw me streaking past.

'What's the matter?' he asked.

'You don't want to know,' I answered, not wanting to alarm the clients. He saw me rushing back armed with my snake-removal gear and knew.

'Are you sure you can handle it alone?'

'Yes. Just keep everybody laughing. I'm an expert,' I said.

I dealt with the asp in the same manner as before, except this time I threw it as far as I could down the slope beyond 'Winter's terrace and told it never to come back again. It too had played doggo, remaining motionless even as I swept it on to the shovel.

I told this story to a friend in La Chaise-Dieu. He turned a little pale on hearing it.

'Where are the gloves normally kept?' he asked me.

'In an outside cupboard up against a wall on the terrace,' I replied.

' It was evening? Slightly cool?' he enquired.

'Yes. Cardigan temperature.'

'Don't think the gloves, however thick, would have protected you against its bite,' he said. 'Those fangs could easily have pierced through them. What saved you,' he continued, 'was the lack of body heat coming through the cool gloves, and the cold surface of the metal shovel. But never do that again! Remember, the *vipère* and the *aspic* can leap at you if they want to attack.' If I had known that, I'd never have been so brave... or stupid.

The couple I'd accompanied down to the entrance were supposed to have stayed for several nights. They left the following morning. I wonder why.

There were so many new experiences we were living through, it was not so much a case of having turned the page on our lives, nor even starting another chapter. It was a completely different book we had opened, and not all the writing within was easy reading.

A pleasant walk on a winter's day through a Christmas-card landscape could end with a scene that caused revulsion. I had taken the path I loved most, to Dents d'Or's farm. In the spring this walk was a delight of colourful wild flowers; in the summer, the wild berries tempted my appetite; and in the autumn, I'd branch off it, climbing further into the woods to gather mushrooms. But this time, with the frozen ground underfoot, my goal was another treasure. Dents d'Or's wife, Janine, made wonderful goat's cheese. We had clients who were eating dinner that evening, and I wanted them to taste some genuine local produce.

I was more than a quarter of a kilometre away when I could hear their pig squealing. The shrill staccato sounds pierced through the crisp, cold air, unnerving me. I walked on for a few more minutes, and the wild screaming began to get fainter. By now, I'd met all of their animals: the ducks, the geese, the chickens, the goats, the rabbits, their two cows. Dents d'Or had sold his splendid team of oxen before I knew the farm. He had proudly shown me the pig while feeding it in its pen one day. All the kitchen scraps, cereals, milk and dried bread were slopped into its trough, and it grunted pleasantly with gratitude. I cannot say that I did not know its destiny. The pig, like all their animals, was not a pet.

I crossed the little stream on an ancient stone bridge to approach the farmyard. It was deserted. The animals were kept indoors when there was snow on the ground. But the dog began barking loudly in their kitchen and alerted Dents d'Or to my arrival. He opened the door and, on seeing who it was, flashed his brilliant smile at me in welcome. After giving me the customary three kisses, he began his usual tirade of never-ending jokes that I couldn't understand while ushering me into the kitchen. Two men I'd never seen before were sitting round the table. What appeared to be a butcher's apron was thrown across it. An assortment of dangerous-looking knives and a saw were spread neatly in a row upon the apron, their grey metal reflecting the neon strip lighting screwed into a beam directly above. One of the men was caressing the blade of a large knife, drawing his thumb down the sharpened edge. He let go of it briefly to shake my hand. The second man just grunted a greeting.

When I told Dents d'Or I'd come for cheese, he led me to the stables and opened the heavy wooden door. Cheese was Janine's department and that was where I'd find her. The interior was meagrely lit; but, even in the gloom, the sight that accosted me flashed brightly like a bulb from a camera to be forever printed on my memory.

The pig was on its side, tied on the two-wheeled wagon that Dents d'Or had dragged happily away from our barn. Two bits of wood had been nailed upright to the plank at both corners at its back. The pig's hind legs were secured to them. There was a cord wound through its mouth and around the snout. The wagon was tipped forward so that the shaft where the head was attached was lower than the plank. Janine sat on a stool near to its head. She was stirring the contents of a metal bucket. From an incision in the pig's neck, black blood squirted to the rhythm of a heartbeat, splashing into the still steaming bucket. The pig's eyes were partially closed and glazed over as in a drunken stupor. Ducks and chickens pecked about on the dirt floor, unperturbed. The bad-tempered billy goat who, out of necessity, was always chained to the far wall, had leapt up and was standing in its manger, looking down suspiciously at the gruesome procedure.

Janine lifted her little round face to me. Her dark button eyes showed surprise. '*Tiens!*' she said. 'What are you doing here?' All the while she continued to stir the blood in the bucket with a long metal spoon.

I had to pretend not to be shocked; that what I was seeing was a normal occurrence in my life. 'I've come for some of your cheese,' I said, suppressing the feeling of nausea that was beginning to take hold of me.

'*Mais non,*' she answered. 'Not at this time of the year. The goats are all pregnant. There'll be no cheese until June.'

The bucket continued to steam. But the spurts from the pig's neck were getting weaker.

203

I said goodbye and backed out of the barn, bumping into Dents d'Or who had been standing close behind me. He had a sly smile on his face. I had the feeling my sensibilities were being tested. He could easily have told me that I'd come during the wrong season for the goat's cheese, and not bothered to take me into the stable. I continued my pretence of *sang-froid*, kissed him three times in farewell and departed taking the same path I had come by.

On my way home, I had to remind myself that it was our decision to come to this part of the world. These people had not come to London. They had not insinuated their ancient traditions upon us. A pig is killed every year for their table. That manner of bleeding and the constant stirring made for the most perfect *boudin noir* (black pudding). Every part of the pig would be processed, salted, dried or freshly consumed. What they were doing was more honest than my seeking cuts of meat, cling-film-wrapped and neatly displayed on a supermarket shelf. They were the real, dedicated carnivores. I was a phony.

Bill was preparing a bread-and-butter pudding for our guests' dessert when I arrived back. I had to tell him of my experience, and did so using dramatic gestures, showing how the poor pig had been tied down with the rope wound round its snout and the gash from which the blood spouted into the bucket. I sat on a stool imitating Janine and her constant stirring. My hyperactive gesticulations were tiring him out.

'Rest your hands and face,' he said, leading me to the sofa. 'Just sit down for a minute and listen to this.'

We'd had a satellite dish installed and could now get BBC radio with a better reception than we ever had back in London. He turned the CD player off and switched to Radio 4. His timing was perfect. The happy theme tune of ordinary folk in an English farming village blared through the speakers. Another episode of *The Archers* was being broadcast to the deepest part of France. I had to laugh at the difference between the two worlds, the juxtaposition of the storylines in that quaint radio soap with the crude reality I had just witnessed. We were definitely not living in Ambridge.

My lack of a hysterical reaction must have met with Dents d'Or's approval. He arrived the following day with a round parcel wrapped in newspaper. It contained a thick coil of *boudin noir*.

That night, I baked it in the oven on a bed of onions and apple wedges with salt, pepper and a powdering of nutmeg. It was the most delicious black pudding Bill and I had ever eaten.

When, a few years later, I took part in the procession that followed Dents d'Or's hearse to the cemetery, I thought back to that incident in the semi-darkness of the stable. How strange, I thought, to remember someone for the brilliance of their golden smile and the black spouting blood of a pig.

Theirs was not the only farm in the vicinity that killed a pig in winter. Relatives and friends who would partake in this tradition came to Bonneval from all over France. When there wasn't enough room for them at the farms, we received the overspill. That was why, the middle weekend of January, we were often fully booked with pig-killers.

After Dents d'Or's passing, I visited Janine more frequently. Except for the animals, she was living alone. Since I had known her, she had had health problems, suffering from severe diabetes and other related illnesses. Perhaps that was why Dents d'Or never made a will, relying on the probability that his wife would die before him. She had been an only child and her parents were dead. With the absence of any near relatives on her side, the inheritance would have been uncomplicated. The house and surrounding land had belonged to him. He could not have presented her with a crueller parting gift than dying intestate.

Not long after he'd been buried, his nearest blood relatives, their husbands and wives descended on Janine to claim the property. They began by removing his car in order to sell it. After forty years of living in the house, she had to suffer her husband's furniture being carted away in front of her eyes, and fight to be able to keep her own. When her parents had died, she'd inherited a house in a nearby town. Upon the sale of the house, Janine was wise enough to have the proceeds notarised as her personal inheritance. The money did not enter into the joint marital estate, thus protecting it from the grasping hands of Dents d'Or's relations, much to their annoyance. She had never been accepted as part of the family and now they wanted her dispatched into a care home.

They had rushed to sign the papers for the inheritance of the farmhouse, outbuildings, another house nearby and the many hectares of land. But it was a poisoned chalice they would drink from. Unknown to them, Dents d'Or had been accepting a supplementary pension from a National Agricultural Fund (*Fond de Solidarité*) for years that he had not been truly entitled to claim. The extent of this chicanery was only discovered when the *notaire* had to determine the probate. He had far more land than he'd declared to the Fund when he had approached them pleading poverty. The money he had been receiving for the past twelve years was, in effect, a loan to be paid back from the deceased's estate. He was more devious than he'd appeared. Janine had been unaware of these dealings. They had separate bank accounts, and he'd certainly never shared this extra income with her. For the forty years they were married, she had never received either a Christmas or a birthday present from him. But other woman had. It had not been the happiest of marriages. If the relatives had not claimed the inheritance, it would have been she who would have been responsible for the whacking £18,000 debt. There was a reason he'd not made out a will: his deceit would have been discovered by the *notaire*. The longer he lived, the more would have been owed. Whoever accepted the inheritance would have had to repay the debt, or the estate would revert to the Fund. He was thrusting two fingers in the air at Janine and his siblings. He'd had no intention of anyone enjoying what he would have left behind.

Under the strictures of the Napoleonic Code which still mostly applied upon his death, the surviving spouse of a childless marriage, and with the absence of a testament, retained fewer rights to the estate than did a blood relative. These outdated laws are slowly changing, thanks to pressure from the European parliament in Brussels. She fought and won the battle to obtain usufruct of the house, which gave her the right to remain in it for the rest of her life; but the *notaire* for those proceedings had cost a great deal of money which she could hardly afford. By law, though, her home now belonged to the relatives and the sooner she vacated it, the sooner they could sell.

Her desire for remaining was prompted by her love for her animals, especially the dog and her goats, a fact the relatives were aware of. 'They are the reason for me to wake in the mornings,' she often said. 'Without them, what would I have to occupy me?' I'd sometimes catch sight of her sitting on a canvas folding chair at the edge of a field, the goats nibbling the grass a distance away, and the old dog lying down at her side. She liked to keep an eye on her charges.

One day one of the pregnant nannies died having had convulsions. The vet had been sent for and diagnosed severe poisoning. The other nannies sickened as well, but they pulled through. At the end of their term, they gave birth to dead kids, all of them hideously malformed. Earlier, on the day that the goat died, the mayor had seen a four-wheel drive suspiciously parked near the top of the field where the goats liked to graze. He had not noted the licence-plate number; but the two men, who quickly returned to their car, averted their faces from him as they drove hastily away. Without proof, Janine could accuse no one. Her water had been piped to the house from a private natural spring; she was frightened that would be poisoned too. Even the mayor was concerned enough to connect the house to the mains, which is fed from a reservoir belonging to the commune. For all of our sakes, I hoped it was well guarded.

Janine's remaining goats continued to be milked for cheese. She adopted another dog which never left her side. Geese were added to her collection of fowl; I kept a healthy distance from them.

She stayed in the house well into the twenty-first century, before passing away having succumbed to a heart condition brought on by her diabetes. During her last years she was often visited by the people of the commune and even from further afield. The aroma of brewing coffee assailed the senses whenever you entered her kitchen. It was the place to go to learn the local gossip, to be warned of a severe winter because of the abundance of hazel-nuts clinging to the twigs, to be advised as to who would honestly supply the precious wood needed for the fires and, of course, to savour her delicious cheese.

Chapter Fifteen

'**B**UT THE PETTICOAT AND SKIRT COME DOWN to my ankles. Why do I have to wear the split bloomers underneath?'

'Because someone may want to examine them.'

'Pardon?'

'You may be asked to stand on a chair.'

'Why?'

'If you are at that height it's easier for someone to look under your skirt.'

'Excuse me? Someone's going to look under my skirt? Who?'

'Not only the dance steps have to be authentic. So does everything else, including the bloomers. People will want to examine the entire costume… that's the tradition.'

'They have to be split bloomers?'

'Yes. In those days women just hoisted their skirts to their knees, spread their legs apart and had a pee while standing.'

'I won't be asked to demonstrate that, though, will I?'

The leader of the traditional Auvergnat folklore-dance group I'd recently joined reflected for a while, and then answered, 'So far, no one's ever asked to see that.'

What on earth had I done? The winter's darkness is long. It can envelop you in a heavy, suffocating shroud. After the hyperactivity with a household full of guests, we were suddenly alone with very little to do. I was not a lady who knitted. I used to be a lady who lunched, who dined, who went to the theatre. I was a lady who partied! The nearest diversion I could find here was to rehearse with the locals the various dances to the 1-2-3 rhythms of the ancient Auvergnat *bourrées*. We women would skip daintily around bottles placed at our feet, while the men leapt up into the air, coming back down and smacking the floor with their wooden clogs. The women danced, making various figures, entwining colourful ribbons or scarves. And the men whacked the floor again with their wooden clogs. Wherever we rehearsed, the floor took a terrible beating from those noisy wooden clogs.

A musician played different tunes for all the separate dances on a small wooden accordion called the *diatonique.* He was eager and played with gusto; but, as I am clinically tone-deaf, I could never distinguish one tune from another. Our leader would call out the dance: *la Crouzade, la Galinette, la Bourrée des Moissons.* The music would start, and I'd always begin a few beats behind until I realised which configurations we were supposed to be dancing.

I bought the material for the costume, and Marie-Jo (from whom I procured the rabbits for supper) sewed it from an authentic pattern. I even found reproduction buttons to sew on to the bodice. Her friends and family searched through old trunks in their attics for what their grandmothers wore and found an original petticoat and the notorious bloomers. I was given a lace *coiffe*, which looked a little like a doily, to wear on my head.

After all of that effort, though, I only did two gigs. The second one took place in the communal hall of a picturesque village in the heart of an agricultural community. When the musicians had finally packed away their instruments, we were offered a glass of wine and were meant to socialise a little with the audience. An elderly man approached me. During his introduction, I could only understand that he was a farmer and had been recently widowed. His Auvergnat accent was so thick, it rendered most of what he said incomprehensible. I was staring into a round, fleshy face that had a cooked beetroot for a nose, and I was certain that one eye was lower than the other. His speech was further impeded by the lack of dentures to fill the dark gaps between his remaining teeth.

Over his shoulder, I could see one of our female dancers being invited to stand on a chair. Women were gathering around her skirt, slipping it up to admire the layered lace of her petticoat. Then the petticoat was lifted, and I could see the women looking up towards the bloomers.

My suitor had begun to ask me indiscreet questions about my marital status. He had also followed my eyes in the direction of the chair. When he turned his face back to me, there was a lascivious glint in his moist, uneven eyes. I didn't wait for any suggestions he may have wanted to propose, and moved quickly to where my car was parked to drive away. Perhaps my reaction was rude and his intentions were entirely honourable; I'll never know. That was the end of my dancing experience.

I took up teaching English in a converted abattoir on Wednesday nights instead. My students were La Chaise-Dieu locals, mostly middle-aged. They only numbered about six at a time, and as someone always brought a bottle of wine, the atmosphere resembled more of a party than a lesson. If any ghosts had lingered from the animals slaughtered there, they probably learned more English than my students did.

Back in London, I had never been a stay-at-home type, and it did not take much to entice me out of the house here. During the winters most of the locals sought some sort of distraction. There were times we'd receive a phone call at nine o'clock at night. A spontaneous gathering at somebody's house had developed into a party. Did we want to come? I'd ask Bill who'd be sitting in his oyster chair which was deep and round, forming a sort of carapace around his body. He would not have heard me. He had not even heard the phone.

The constant sound of his music, which was overriding my thoughts, had begun to irritate me. I never noticed it so much in London, perhaps because of our frequent separations and the social life we'd led. We didn't seem to be indoors that much. I complained, and so he obliged me by listening to the symphonies in his head with a finger from his left hand plugged into his good ear, insulating him from external noise. His right hand waved about as if conducting an orchestra.

'Darling, we've been invited to a party.'

No response.

'Darling, it's René. He wants to invite us for dinner.'

No response.

'Darling!!'

Finally, his eyes would catch mine. 'What?' he'd shout above the din in his head. The symphony would be put on hold; his ear would be slowly unplugged.

'We've been invited out tonight.'

'You go.' The finger would be stuck back into his ear, the right hand repositioned, and the music in his head would continue from where it had left off.

It was not an easy sight to glimpse your lover so. But it could not have been easy for him either to watch me go out of the door and see the glow of my rear lights as I'd drive away, determined to have fun.

I had found playmates. After the gruelling workdays during the season, I felt I deserved a reward. Unfortunately, Bill had very little in common with the local hellraisers. I had met most of them at René's equestrian centre. It had not taken me long to follow the horse droppings and find his establishment. Thereafter I became a regular customer, and was allowed to take his horses out on my own.

Bill had always indulged this passion of mine. We had an understanding that, wherever I visited him on his filming locations, one of his assistants had to reconnoitre the nearby riding facilities for me. That was how I managed to gallop across the Yorkshire dales, through the New Forest, on the sandy tracks of the African plains and leap over stone fences in Ireland.

But I lingered here after my rides, usually meeting friends in René's adjacent bar. I should have gone home and drunk my beer there instead of dallying and gossiping with people who would later ring up and invite me to their homes. And I would go, and return to a dark house where only the cats would greet me. They'd leap off the sofa where they had been scattered like cushions and make their way slowly to the door, expecting me to lead them on their nightly promenade.

A distance more than a mere rift was widening between us. Bill was happy to succumb to the inactivity of winter, ensconced in his oyster chair, moving only to put another log on the fire. He'd begun to paint snails: wonderful, witty, cartoon snails with bulbous noses and arms. A man who had never remembered a birthday suddenly made notes in a calendar. All our friends, in London and France, were delighted to receive personalised cards starring his snails for birthdays, christenings, marriages. I stopped buying Christmas cards. Bill designed them, with his snails as baubles decorating the Christmas tree; Rudolph the red-nosed snail; the three snail magi crossing the desert, following the star of Bethlehem... alas, arriving too late.

Bill had always needed to express himself within an artistic medium. As a director, he was closely involved in the design and 'look' of his production. While he was painting the doors, the bath panels and certain wall hangings here, his need to satisfy that passion was fulfilled. If I had let him have his way, he'd have gone on to paint murals in all of the rooms. But there wasn't enough time, and anyway the colours we had chosen for the interiors were all that was necessary to evoke the four seasons. We didn't need, as he wanted to depict, a blizzard on 'Winter's walls. There were no grand scenes left for him to paint, and so his cards occupied him.

I'm sure his obsession with snails came subconsciously from the chair that enveloped him, almost swallowed him; the chair to which he retreated from the world. It became more and more difficult to make him accept an invitation. Even Patrick and Marie-Christine, Li-li and Kri-kri or our Lyonais friends had to get used to seeing me alone.

When I came back from a visit to my mother, I found a sign pinned to our front door. 'This is the house of William the hermit. Do not enter!!' It was written in French. While I was away, not a soul dared to knock on the door.

Patrick did, though, interest Bill in a project which would once again involve his artistic expertise. Having decorated the many surfaces of both barns, we found we had piles of different coloured tiles remaining. Bill's solution to this over-ordering was to throw them on the floor until they shattered into small pieces. He then created out of these multi-coloured shards two magnificent wall mosaics. In the large dining room, he designed two laburnum trees with pendulous golden racemes hanging from the branches through which peeked (if you looked closely) three blue-eyed ginger cats. In the en-suite bathroom of the newly created bedroom below, he fashioned with more broken tiles an array of wayward, blousy tulips to go with the theme of that room.

Patrick had been very impressed when he saw these mosaics, and suggested he do a large one in the entrance of a retirement home that he was designing just outside of La Chaise-Dieu. A meeting was called at our place for the trustees to examine Bill's work. They were thrilled and offered him the assignment. We bought more tiles for him to shatter. They were chosen for the colours of a certain view of La Chaise-Dieu, depicting the Clementine tower, built to honour the pope who is buried there. I drove him to the building every morning and picked him up for lunch. He'd be dropped off again in the early afternoon to continue until about four when I'd bring him home. It was January 1998, and the entrance was still a building site. The glass doors were not yet in situ; he was working in freezing cold conditions.

Bill began to complain of a numbness in the fingers of his left hand, as well as an area above the left side of his upper lip, including the nostril and a part of his cheek. He blamed it on the cement he was using to glue the tiles on the wall, saying he must have wiped his runny nose with a hand which still carried a residue of the cement. I read the tin very carefully, looking for certain cautions. Did one have to use gloves when applying the product?

There was no such warning on the tin. Bill was prepared to sue the manufacturers. But I think it was the first sign of what was to come.

I remembered a time when, if we walked somewhere together, I'd have to trot at his side to keep up. He was walking much slower now, as if he couldn't quite feel the ground beneath his feet. When we worked that summer's season, Bill pushed the tables on the terrace ever nearer to the doors, so that he'd need to make the fewest possible steps when serving breakfast. It was another sign I should have read. He used to walk the three miles to work from our flat in West Kensington to the BBC in White City; now every step became an effort.

He had lost his appetite; not that he'd ever been a great eater, but he used to enjoy food. Now he couldn't even bear to watch me eat, much less the guests. Anything to do with eating habits could provoke a fit of ill temper. He'd spy from the kitchen window someone spooning my home-made jam directly into their mouth. 'That's disgusting!' he'd shout almost loudly enough to be heard. I didn't find it a pleasant sight either… but hey, I make good jam.

More than three sugar lumps dropped into a coffee cup would bring on a remark like: 'Why don't you just pour your coffee into the sugar bowl, and be done with it?'

He helped clear the tables, as I stuffed the settings into the dishwasher. Then he'd wipe the table's surface clean. This job usually invoked most of his anger. He had to deal with the *crumbs.*

'Swine! They have perfectly good plates. Why can't they use them!?'

I'd be called to witness his sweepings under the table.

'Look! Look at that under their chairs!! They're meant to butter their baguettes, not batter them to smithereens!!!'

We were supposed to be building a reputation as smiling, cheerful, gracious hosts. No amount of work was too much for us in order to please. I was climbing a mountain, hauling a boulder behind me.

Bill had almost completely given up on dinner, only joining us at the table if there were guests he wanted to socialise with. I could put three peas on his plate and he'd only eat the one, washing it down with red wine, lest it got stuck in his throat like a pill.

Our 1998 season found us working at almost full capacity. Many of our clients were people who'd returned, or those who came via word of mouth. By the end of August, we were already exhausted. September and October bookings were better than ever with groups of walkers, cyclists and the seekers of the surrounding forests' treasures of wild mushrooms.

We closed at the beginning of November. Bill's family was coming on a five-day visit on the eighteenth: his son, Daniel, with his fiancée, Lucy, whom we would meet for the first time; his daughter, Joanna; and their mother, Jill, Bill's ex-wife.

French television news had encouraged its audience to enjoy a meteorite shower on the sixth of November between the hours of four and six a.m. If the sky was clear, one would be rewarded with a spectacular display. I looked forward to this phenomenon, and for once didn't mind waking at that ungodly hour. I was hoping to share those moments with Bill… holding hands and wishing together on the shooting stars. I needed to be reminded of how we used to be.

He woke me at four. I dressed quickly for the cold, and then saw him returning to bed, leaving me to go into the night alone.

This minor rebuttal caused a major moment of despair. The glittering shower, the flashes of light searing through a black sky, only made me weep. I saw them as bright smudges through my tears. I couldn't even wish happiness for my mother. She had died earlier that year, my dragon woman, my confidante. I called for her like a lost child, and could only hope she had found peace within the ether. And as for Bill? The love of my life? My hero? I was too bitter to wish him well. I behaved like a woman scorned.

The temperature had dropped to minus 18 degrees Celsius the morning I drove to Saint-Étienne to pick the family up from the airport. There were moments I worried that I wouldn't arrive. The car kept losing power. The diesel was freezing, and it wasn't until I descended to the comparative warmth of the lower altitudes that the engine obeyed the pressure from my foot on the accelerator.

They had already gone through customs and were waiting inside the entrance of the terminal, huddled around their suitcases, when I drove up.

'How's Dad?' Joanna was the first to ask.

'He'll be all the better, hopefully, for seeing you,' I replied. Bill may not have been demonstrative towards them, but there was never any doubt in my mind of his love and pride for his children, who were now in their early thirties.

That night over dinner, the living room came back to life. The symphonics were stilled and replaced with lively chatter. Bill's posture had been transformed from the usual slumping in his chair, to become positive, upright, embracing. That good mood did not last for very long.

November the twenty-third, the day before their departure, we went to a restaurant in La Chaise-Dieu. It was Bill's decision not to join us. On our way back after the lunch, I stopped at the retirement home to show them Bill's mosaics on the two walls of its entrance. We stood for a while, admiring his work, not returning home until four o'clock. As I opened the door, Bill was just moving away from the fire, having positioned a log. He was making his way towards the sofa to sit down. I apologised for our lateness, giving the excuse of having broken the journey home to show everyone his artwork. His mood was dark and brooding.

Daniel went down to the suite to tend to the stove. Jo and Jill took Lucy off to the Four Seasons to show her the rooms. I stood at the sink of our open-plan kitchen, washing up the remnants of the morning's breakfast dishes, continuing to speak to Bill, trying to lift his mood. The kitchen was behind the sofa, so I was speaking to the back of his head as he gazed into the fire, drinking from a glass of scotch which he held in his right hand.

'They really admired your mosaics,' I said enthusiastically.

'And so they should,' he replied. His tone was almost aggressive. Those were the last words I would clearly understand him to say for a frightening time. He continued to talk, but his speech had become almost incomprehensible. It was not an inebriated slurring, but more as if he was talking with a wad of cotton wool in his mouth. An instinctive alarm-bell rang in my mind. I left the sink and rushed to face him, standing with my back to the fire.

'Say something! Talk to me! Talk to me!' I pleaded. I wanted to study him as he spoke.

'Whahdjawahnmedozay?' he replied, looking up at me as if I'd gone mad. The left side of his face was immobile, drooping.

'You're not speaking correctly. And the left side of your face isn't moving. I think you've had a stroke,' I said in a panic.

He managed to place the glass on the table in front of him with his right hand, and then with that hand he gripped his left arm.

'Icandfeelmyleftarm,' he muttered, '... ormylegeither.'

There was no doubt. He'd suffered a stroke. The image I'd had of him as we entered from lunch, moving away from the fire to go to sit down, played havoc in my mind. If the stroke had happened only a moment earlier, we'd have come home to find him lying across the flames.

There were emergency numbers I could ring; but, unlike the UK's universal 999, there were several here that ran through my head. Was it 12,

15, 17, 18? I was too frantic to remember the correct one for this particular emergency.

Placing cushions around him so that he wouldn't fall, I urged him not to move and rushed out of the house to run up to the *auberge*.

Jean-Pierre was about to get into his car when he saw me hurrying towards him. The expression on my face must have told him something because he looked at me with intense concern.

'What's the matter?' he asked.

'It's Bill!' My French completely left me. I didn't know the word for stroke. 'An attack! He's had an attack!' I pulled one side of my face lower than the other.

'Go back to him. I'll make all the necessary calls,' he said and then to reassure me, 'The *pompiers* will be there shortly.' I saw him go inside to telephone and ran back down the hill.

Before entering the house, I saw Jill, Dan, Lucy and Jo exiting from the Four Seasons. They were happily commenting on the decor of the rooms. I walked down the steps to meet them. Once again, my expression must have been a warning. They became silent, and four faces with wide questioning eyes stared at me.

'Now don't worry,' I began, trying to assume a calm tone of voice. 'Dad has had a stroke. But the emergency services are on their way. He'll be all right,' I added with more confidence than I felt.

They all gasped with shock, and Jo raised her hands to her face. She had begun to cry. All four looked pale and anxious as I led them up the steps and through our front door. Bill was still sitting upright as I'd left him. It was natural for them to surround him, to show him their concern; but Bill made it clear he did not want an audience. The women left, tiptoeing down to the suite, leaving Daniel hovering discreetly at the top of the stairs in case we needed his help. Jean-Pierre came down briefly, looked at Bill's face and whispered to me that my diagnosis had been correct. Bill made it obvious that he didn't want him there, staring angrily at him until Jean-Pierre quietly left.

What seemed like an eternity, but was only a quarter of an hour later, I saw through the window the bulky figures of the *pompiers* trotting down the hill, and opened the door. Four huge, uniformed men entered the living room. I recognised some of their faces as locals we had seen about in the bars of La Chaise-Dieu. We had sometimes heard the howl of the siren which gathered the volunteers, and saw them rushing to get into their cars to go to the station and to their next emergency. I had never dreamed that the siren would howl for us one day.

Up until then, I'd always thought our living room was a spacious area, but the size of these men shrank it to a broom cupboard. I don't know what they had been told; whether Bill was a two-ton giant who had to be subdued, for the brigade to have sent the biggest, strongest, widest firemen in the service. All manner of furniture was moved and shoved towards the dining area, leaving only the sofa with Bill sitting on it in centre stage, as it were.

The *pompiers* had parked their ambulance further up the hill, leaving a clear space in front of the house. Shortly after their arrival, I saw a little white car come down the path and come to a stop opposite our door. It contained a driver and a passenger with a mop of wild, grey hair, who seemed to be making an incredible effort to exit the car. His movements were slow and clumsy as he struggled to open the door. The driver ran to the passenger side to help the man out, pulling his legs around so that they would touch the ground. Two crutches jutted out of the car, and the driver lifted the man to his feet; whereupon, with the help of his crutches, the man limped on precariously bowed legs to our door. He was the doctor. And it was only a few days after he had undergone an operation for a double hip replacement. We gave him full marks for dedication to his profession.

The doctor wobbled across the threshold, leaning heavily on the crutches. His grey hair burst forth like an explosion, forming a corona around his head. Although I'd later discover that he was not born locally, he must have had some Auvergnat genes, as his large dark eyes were so impossibly wide apart that they were almost set into his temples.

The incredible bulks made room for the doctor to approach Bill. One of them took his crutches while another found a chair for him to sit facing the patient.

'What's your name?' he asked in French, using the informal *tu*. His voice was low and as soft as the murmuring of a brook.

Bill understood the question and answered, 'Bill'.

The doctor lifted Bill's right wrist and felt his pulse.

After a moment he said gently, 'Ah, Billy, you have had a little clot that has gone to your brain.' As he only spoke French, I listened attentively, trying to remember the terms he used. The word for clot (*caillot*) sounded to my ears like pebble (*caillou*). It made a strange image, to think of a little stone lodged in one's head. I knew my dictionary would have to be scoured through again.

The driver had carried the medical case from the car and placed it within the doctor's reach. He removed a stethoscope, plugged the tubes into his ears and placed the metal disc on the right side of Bill's neck.

'It has travelled up through your carotid artery.' I realised he was listening to the blood flow within an artery but, once again, it sounded as if he was talking about carrots. We possessed the *Reader's Digest Medical Adviser*; it, too, would have to be scoured through. He then withdrew several plastic boxes from the case. They all contained hermetically sealed needles and tubes to take blood samples. By the time he filled all the different vials, Bill remarked he had extracted an armful of blood. I noticed to my relief that, although his speech was still muffled, at least his sense of humour had returned.

The gentle giants, who had been standing around in a respectful silence, brought the stretcher which would carry Bill to the ambulance. I was told to follow them to the emergency department of Le Puy's Emile Roux hospital.

Daniel and Jo accompanied me. We left Jill behind with Lucy's comforting arm around her shoulder. She may have been divorced from Bill, but they had made two wonderful children together which bound them forever in a relationship of mutual affection and concern.

On route to Le Puy, the ambulance stopped and parked on the side of the road to meet with the SAMU (emergency medical service) vehicle, coming to us from the opposite direction. Bill was transferred into its back. In case any translations were necessary, I also stepped into its interior, and was amazingly impressed with the equipment this mini reanimation theatre on wheels possessed. A male nurse and a young doctor trained for all manner of emergencies examined Bill. The doctor's English was quite adequate. He scraped the soles of Bill's feet with what looked like a metal file, to study which way the tickling would affect his toes.

'Yes, your 'usband 'as suffered a stroke,' the English speaker said in a sweet accent to me.

'You can tell by just tickling his feet?' I asked, astounded.

'It is an instinctive reaction,' he explained. 'Normally, the toes would curl inwards when the foot is tickled. But if you 'ave 'ad a stroke, the toes stretch upwards. It is the classic symptom. We know it as the sign of Babinski.'

You live and learn.

Bill watched the handling of his feet in fascination. I could tell he was recovering. 'All this foot tickling has made me want to have a pee,' he said. The young doctor opened a drawer built into the side of the van and extracted a plastic bottle in the shape of a decapitated duck which he positioned perfectly for Bill to relieve himself.

Satisfied that Bill had had all the necessary attention for the time being, the doctor allowed him to be transferred back into the *pompiers'* ambulance to be taken to the hospital.

'If there are no more crucial calls, I will visit you in Emergency,' the doctor said to Bill as a farewell. 'It is not often we have an English patient. I can practise the language and translate for you.' In a matter of an hour, we'd met two different doctors with the most comforting bedside manners ever.

At the entrance to the emergency department, Bill was unloaded from the ambulance, placed on a gurney and moved to a cubicle. The children and I were allowed to remain at his side. Bill had begun to speak more clearly and had regained considerable movement in his left arm. This amelioration caused him to demand that I take him home. What had happened earlier was only a momentary aberration and he felt perfectly well enough to be driven back to the house. It took a lot of persuasion from all of us to keep him horizontal, and we were grateful when two white-smocked male nurses came to wheel him away. We were told to wait in reception and watched him disappear through the double swing-doors into a dimly lit corridor beyond. A little over an hour and several nails bitten to the quick later, a nurse called us by name and told us we could return to Bill's side.

Two doctors arrived. One of them was the English speaker from the SAMU vehicle. Bill had been given an emergency brain scan, ultrasound imaging of the arteries around his heart and an ECG.

The results of the tests were very hopeful, but the scan had shown that this had not been Bill's first stroke. My mind went back to the numbness he had felt on the left side of his face and in his fingers when doing the mosaics in the retirement home.

'Can you tell when he had the previous stroke?' I asked. 'How long ago?'

'No,' I was told, 'but he has definitely suffered one before.'

I could only imagine it had happened then, and it was that which had affected his walking and, possibly, his moods.

We left him that night ensconced in a room on the cardiology ward, and bent over his bed to kiss him goodnight. I promised to return the next day.

Jo and Dan were flying back to London the following morning; for them, it was an emotional farewell.

Something strange but wonderful happened on the way home. I had remembered the day as cold, grey and overcast. But now, late at night, the sky was a velvet black with tiny bright specks twinkling against the darkness. As we drove up from St-Paulien to the higher plateau of Bellevue-la-Montagne, an unexpected blaze of a shooting star streaked its way in an arc across the entire breadth of the windscreen. Jo, sitting next to me, sucked in a breath of surprise. Even Daniel, in the back of the car, could see the searing glow tearing through the sky. For a few minutes none of us spoke. We all made a wish. I was grateful for that second chance.

Daniel didn't leave with the others the next day. He hugged Lucy in a tearful goodbye at the airport. They all had jobs to return to, whereas his artist's studio had no such constraints. The canvases could wait. If necessary, when returning home he would paint late into the night to prepare his work for the next exhibition.

I was relieved and happy to have his company for a few more days. We waved and blew kisses through the glass partitions of Saint-Étienne's small airport terminal, and kept sight of the three women as they climbed the steps to the fuselage of the aeroplane parked on the tarmac only a few yards away. We watched the plane lift safely into the sky, and then drove to the hospital in Le Puy.

We were not prepared for the sight that met us. All the advances Bill had made the previous night – his speech, the movement in his left arm – seemed to have regressed. Transparent spaghetti attached to drips sprouted from his arms. More tubes hung down from under the blankets, coiling into a plastic bag hooked to the underside of the bed.

Bill could hardly talk. And when he did, it was worrying. He muttered incoherently that he'd been taken down into the bowels of the hospital for further tests and been left on a gurney in a dark corridor to wait outside one of the rooms. He was adamant that there must have been another English patient because he could hear, wafting through the corridor, the theme tune to *The Archers*. Daniel and I figured later that it must have been his imagination, as the examinations would have taken place in the morning, before our arrival, and *The Archers* is heard at three p.m. on the radio in France.

We were told by the staff nurses not to remain very long. I asked what the drips were for and it was explained that, after the results of the blood tests, he was being given supplementary treatment: a cocktail of vitamins and some sedatives. It was obvious our presence and his efforts to converse were tiring him.

I said goodbye and kissed him gently on the lips. Dan squeezed his hand and we moved to the door. 'Dominoes,' we heard him say, which turned us around. '... And pencils... paper... Christmas.'

Those were the sweetest words I'd heard him speak for a very long time. He was going to fight his way to a recovery. I knew he meant his watercolour pencils, and that he was determined to do our Christmas cards. But the dominoes? Was that what we would play on our next visit?

Driving home, Daniel mentioned music. We should buy him a mini-Walkman so he could listen to his favourite CDs. We did exactly that in the afternoon.

The following day, armed with his requests, we returned to the hospital. I placed the pencils and the paper in a drawer of his bedside table. He was pleased with the Walkman and the music Daniel had chosen for him to listen to. We watched as he tried to come to grips with placing a CD into the player. For the time being, with only the use of his right hand, it was a difficult manoeuvre. I put the box of dominoes on the tray that was placed across the bed. He opened it and, with his left hand, began to remove the small rectangular pieces with their little black dots to position them in rows in front of him. It was not easy for his hand, much less his fingers, to obey the commands from his brain to place the dominoes exactly as he wanted them. Some tipped over. It was agonising to watch as, with intense concentration, he tried to move his hand to pick up those pieces lying flat on the tray. They slipped through his fingers like little bars of wet soap.

Less than forty-eight hours had passed since his stroke. Even with sedatives, Bill was already showing an intense strength of will to overcome his paralysis. I had a feeling I would be more proud of him for that achievement than for any critical acclaim that his directorial successes may have brought him in the past.

Chapter Sixteen

I FOLLOWED A WOMAN WHO WAS WEARING a white nurse's smock down the corridor of the cardiology ward on my way to Bill's room. The corridor was crowded with empty gurneys, cleaning trolleys and wagons upon which starched white sheets had been stacked. It was late morning and there was a general hustle and bustle as the cleaners were mopping the floors and preparing the beds for future occupancies.

The woman was walking very slowly, with her left hand sliding along a rail which stretched the length of both walls except for the insets of the doors to the rooms. Each time the rail stopped, she reached her arm out to feel the empty space and then, having passed it, she'd place her hand on the rail again. I wanted to move faster, but because of the obstructions in the corridor, I couldn't overtake her. She bumped into one of the wagons which had been parked in her path, and carefully felt her way around it. It was then that I realised I was walking behind a woman who was blind, and wondered how it was she'd become a nurse.

Bill's room was the fourth on the left. I was surprised to see her stop, gently tap on his door and enter. By then, I was immediately behind her. She must have sensed my presence, because she kept the door open for me.

I went directly to the bed and kissed Bill 'hello'.

'Have you met my physiotherapist?' he asked. His speech was completely back to normal.

I turned to look at the woman, who was standing a few metres from the bed. She did not have a white cane, nor was she wearing glasses. There was a shy smile on her lips, and her eyes, although not entirely focused, were trained upon me nevertheless. One is so accustomed to shaking hands in

France upon meeting a stranger that I moved without thinking towards her with an outstretched arm which she, of course, could not see. Realising my mistake, I lifted her right wrist until she found my hand, and so I shook the hand of the woman who would work the first few miracles to put Bill back on two feet.

She was remarkable; with a memory for feeling so acute that she could perceive the slightest improvement in a muscular reaction, or the lifting of a finger or a foot half an inch higher than the previous day. She could test the grip of Bill's left hand, and pronounce it an ounce in pressure more powerful than the last time he'd squeezed her hand.

I tried to be there for all of her sessions with him, and watched with admiration her gentle manipulations of his affected limbs. She never spoke of the cause for her blindness, only the advantages her lack of sight had produced in developing her other senses.

'I'm not the only one,' she told us one day. 'The health service has come to recognise our unique abilities and is training more like me to be of service.'

I couldn't help thinking, with the Government providing for her training, she was able to practise a profession which made a greater contribution to society than the tuning of pianos.

We were incredibly impressed with her, and it was she who instilled in Bill the confidence to take, with her support and guidance, his first few steps. Only two weeks after his admittance to Emile Roux, and upon her recommendation, a space was found for him at the rehabilitation centre situated in a newly built block within the grounds of the hospital. We thanked the doctors and the nurses on the cardiology ward for their good humour, kindness and excellent care. They were happy he was well enough to leave them, but regretted no longer to be treating the man whom they had come affectionately to call 'The English Patient'.

In the rehabilitation centre, Bill was placed in a room that he shared with a French airline pilot. His name was Paul. They were of a similar age, and Paul had also suffered a stroke, although his affected the right-hand side. Inexplicably, our brains work in opposing directions: the left lobes commanding the right limbs, and the right lobes, the left limbs. Language and some artistic capabilities are situated in the left side of the brain. Bill had luck in his misfortune, in that the damage happened in the right lobe. His speech came back to normal, and his artistic talents were not affected.

I would find out later that Bill's stroke was not caused by a clot in the brain but rather from a sudden and prolonged lack of oxygen due to an obstruction in his right carotid artery. The doctors prescribed medication, which he would have to take for the rest of his life, to ease the blood flow through that artery. It was a little round pink pill; and no, it did not have pride of place next to his breakfast setting. He managed to swallow it discreetly.

He and Paul had a wonderful relationship. As a pilot, Paul had had to learn some English, and although he spoke with difficulty, they understood each other well enough to laugh together. Paul was released before Bill, having begun his rehabilitation much earlier. They said an optimistic goodbye to one another; and on Bill's birthday, the following March, we received a surprise visit from him in the company of his wife. His manner of walking had improved miraculously. Only when he spoke did one notice the residual effect of the stroke. I curse my untidiness: his phone number was on a slip of paper which has gone astray. Beyond that visit, we have not kept in touch.

December brought blizzards, which would continue into January. I was still driving the same car I'd imported into France and began calling it 'The Intrepid'. Going to visit Bill was an 80 km return journey which I did every day for eight weeks. We'd been given a Breton spaniel by the owners of the Tremblant hotel in La Chaise-Dieu. We called her Olive. It was the first dog Bill had ever had. She accompanied me like a co-pilot on these journeys, with her front paws on the dashboard and her nose stuck against the windscreen, sniffing the external air being blown through the demister. I drove at a steady 60 kph where I thought it was safe. Even then, I'd be passed by cars doing twice my speed. Olive would follow these with her eyes, and then turn back to me with an expression as if to say, 'What idiots!' She could feel the slightest slide when my tyres crossed a particularly bad patch of tightly packed icy snow. I'd regain control and her look to me then would read, 'Phew! That was close.'

Nearing the hospital gates, she'd begin to whine, anxiously anticipating her greeting with Bill. He'd be waiting just inside the entrance of the rehabilitation centre in his wheelchair. I'd let her out of the car and she'd rush towards the automatic door which would open for her. By the time I joined them, Olive would have leapt into his lap and was happily kissing his face. None of the staff seemed to mind this ritual, not even when Bill had not completed the exercises in the large gymnasium and her little nails could be heard clattering across the polished wooden floor in her eagerness to find him. Without her company at home and on those daily journeys, I could have sunk easily into a deep depression.

The house was empty without Bill. I even missed his music. Night-times were the worst, when my mind would travel to that land between reality and dreams. Not quite awake, not quite asleep, I'd blame myself for the stroke; my lack of vigilance, my lack of understanding. The move away from everything he'd ever known must have been more difficult for him than I'd realised. I'd led the life of a gypsy, a butterfly. He was deeply rooted into the English way of life: cricket, rugby, the pub, the BBC. I had never been anywhere long enough to grow roots. A wind could blow me anywhere, and I'd settle where I landed. Perhaps the lack of all that was familiar to him had caused the stress which led to the stroke. He'd been a great communicator, raconteur, someone who always found the perfect line to set sides splitting with laughter. These talents were disabled through his lack of French. It was no wonder he had glued himself to his chair, listening to the familiar sounds of his music and the BBC, drinking too much scotch. He had lost his identity. These were the thoughts that tortured me throughout the night. But sometimes, while lying in bed, I was sure I could hear sounds of the music from Rosalie's old café, like a captured echo being slowly released from the stone. It gave me heart.

Very gradually, visit after visit, I began to notice an improvement in his condition. The first day that Olive and I found him standing outside the building leaning on a cane, waiting for us, made me weep with emotion. The therapists had deemed it possible to remove his wheelchair and replace it with a walking stick. On further visits, I'd find him practising moving up and down the stairs. His balance was returning.

I was given permission to bring him home for Christmas. He was allowed to leave on the twenty-fourth of December, but had to be returned the evening of the twenty-sixth. I festooned the living room with fir branches that I cut from the trees in the surrounding forests. Baubles and lights were hung from them and in all of the windows. It was a lonely job, not having Bill to direct me.

Dan and Lucy were coming, along with Jeremy, Jill and their daughter. The holiday was such a success, we managed to kidnap him again for New Year's Eve. It seemed everyone we'd ever known phoned to ask his news and to wish him well. It was a time we wallowed in the wealth of our friends; not that they were rich, but that we were rich to have them.

Back at the centre, Bill continued to draw, sketching scenes from his bedroom window. But one picture in particular delighted the staff. He drew a cartoon of the gymnasium with the patients behaving like circus performers. They were swinging from trapezes. Some were juggling or crossing a tightrope. Others were doing all manner of acrobatics while the staff of physiotherapists lounged about, arms crossed at their chests, leaning against a wall, bored with nothing to do. He gave it to them as a gift. They insisted on having it framed, and as far as I know it still hangs in pride of place on the wall of the corridor that leads to the gymnasium.

His progress was being assessed every day. One of the final challenges he was given to evaluate his readiness to go home permanently was a particular test. He was given a pencil and asked to draw concentric circles, like a whorl. The therapist suggested that he think of a snail's shell. Well… quicker than a flash, Bill grabbed the pencil and drew one of his famous snails. It had a smiling face with huge eyes and a bulbous nose. One of its hands was holding a placard which read GOING HOME BY ESCARGOT EXPRESS. He passed the test. I went to fetch him home in the second week of February.

Many of the staff were gathered in the reception area to say goodbye. One of them retrieved ceremoniously the walking stick from Bill. We thanked them for their magnificent work. He faced me and put an arm around my waist. I lifted my left hand on to his shoulder. My right hand was clasped by his left and held up in the air as we waltzed slowly across the tiled floor and out of the sliding doors into a sparklingly bright, sunny morning.

Bill's recuperation continued when he came home. He was offered twice-weekly home visits from a local physiotherapist over a duration of six months. Even our French friends were impressed with the care the state health system was affording him.

By April 1999, Bill was eager for us to reopen. Except for a slight paralysis which persisted in his left leg, his rehabilitation was almost complete. He cut a handsome figure, leaning on a cane. It gave him a certain gravitas and earned him enormous respect. His daughter, Jo, bought him a walking stick with a bicycle bell attached to it. He loved ringing it on a crowded pavement and delighted in seeing everyone scattering out of his way. Simple pleasures.

We were now appearing in a well-known English B&B guide, and would become acquainted with the best and the worst of British tourists. Most, of course, were delightful, whose company we enjoyed and even cherished; but there were those whose presence we were quite happy to see the back of. It was through that guide that we experienced a phenomenon that, with the law of averages, we'd always expected but had hitherto managed to avoid, namely: *The Families From Hell!*

We received a reservation for one night in mid-August for two couples with five children between them. I was told on the phone that they'd be coming in two cars from Barcelona. I warned the man I was speaking to that it was a very long drive, especially with children, and advised him to find accommodation further south in France. My concern was pooh-poohed. In due course, we received a cheque in the post as a deposit, with a letter confirming the date and the sleeping arrangements. I should have been warned by the handwriting. It was the same illegible scrawl one associates with a doctor's prescription.

One family opted for the 'Autumn' room which normally only sleeps three people. But I was assured that their two children aged six and eight could easily share the spare single bed. The other couple who had three children aged two, four and six reserved the suite, where the children would share the futon in the salon and the parents sleep in the adjoining bedroom. They were looking for the cheapest possible formula, and also ordered a meal in the evening.

We received a phone call at nine in the morning the day they were due to arrive, telling us they were just leaving their accommodation in Barcelona and should be with us at five o'clock in the afternoon. Fat chance, I thought.

At 7:30 p.m., the two cars came into view and parked laboriously a few yards from the house. Even at our altitude of 850 metres, it had been a blisteringly hot day. I did not envy them their drive. Walking to the nearest car with a smile in welcome on my face, I was accosted by a 'B' movie version of a Vanessa Redgrave lookalike screaming like a banshee from the opened passenger window, 'Where's your bloody paddling pool?!!'

Not a 'hello', or a 'how do you do'; just hysterical screaming, and that was only the mother. The noise the children were making could have caused a landslide.

'I'm terribly sorry,' I answered politely, 'but we don't have a paddling pool.'

'What do you mean, you don't have a paddling pool?!! I promised the children a swim!!'

By now the children had leapt out of the two cars and were running amok, frightening Olive, the cats, the snakes in the grass.

'There is a river at the bottom of our fields,' I said, while thinking evilly, *... and it's just deep enough for the kids to drown in.*

The husbands and the other wife muttered a perfunctory greeting and busied themselves removing cases from the boots. The 'B' version Ms Redgrave got out of the car. Her bawling two-year-old was stuck like a brooch to her heaving chest. She glared unforgivingly at me for not having a paddling pool.

The dinner was utter mayhem. We were entertaining two other couples, both French, who smiled indulgently as the children screeched, squealed, kicked each other and, when not throwing the cutlery about, used it as drumsticks to beat on their plates, the glasses or Bill's beautifully painted tabletop.

'I don't suppose we should be allowing the children to behave like this,' said the Vanessa Redgrave reject.

'We would prefer it if they calmed down,' I answered between gritted teeth while forcing our antique brass candle-snuffer out of the tenacious grip of the two-year-old child who was smashing it against a rather beautiful porcelain serving-dish.

The French didn't complain. They continued to chew their food and nod benignly at the antics of the little monsters. They either had a saintly understanding of children, or had become so traumatised that they'd sunk into a state of bovine placidity.

Bill and I were extremely relieved when three of the English adults, who had never even attempted to communicate with our French guests, removed themselves with the children from the dining room to continue their meal on the terrace. It meant a little more work for us, rushing between the two tables, but we were grateful for the comparative peace in which we were allowed to finish the meal. I didn't even mind the sharp calls of, 'Madame!' or the loud snapping of fingers to draw my attention when they wanted their carafes of wine replenished. At least one of the husbands deigned to remain at our table, and made an effort to converse in schoolboy French with our other guests.

In mid-August it is still quite light even after nine o'clock. The children scattered from the table, and were now allowed to run rampage through the grounds surrounding the house.

I had joined an equine benevolent association in the hope of being able to adopt, one day, a suitable horse. With my luck, I was offered a donkey instead: a grey, shaggy, sway-backed, elderly lady called 'Desirée'. We shortened her name to Daisy. She was a joy and a pleasure to keep. Daisy adored children. She would lower her head gently to them to have her muzzle tickled, and stand like that for ages, allowing their little hands to run through her long wispy coat. The high-pitched shouting from the children brought her out of her shelter to stand near the fence from where she gave a mournful, gasping bray.

There was a glorious calm as the children went to discover the source of that bagpipe-like noise. I had heard her as well and went out to the terrace to tell the parents to warn the children not to touch the electric fencing. I'd be there shortly to introduce them to Daisy.

Too late. A terrifying scream emitted from the field below. The current is minimal, the electric shock being more a surprise than painful. It worked wonders, though. After the initial bawling, that child, at least, kept quiet for a while. Daisy made a dash back to her shelter.

It must have been well after midnight when the hysterical energy of the children, brought on by the day's uncomfortable journey, finally ebbed away and we were all allowed to sleep.

I had expected to hear noise in the morning from the suite when the three children woke up, but all was surprisingly quiet. All five were herded like geese on to the terrace for breakfast, which proceeded in a manner only marginally more civilised than the previous evening.

Before leaving, the two women came to ask Bill if we sold plastic bottles of mineral water.

'I'm afraid not, but you're welcome to help yourselves from the tap,' Bill told them.

'Good God! Never! We only buy mineral water,' they gasped in horror, and then mentioned certain specific French brands.

'You buy those brands? Haven't you read about them?' I could tell Bill was entering one of his Piscean moods.

'What do you mean?' they both asked.

'You get them in plastic bottles, don't you?'

'Of course. They're easier to carry.'

'And you keep them in the car?'

'Yes, of course.'

'And the car heats up?'

'Well, yes. That's why the children need a drink.'

'You give that water to your children?! I don't believe it! You're poisoning them!'

'What?'

'Don't you know, there's a dangerous chemical reaction with those brands of water when they come into contact with plastic heated over 25 degrees Celsius?' I was busying myself elsewhere but could hear every word he was saying. Any moment now he was going to convince the women that their children had been drinking the heavy water required in the production of the atomic bomb.

'We've never heard about any dangers from this water,' they said, but they looked very worried. 'And that's strange,' they continued, 'because we're all doctors.' That explained a lot to me.

'What? Well, don't you ever read *The Lancet*?' Bill asked in an admonishing tone. 'There was a huge article. It even made headline news on the BBC.'

'When?'

'Just recently. You were probably in Barcelona. Anyway, there's a little supermarket in La Chaise-Dieu. Buy them some Coca-Cola instead.'

The two mothers left with anxious expressions and got into their respective cars. God only knows what they told their husbands, and what they bought as refreshments for their route.

I would have scolded Bill for that enormous lie, only for the sake of the children, but the condition in which I found the room 'Autumn' when I went to clean it more than justified his flight of fancy. It was beyond description. Suffice it to say, if Attila the Hun and a few of his horde had recently vacated it, they'd have left less devastation. It was impossible that adults, if they had been present, would ever have allowed their children to wreck such havoc in a room. I think that explained why the suite was so quiet. The two couples must have dumped all of the children into 'Autumn' with the eight-year-old as guardian, and escaped to sleep separately in the suite for a peaceful night's rest. Bloody doctors.

Nevertheless, the rooms were prepared to an immaculate state awaiting the arrival of our next guests. The welcoming smile in greeting was ready. A new couple descended the gravelled steps. They introduced themselves and I knew that another experience with two different members of the human race was about to begin.

*

A Late Chapter

MANY YEARS HAVE PASSED SINCE THESE EVENTS. We had to close the guest house in 2002 because of further difficulties with Bill's health, and I used the hiatus for writing this book. We reopened the following year but much had changed. The *aubergiste* and his family moved away. Jean-Pierre must have been in a hurry because a large stash of cash wrapped in a plastic bag was found in one of the restaurant's freezers. They moved to another department in the north where Anna Magnani and her three older daughters ran a restaurant. Jean-Pierre was excluded from the venture in any professional capacity. When we welcomed people again, I only served an evening meal at the weekends. Bill was becoming weaker and I found I needed more time to spend with him.

When he'd had his stroke, the doctor who arrived on crutches, who had given him emergency treatment and taken the 'armful' of blood for analysis, had also asked for PSA results for the condition of his prostate. The count was elevated. I had shown the results to the doctors on the cardiology ward where he was being looked after but they were not in the least perturbed, stating that for his age it was not high enough to be a cause of concern. A year later, he underwent a biopsy and it became so.

At a meeting between only the urologist and myself, I was told to avoid telling him the truth. In some cases, doctors in France deem it advantageous for a patient to remain ignorant of the gravity of their condition. In Bill's case, he was one hundred per cent correct. Since I had known him, I recognised his tendency to behave like an ostrich, preferring to hide his head in the sand when difficult, personal problems arose. The consultant told me exactly what would happen, how the illness would proceed and his estimated life expectancy during the treatment. Operating in Bill's condition was out of the question, as was radio- or chemotherapy. The best procedure was hormonal. Bill was a very intelligent man, but I'm sure he was grateful to hear my rationalisations when certain pains became pronounced and morphine patches were prescribed which were regularly augmented in strength.

Eventually, at the very beginning of January 2006, Bill was having problems breathing. I rang our locum doctor who had become a friend. He arrived quickly, diagnosed a serious lung infection and called for an ambulance. Once again, a tearful Billy was removed to A&E at the hospital in Le Puy. It being the season for flu, there was serious overcrowding. He was eventually found a bed in the endocrinology ward which deals with glandular disorders. The ward was situated in the last remaining building not yet modernised in the hospital grounds. He was placed in a room that he shared with a man suffering with extreme diabetes.

Bill's son Daniel flew out to join me and, when we next visited, we found him hallucinating and behind a barrier of bars keeping him enclosed on the mattress. The diabetes sufferer told us that during the night Bill had tried to leave his bed. He had fallen and cut himself. The diabetic rang the emergency bell and a nurse arrived to put him back into the bed but did not notice the wound. I examined the deep gash on his left arm. It had not even been treated with an antiseptic. This was so unusual. Through previous experience, I'd had enormous confidence in the French health system; but, having met the ward's administrator, I began to feel uneasy. He made his dislike for the English very obvious. *'Je déteste les Anglais!'* was how he welcomed Bill on to his ward. To begin with, I doubted Bill's version, remembering the hallucinations. But when I met him personally to demand that something be done about the gash on his arm, there was no doubt about his animosity. He was not prepared for an English wife who spoke fluent French and while he tried to ignore me, a doctor found me standing, glaring at the man from the entrance to the office, and asked me why I was there. The doctor then followed me to Bill's bedside and examined the arm. He was horrified at the lack of treatment. Nurses quickly arrived with unguents and bandages.

I threatened to remove Bill from the ward, even from the hospital; but Roland, our friendly doctor, advised me against doing so lest the hospital administration discharged themselves from any liability. He would make arrangements to have Bill transferred to our local cottage hospital in Craponne, only thirteen kilometres from Bonneval. He was found a large bright room and I could visit him without restraint. The lungs were treated with double doses of antibiotics, but it was more the cancer that had progressed. Within weeks, he was put on to impossibly high measures of morphine, delivered into his veins via a pump.

I visited as usual on the fifth of March and found Bill in a catatonic state. In a fit of tearful hysterics I approached the treating doctor (Roland was away on a skiing holiday) who tried to calm me down with a palliative dose of soothing words. I wanted to be able to communicate with Bill, and the doctor promised to lower the amount of morphine for a short while to make that possible for the following day; but it was the nurses who advised me to call his children. I spoke to Daniel who in turn called Jo, but it was more difficult for her to leave quickly and catch a plane as she was working nine to five. Daniel went online immediately, and by chance found an early-morning flight. At six o'clock the next morning the doctor in charge rang me. I should come right away. Bill's flesh was beginning to marble which, I was told, was a sign of imminent death. Daniel had rung me the night before and figured he'd be in Craponne by ten a.m.

By this time, we had another dog who had been abandoned and found his way to our door. As we already had Olive, we named him Popeye. I quickly dressed and drove with both dogs to the hospital. Leaving them in the car, I ran up the stairs to Bill's room. He was barely conscious but I was able to hold him and whisper words of love into his ear. Because Daniel didn't know where the hospital was, I'd arranged to meet him in a café/bar called 'Le Cézanne' to collect him. I left Bill for a moment, telling him I would return with a wonderful surprise. As it happened, we crossed paths without seeing each other. Daniel had arrived slightly earlier than expected and Bruno, the *patron* of 'Le Cézanne', had explained how to get to the hospital. When I returned to the room I saw Bill with a radiant smile on his face and holding Daniel's outstretched hand. They spoke for a short while with Bill becoming weaker and then slipping slowly out of consciousness.

Now I had a problem with the dogs. They had been locked in the car for over four hours. We did not know how long this process to Bill's final breath would take. They had to be driven back to Bonneval. I'd bought a CD player for his stay and had much of his favourite music. Just before leaving, I placed a disc into the player without even looking at it and hurried to the car. Although it was the beginning of March, there had been a blizzard which meant my taking the long way home, staying on the wider routes which had been cleared of snow. Once home and having dealt with the dogs' needs, I got back into the car for the return journey to the hospital. I was speeding again on the main road which passed through a village called Fontannes. A hundred metres outside the village, I crossed some railway tracks. Suddenly, I felt Bill next to me. The sensation was so strong that I looked at the passenger seat expecting him to be there and shouted, 'You can't be here! I left you in the hospital with Daniel.'

I drove on even faster, and upon arriving ran up the stairs to his ward. The nurses were waiting for me. They gave me the sad news. '*Il est parti. Il a choisi de mourir sans vous.*' (He's gone. He chose to die without you.) It was not the first time I'd heard this sentiment expressed here: that the dying choose when and with whom they pass out of this world. I found it unbearably cruel to be told such a myth, but was assured by the nurses that he wanted to spare me the pain.

I rushed into the room and found him lying peacefully as if asleep. Daniel and I embraced, comforting one another. I learned that my experience when crossing the tracks had corresponded to the time of his death; and then Dan told me of another coincidence. The disc I'd chosen to play when hurrying away and without realising was Copland's ballet of *Billy the Kid*. Daniel played the disc again to recognise and determine at which part of the ballet Bill had died. He took his very last breath during the movement named 'Billy's Death'. When I spoke about him to others I called him Bill or Mr Hays, but when we were alone I always called him Billy. And he loved it.

He was cremated near to Saint-Étienne in a newly built crematorium which took pride of place in a part of the cemetery fittingly named *Côté Chaud*, which in English means the hot side. He'd have loved that too.

Besides Dan and Jo and their partners, many friends flew out from England to attend. Amongst them were Jeremy Nicholas and Bryan Pringle, two of my accomplices when finding the Auberge Valentin. Two of our great friends, the actors John Woodvine and Lynn Farleigh, were there. John sang an emotional number from Alan Plater's play with music *Close the Coalhouse Door* which Bill directed to great success so many years ago. Jeremy had his wife Jilly and daughter, Rosie, in tow. Rosie was Bill's and my god-daughter. I remembered the baptismal ritual where Bill, a committed atheist, had to renounce the devil. He performed his lines with élan.

The farewell was a moving ceremony, even though, as he would have wished, God and the hereafter were never mentioned; but the immediate aftermath was bizarre. The congregation was invited into an anteroom which had a large screen on one of its walls. We were to witness the actual cremation which would take place in another part of the cemetery grounds. As the crematorium was new, and with the French opting more for burial, the manager/master of ceremonies wanted to have the process explained in the hope of impressing a possible new clientele.

As I was the only person present who was fairly bilingual, it fell to me to do the translations. Some of my French friends were horrified but too polite to intervene; and one of them, a dear friend called Anick who adored Bill, almost fainted as I described the moving image on the screen in English, translating from the manager's commentary. I had to explain to my audience that when the incinerator door opened, the extreme heat from within, literally radiating towards the exterior, would consume the coffin as it made its slow approach to the glowing entrance. I have forgotten the precise temperature that was mentioned of the flames that would envelop the coffin, but it was told to me exactly, as was the reason for this extreme heat: the human body was essentially 80% liquid. The master of ceremonies seemed to imply that at lower temperatures the body would simply roast and that would take a long time, not to mention the condition of the remains which we would in due course be given in an urn. He did not exactly say that, but it was left to our imagination. We had been given a science lesson in human incineration. All the while, I translated faithfully his tutorial. It was as if I was playing the part of a foreign correspondent.

I'd placed a lit candle in the form of a snail on the back of the coffin. As it entered deeper and deeper into the furnace, the snail suddenly exploded and the coffin disappeared with a bright light which was then swallowed into the interior and the metal doors closed. Billy had made his exit.

When we were ushered out of the anteroom the manager shook our hands, thanking everyone, saying he hoped the experience had been helpful and educational. We were encouraged to pass the word around to family and friends. I was complimented for my bravery in not breaking down ('*Vous êtes courageuse, Madame!*'). But I had the feeling we were being treated as future customers and he was looking forward to welcoming us again, dead or alive.

After sharing out some of Bill's ashes with Dan and Jo to smuggle back in plastic bags to England (it being against the law unless signed permissions are granted by the Prefecture) for them to scatter where they wished, we had a little ceremony to cast most of the remaining ashes from the arched stone bridge which spans the Dorette and was Bill's favourite sight.

Bonneval's gentle stream, the Dorette, snakes its way into the Dore which in its turn flows into the wild salmon-spawning river, the Allier, and the Allier joins the Loire which empties into the Atlantic; but not before winding its way through some of France's most cherished vineyards, which we thought would make the voyage for Bill's ashes more pleasurable before finally being taken and dispersed by the tides on Britain's shores.

In the ensuing weeks, I felt very much alone and the thought of continuing to work the guesthouse without Bill was abhorrent to me. He may not have been able to help me much with physical tasks but his presence, advice and humour made up for that lack. I told the mayor that I was stopping, closing and maybe even selling. He would not hear of it. *'Ne pas fermez! Continuez! C'est important pour vous. Bonneval vous aidera!'* (Don't close! Continue! It's important for you. Bonneval will help you.) And it did. The mayor, Paul Bard, who had been there from the very beginning of our adventure, obtained agreement from the municipal council to pay a woman to help me run the establishment as before. Her name was Catherine. In order to avoid confusion, I decided that as I was by far the elder and had possessed my name many more years than she, I would continue to use Catherine and she would have to be called Kati. We became best friends. Also born, as Bill, under the sign of Pisces, renowned for their sense of humour, she helped me overcome my loss by our moments of shared laughter.

The barn that housed the Four Seasons was eventually sold to the municipality, still under the leadership of Paul Bard. The money I received has enabled me to continue to live in the old *auberge* sweetly called 'Valentin' where I am cosseted by fond memories, friends and, as I write, three cats who recognise the sound of my car and welcome me home as if they were dogs. Sadly, my constant companion, Olive, is no longer at my side. But I know all those I loved who had the audacity to leave me, I will see again in that other world. No rush, though; I'm pretty patient and still enjoying being here, leading a blessed life regardless of the tragedies, because laughter is never far away.

It is autumn here and when I walk the many forest paths near me, I marvel at the striking colours: the crimsons, rusts, golds and pale yellows bursting through the dark greens of the sweet-scented pines. This is why I'm here, and I drink a toast in gratitude to the French God who adheres to custom and takes himself out to lunch. Yet I can't help but wonder, where on earth does he eat? There are placards on properties that boast, 'Napoleon slept here'! But I've never heard of a sign, 'God has eaten here'! What a coup for a Michelin restaurant that would be.

Alisha April

Undercover Millionär

Verbotene Liebe